URBAN SOCIAL CONFLICT

URBAN SOCIAL CONFLICT

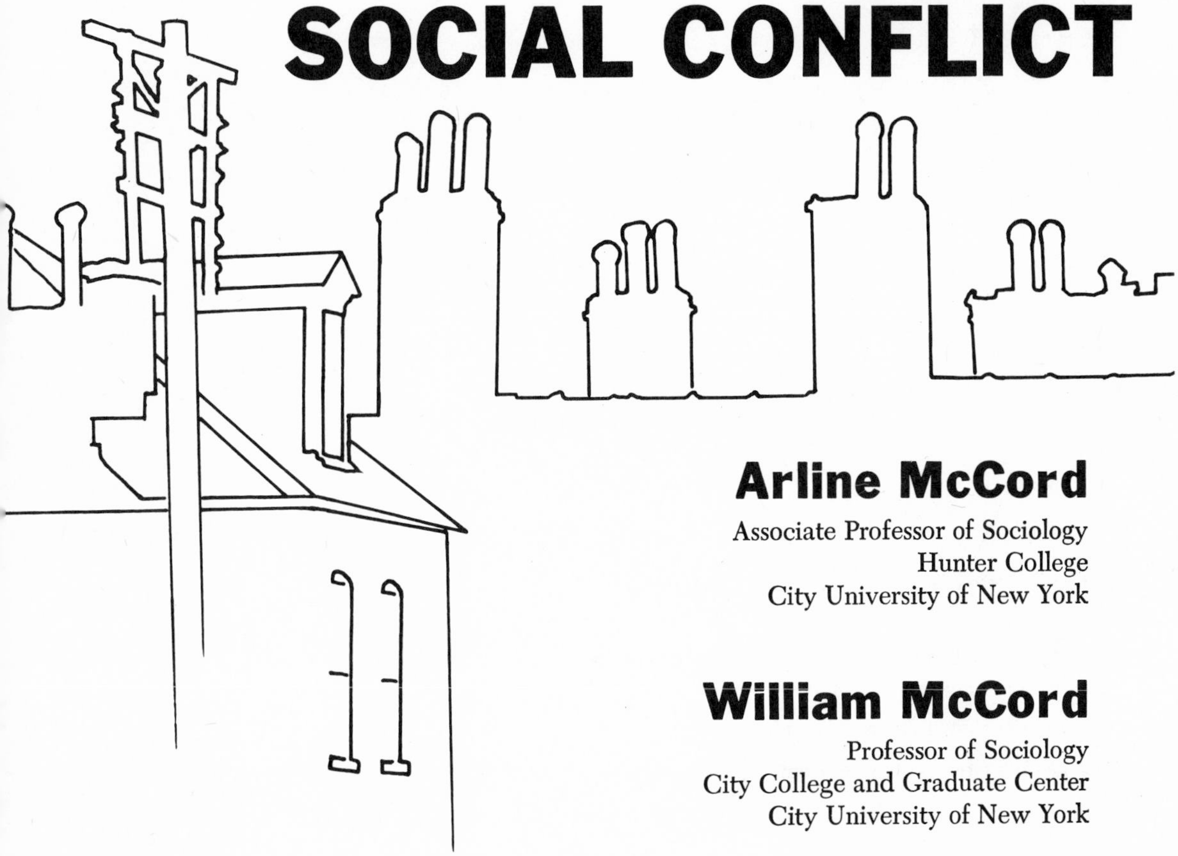

Arline McCord
Associate Professor of Sociology
Hunter College
City University of New York

William McCord
Professor of Sociology
City College and Graduate Center
City University of New York

The C. V. Mosby Company
Saint Louis 1977

COVER DESIGN:

Black and white silhouette of the urban skyline
courtesy Susan Sanders Block

Color transparency of bursting fireworks,
suggesting conflict, by Jack Zehrt

Printed in the United States of America

Distributed in Great Britain by Henry Kimpton, London

Library of Congress Cataloging in Publication Data

McCord, Arline F
Urban social conflict.

Bibliography: p.
Includes index.
1. Sociology, Urban—Addresses, essays, lectures.
2. Social conflict—Addresses, essays, lectures.
3. Cities and towns—United States—Addresses, essays, lectures. I. McCord, William Maxwell, 1930- joint author. II. Title.
HT151.M25 301.36 76-26697
ISBN 0-8016-3220-X

VH/VH/VH 9 8 7 6 5 4 3 2 1

Dedication

On December 7, 1941, an American pilot, Don C. McCord, flew his squadron into Hawaii. They came in low, under the clouds, since the United States Army Air Force had decided to disarm the airplanes and fill them with gasoline during their flight from California. Unable to land at Pearl Harbor because of the Japanese attack in progress at the time, McCord shot down one Zero with his .45-caliber pistol. He landed safely on another island. He was killed some months later after having flown more than his twenty required missions. His luck ran out, someplace off New Guinea, when he was twenty-three years of age. His life's ambition: to write the "Great American Novel" in a secluded village in upper Vermont.

Early in December, 1941, in Seattle, Washington, George S. Fujii was awakened to the knock of the FBI at his door. The agents arrested him as an "enemy alien." He was sent to Montana, New Mexico, and then Texas. He did not see his wife and two young children for over two years. They had been sent to California and eventually to Texas.

Like so many immigrants before him, Mr. Fujii had come to America from Japan with the hope of fulfilling the dream of opportunity. After years of work, his hopes were smashed. He spent four years in camps. He suffered as soldiers with fixed bayonets forced him to obey their will; he helplessly witnessed the confiscation of property he had earned by his own labor and sweat.

Neither Don McCord nor George Fujii were guilty of having committed crimes. Both were individuals, like countless thousands before and after them, caught as victims of conflict between ideas, people, and nations. McCord's sentence: death. Fujii's sentence: imprisonment and humiliation.

Many who read this book will not remember Pearl Harbor. Nor will a majority recall the "great betrayal" when America sent more than 100,000 Japanese Americans to detention centers. Most of these people were American citizens: not one was convicted of any act contrary to the interests of the United States.

We remember Don C. McCord, a brother, and George S. Fujii, a father. And thus we have written this book.

Our hope is that we may share with others our understanding of the nature of some forms of human strife; its suffering, its violence, and ironically, perhaps even its benefits.

Arline Fujii McCord
William McCord

Acknowledgments

We wish to express our gratitude to the following critics who read the manuscript at various stages of its development and who supplied many useful insights and criticisms.

JAMES H. LAUE

Director, Center of Community
and Metropolitan Studies,
University of Missouri,
St. Louis, Missouri

PAT HAYNES

Instructor, Department of Sociology,
Illinois State University,
Normal, Illinois

STEVEN VAGO

Chairman, Department of Sociology,
St. Louis University,
St. Louis, Missouri

JOHN J. LENNON

Professor of Sociology,
University of Arkansas,
Little Rock, Arkansas

NATHAN KANTROWITZ

Professor of Sociology,
Kent State University,
Kent, Ohio

JOHN D. KASARDA

Associate Professor of Sociology,
Florida Atlantic University,
Boca Raton, Florida

JAMES A. GESCHWENDER

Chairman and Professor,
Department of Sociology,
State University of New York,
Binghamton, New York

EVERETT HUGHES

Professor, Department of Sociology,
Boston College,
Chestnut Hill, Massachusetts

Contents

part I

INTRODUCTION TO THE CITY

chapter 1

Strife as the human condition

Life is a battle and a sojourning . . . in a strange land.

Marcus Aurelius

URBAN GROWTH

Although cities had been well established on every continent, except Australia, by the early centuries of the Christian era,[1] historians may well record their growth and development as the most important fact of the modern period. The widespread nature of urban growth can be noted in the population statistics of many of the world's largest cities. Paris, for example, grew from a mere 0.5 million people in 1801 to 7.8 million in 1960, and 9.2 million in 1970–71. The population of Tokyo and the surrounding Yokohama area expanded from 1.4 million in 1795 to 13.6 million in 1960 and 14.7 million in 1970–71. New York and its metropolitan area also experienced a staggering population increase, moving from 0.6 million people in 1800 to 16.2 million in 1970–71.[2] Further, statistics from several countries including Finland, Denmark, Belgium, West Germany, Venezuela, Sweden, Mexico, the Soviet Union, Japan, Poland, Canada, and Switzerland clearly support the urbanizing trend. Only one-fourth of the total population of each of these nations live in small or medium cities, that is, cities with less than 100,000 population.[3]

The rapidity of growing urban density can also be expressed in global terms. Within slightly more than two decades (1950–70) large cities increased from 16 percent to 23 percent of the world's population.[4] Large cities are defined as those with more than 100,000 population, with the amount of urban growth around the world varying by region. Most of the highly urbanized nations in 1950 continued their urbanizing trends in the 1970s. Japan was 37.4 percent urban in 1950. By 1970 it was 83.3 percent urban, representing a change of 45.9 percent. Similarly, the Soviet Union, Canada, and the United States shifted toward urban populations by 29.8, 13.0, and 11.2 percent respectively, making each of them over three quarters urbanized.[5]

Of course, statistics on the relative shift of population to urban areas do not tell the full story of urbanization. In nations where the relative growth of the urban population is small compared to the growth of rural populations, the statistics reflect a very low rate of change. This is true even though cities may be flourishing and population density increasing rapidly. An example is provided in India, where 17.1 percent of the population resided in cities in 1950, increasing only to 18.8 percent urban in 1970. Yet Calcutta and Bombay represent two of the world's fastest growing cities.[6] The reason for the relatively small rate of urban growth reflected in the statistics is an increase in rural population.

Moreover, even a full study of population growth, shifts, distribution, and densities, though important, constitutes only one segment of the story of urban development. Of predominant concern to many social scientists are the implications of population studies for the quality of life experienced by individuals, the development of different social environments, and the creation and alteration of political and economic balances. With this introduction to some facts of urban growth, let us turn to the main focus of this volume.

THE PROBLEM: CONFLICT AND URBAN LIFE

The basic premise of this work simply stated is that *strife is an essential governing element of the human condition: technological change and urbanization, however, have served to change the nature of social conflict and, at times, to intensify its violence.*

The primary concern of this book is with social rather than individual strife. This is so in spite of the realization that everyone is caught up in a concentric system of intrapsychic and intrafamilial conflicts, as well as conflicts between members of primary and secondary groups within institutions, neighborhoods, communities, and regions. The various layers of problems are at times inseparable; however, individual and social conflict come together in the decision-making process. Many of the decisions made by individuals concerning the situations that confront them affect others to some degree. A specific resolve, rather than answering problems, usually opens the door to more contradictions that must eventually be decided upon. There are, in other words, few times when a single decision solves a problem. There are even fewer instances when an individual is able to make the most desirable resolution for everyone involved, with even partial awareness of the variety of logical alternative consequences or solutions. It is the nature of urbanism to exaggerate this ambiguity.

The omission of an extended discussion of individual strife does not preclude its consideration. It is important to consider the role of some individuals in creating ideas and mobilizing support for changing the social structure. Further, consideration of the impact of urban life on the attitudes, behavior, and values of individuals is important, especially as they rebound and have implications for the social structure.

It is recognized that the statement of the basic assumption is at odds with the work of many distinguished thinkers. For example, we obviously disagree with Gordon Allport and Abraham Maslow,[7] who viewed love, cooperation, or self-actualization as mankind's principal motivating force. Although these feelings have served as the bases of interaction of many social relationships, even these types of relations have inherent in them potential intense conflict.

We differ also from such great thinkers as Hegel and Marx,[8] although these men considered strife as the essence of human life. Both hoped that strife would eventually end. Hegel pictured society as involved in an unfolding dialectic moving toward utopia. This occurred, according to his writings, through a perfect merger of individuality and authority. Marx thought that the elimination of class distinctions would signal the end to social conflict.

Conflict, then, can be thought of as endemic to all social relations. This, however, is not reason to despair. Although alienation and frustration will always serve to set some men against others, at times it can also move people to work together and lead to innovations.

Conflict defined

The inevitability of conflict derives from mankind's innumerable and changing needs: if starvation is ended, men will fight for prestige; if one power system is destroyed, another emerges; if authority is eradicated, men will compete for precedence. There will always be a scarcity of "commodities"—whether it be money, prestige, power, love—that will continue to set man against man. Therefore, all men will experience some form of conflict during their lifetime.

Fighting for the control of some scarce resource is a most obvious type of strife. John Howard, in his recently published work *The*

Cutting Edge,[9] labeled this type of strife *substantive conflict*. He also noted three other bases of conflict: conflict over *symbolic issues*, as in the refusal to pledge allegiance to the national flag; the *conflict of ideologies*, such as racism or sexism, which have been created to justify the advantages of various groups; and *cultural conflict*, deriving from differences in life-styles and values, as in the rejection of middle-class life-styles by many American youths in the 1960s.

Regardless of the bases, conflict can be strident and violent, or subtle. More subtle forms can be found in the decision processes and activities that follow when equally desirable (or undesirable) lines of action or goals are present. By strife we refer to situations where (1) contradictory goals are sought by two or more persons; (2) where individuals (or groups) pursue the same goal by contradictory means; or (3) where two individuals or groups pursue the same goals, but only one party may win. Our definition of strife, then, includes any of the four types of conflict identified by John Howard.

Strife has differed in its manifestation, scope, intensity, and consequence over the various periods of the world's history. Stirred by the Enlightenment, the French Revolution, and industrialism, widespread violent strife has been the hallmark of the last two hundred years. Emerging social classes engaged in revolutions designed to overthrow the status quo. The spirit of nationalism spawned two world wars. Colonial revolts, independence movements, riots, and labor conflicts have seared the twentieth century. As evidence presented in chapter 3 indicates, on a personal and interpersonal level, drug addiction, delinquency, and crime, as well as familial disorganization, have risen exactly in pace with technological progress and modern urbanism.

Associating conflict and urban life

Perhaps these historical facts, in part, account for the feeling that strife in urban areas has been the handmaiden of what in Western thought is considered progress. As such, the idea of progress itself, as well as nefarious activities and "undesirable" change, has been commonly associated with the development of cities.

Romantically, almost yearningly, many members of modern societies look to the past and a farming or rural existence as a glorified life-style. Even current generations of American intellectuals rediscover Turner's frontier thesis, originally posited in 1893, if only to modify or later reject it.[10] Turner's interpretation of American life began with men who lived in cabins, sod huts, and farmhouses of the "Great West."[11] As one historian has pointed out, " . . . whether as part of the activity of the French and Spanish from New Orleans, or of the English and Americans operating from the Atlantic seaboard, the establishment of towns preceded the breaking of soil in the transmontane West."[12]

In commenting on the role of urban areas in American history, Richard Wade[13] reminded us that it was in the cities the impetus of revolt from the mother country began and spread. The ideology of the rebel cause and notions of the Enlightenment, for example, came through the cities of the Eastern seaboard, which had libraries and newspapers to receive and spread them. Arthur Schlesinger has written: "Boston's primacy as the 'Cradle of Liberty' may well have sprung from her lagging progress in relation to other ports, inciting her at any cost to remove the obstacles that Parliament was thrusting in her way."[14]

The American experience was not unique. Athens, although condoning slavery, was the birthplace of philosophy and democracy. Venice, while sending her fleet on depredations throughout the world, created the Renaissance. Although famine had spread through France's hinterlands immediately preceding the French Revolution, it required the urban men of Paris to overthrow the old regime. And it was in the sweatshops of Manchester and London—not on the North-west Frontier of India—where the colonial roots of the British Empire were laid. In short, with very few exceptions, cities have been the mainsprings of all forms of social and cultural change.

During the period of urban growth and development, then, when many individuals and groups felt rootless, discontented, and socially disorganized, others experienced unprecedented freedom and creative activity. Even as men killed each other, science blossomed, the masses achieved their highest level of living, and the arts continued to flourish.

Beginning from the assumption that conflict is inevitable in human existence, the questions examined in this book are these:

- What characteristics of urbanization or life in urban settings have contributed to the development of conflict?
- What factors in urban life have affected the intensity and manifestations of underlying strife?
- What factors in urban life have affected the nature of conflict resolution?

In an attempt to answer these questions, this book is divided into an examination of conditions related to three different forms of urban conflict: reform movements, riots, and revolutionary action. These three types of social conflict were chosen as germane, for they are uniquely urban in nature. Successful reform movements in America—abolitionism, the suffragette movement, and the spread of public education—all originated among people imbued with an urbane set of ideas. *Riots,* whether inspired by resistance to the draft, labor conflict, or ethnic tensions, have been limited primarily to urban areas. *Revolutions*—the Russian, French, and American—began in cities and were not the result of peasant, serf, or slave uprisings. Even the Chinese Revolution (which eventually drew support from the peasantry) began in cities like Shanghai and was directed by well-educated, urban men such as Mao and Chou.

Of course, conflict as it has been defined need not involve an extensive attempt at social change as in a reform movement or revolution, nor as much violence as a riot. In fact, the most common conflict-filled situations in urban areas may be described in the detailing of otherwise mundane decisions at meetings of boards of education,[15] city councils, welfare agencies,[16] and judicial bodies.[17] This is true in spite of the fact that specific decisions may be reached on the basis of compromise by individuals with different positions on the same issue, thus lending an appearance of a high degree of consensus. Yet, on a broader scale, the implementation of a given decision can serve to create new (or exacerbate old) lines of difference between people. For example, in Detroit, Michigan, federal judges ruled that the mayor could not release policemen from their jobs on the basis of seniority.[18] This procedure, which would have followed standard bureaucratic procedures, would have adversely affected the advances made by women and black people in this occupation during the latter part of the 1960s. The mayor, however, was pressured to reduce municipal services because of the severe economic recession of the 1970s. White policemen with seniority, it appeared, would be the victims of the cutback.

Tension mounted in Detroit as more than a thousand off-duty policemen picketed the courthouse. Racial polarization, which had diminished to some degree in recent years, again came to the fore. The appearance of one black policeman served as the impetus for threats, racial epithets, and the drawing of firearms.[19] Although only a relatively minor confrontation between black and white policemen occurred in this instance (placed in the context of the more general social movements of the 1960s, the economic stresses of the 1970s, and Detroit's history of racial violence),[20] it is easy to understand the inflammatory nature of one decision.

PLAN OF THE BOOK

A review of some thoughts on conflict by various social scientists and philosophers is presented in part I. In addition, the conditions of urban settings that have created some of the potential lines of divisiveness between urban peoples are explored.

Violent action usually occurs as a result of a series of recognized injustices. Yet injustice, by itself, cannot be used as an effective predictor of any social act. Years, at times extending into decades, may elapse before the legitimacy of authority is questioned. It is important, therefore, to learn the specific pattern of events through a historical perspective in order to understand a specific situation. In large part, the focus of the nine cases presented in part II of this book is aimed at this task. Each of the cases, although representative of different outcomes in terms of success or failure, extensiveness of proposed change, and degree of violence, is described by the following category of events:

1. *The setting of the social conflict* includes historical, political, and economic factors, the history of violent action, differentiation, and stratification of the various urban populations and their aspirations. The facts presented in this section of each case develop a rather static, but crucial, element in the understanding of the particular conflict situation under consideration. Aside from providing a clue as to the preconditions of social action, it is only against this background that the results of conflict in terms of long- or short-term social change can be assessed.

2. *The precipitants to action* involve the type of social control used by those in power, the role of possible third parties, and the political or economic shifts related to change in the preexisting lines of differentiation and stratification. Included in this portion of each case are the social facts that more immediately preceded the articulation of discontent, the feelings of injustice, and the questioning of authority.

3. *The action*—reform movements, a riot, or a revolution—is represented as a chronological flow of events. This portion of each case history develops the shape and form of collective behavior or social movement as it emerges from the social context. A detailed report of this phase of the social action allows understanding of the nature of the discontent from the point of view of particular participants.

4. Finally, the *results of the social conflict* are described. At times this can be done only in terms of possible alternatives, since some cases are not yet completed. On a general level, strife may eventuate in many different ways: in the defeat of one party, compromise, withdrawal, conversion, intervention by an outside group, or a transformation into another type of conflict.

Although severely limited in number, the generalized nature of answers to the questions posed about urban conflict is derived from the use of these categories of observation for each case. The interrelationship of the various categories of descriptions over the nine cases presented in this book provides the comparative base from which interpretation is made. Moreover, supportive evidence also is provided in most instances from other situations which are not presented in detailed case history form.

Werkmeister noted the following in regard to the use of idiosyncratic or unique cases and generalization in social science:

> In the social sciences more than in any other field of investigation, it is important to keep in mind that the individual event, situation, or process occurs only within a much wider context; that there exists a reciprocal relation between the context and any event included therein; that neither the context nor the event can be understood in itself, and that an adequate interpretation of either must always involve an interpretation of its functional correlation with the other. In such an interpretation, the opposition between the individual or the unique and the general or the recurrent can be overcome.[21]

The limitation of number of cases is pragmatically based on the decision to present the historical circumstances of each situation. Only through a detailed historical analysis of particular situations can the determination of the specific patterning, if any, of such conflict be made. Further, only through case history analysis can the type of conflict associated with particular urban conditions be discerned.

A METHODOLOGICAL NOTE

Curiosity and the vagaries of fortune have led us into courts, prisons, schools, and urban ghettos. We have witnessed such diverse events as the educational reform movement in New York City, the Watts riot, the attempted reforms in Mississippi, the Ulster revolt, and the Egyptian revolution. In the development of the cases pertaining to the Meiji Reformation, Cuba, and East Saint Louis, many authoritative sources were used. In large part this book is an outgrowth of experiences, direct and vicarious, that led us to question the elements common to the varieties of people and situations we have encountered.

This methodological note is appended in order to provide an understanding of the selected research processes used, as well as some of the problems encountered and represented in the development of case histories of conflict situations.

Entry

Entry into the various situations was obtained through the assumption of different research roles. At times, observation was conducted as complete participants. At other times, entry was obtained through the more traditional role of participant as observer. Both research roles have been described by Norman K. Denzin. He wrote:

> [In the instance of the complete participant] the observer is wholly concealed, his scientific intents are not made known, and he attempts to become a full-fledged member of the group under investigation.[22]

The example provided by Denzin of this type of research is that of Festinger, Riecken, and Schachter[23] as they studied a group predicting the destruction of the world.

Denzin differentiated the complete participant role from the participant as observer role in the following manner:

> . . . unlike complete participants, the participant as observer makes his presence as an investigator known and attempts to form a series of relationships with his subjects such that they serve both as respondents and informants.[24]

This researcher role is more commonly used by those conducting community or organizational studies.[25]

Although there is some similarity between the nature of the participation described by Denzin and our research role, important differences also should be noted. Conflict abounded in all of our research situations. Further, at times entry was gained through sponsorship. Hence, commitments were at times necessitated prior to entering the research setting, and records were kept surreptitiously while working either as professional advisors to the mayor in Houston, advisors to the Aswan Dam project in Egypt, or as members of the Council of Federated Organizations (COFO), which was directed toward registering blacks to vote and school desegregation in Mississippi. The problem of value commitment and the hidden recording of data opens the door to sensitive questions pertaining to the ethics of this type of social science research and objectivity. Each of these points deserves attention.

Moreover, whether entry to a research situation is made as an advisor, a member of an adversary group, or even mere observer, the researcher role is subject to many strains. For example, the researcher may be confronted with contradictory role demands. That is, personal expectations and values may conflict with the group which the researcher has chosen to study. Perhaps this problem can best be explicated with an example of the unexpected and subtle nature of the situation we encountered in Egypt.

In 1964 and 1965 the Ford Foundation financed a team of researchers (including a variety of social scientists) to investigate the potential development of the Aswan Province in Egypt.[26] The project was approached initially with many of the standard tools of social science research: a survey of the population, economic projections of the future of Aswan, interviews with highly placed individuals, and so on.

It soon became apparent from the ensuing investigation that the major industry in Aswan was the smuggling of illicit goods (liquor, cigarettes, radios) from Sudan. To move the 125,000 people who lived in Aswan to a new location in order to build the dam would have meant the death of their trade. Further, the people were not trained as farmers and could not be expected to cultivate land easily. The central government, however, wished to move the people in order to build a new city. The researchers had to make a choice: either leave the city's population to its own devices, or help transform it by edict entailing the destruction of many who would be prosecuted because smuggling was illegal. What would have been in the best public interest?

The resolution of a problem such as this is a personal one and cannot be prescribed through doctrinaire means. At best, perhaps, as Denzin has noted:

> . . . he [the participant] will achieve a sense of heightened self-awareness, an introspective attitude toward his own activities.[27]

There were many complicating factors in the Aswan Dam project too numerous to detail here. However, the frustration of the researchers is evidenced in the fact that no formal report was ever filed by any of the social scientists.

Research ethics

The problem of research ethics has not been consensually defined by social scientists. At one extreme the issue has led to the rejection of any study conducted without the explicit knowledge and consent of the subject.[28] In Mississippi much of the interviewing had to be done secretively since blacks were afraid to be seen talking with white people from the "outside"; and white people would have been hesitant to openly discuss feelings toward the black community and their plans for maintaining white supremacy to outside reporters who might have been members of the FBI. As a result, the research objectives had to remain hidden.

In Ireland, on the other hand, an attempt was made to interview various parties to the conflict. Fortunately, most Irishmen were not threatened by being interviewed by Americans. Our Irish surname allowed some advantage. Hence, our objectives could be made known.

It is our general position that any investigation, secretive or open, that does not result in damage, either physical or reputational, to the subject of research is justifiable. Data, however, must meet with the canons of objectivity set by the social sciences.

Values

Objectivity in social science has been identified with Max Weber's discussion of ethical neutrality in research. The problem of value neutrality, however, is not simply recording all facts, or complete value detachment. In some instances, as in the study of Watts, Houston, educational reform, and the women's movement, we, as Americans, have value commitments provided by the Declaration of Independence. To again cite Werkmeister:

> . . . [one] may not accept the creed (i.e., the Declaration of Independence) as our own value commitment—in which case we may encounter no race problem; but if we, as a nation, do accept it, as interpreted in recent decisions of our Supreme Court, then we have a value premise from which to evaluate without emotional bias all relevant facts of individual and group behavior. Indeed, the principle of self-consistency requires that we do make such an evaluation.[29]

The important element of "objectivity," then, would appear to be to record facts, which may or may not be in harmony with the value commitments, rather than merely recording facts without awareness of values at all.

Research techniques

Observation, interviews, and the study of documents and statistical records constitute the three basic research techniques used to develop the cases presented from our own data. There are many authoritative sources that may be used to learn specific techniques involved in these modes of data collection.[30] Nonetheless, special circumstances confront most persons conducting research in a conflict or crisis situation.

Establishing contacts and sampling population

Once an outline of major participants is drawn up, the researcher must spend some time establishing contact and rapport with persons willing to contact appropriate individuals and organizations. Needless to say, it is easier to establish useful relationships when the researcher has spent a long period of time in a place and is known by members of the community. Having lived in Egypt for more than a year, and in Houston for over three years, allowed us a greater range of persons to contact, as well as more diverse sources of data to tap. In addition to our own observations and interviews, data was available from other on-going research by economists and political scientists.

The preplanning for data collection in Ireland (where we spent approximately two weeks on each of two separate visits) and Mississippi (where a period of three months was spent) was conducted prior to visiting the research site. Although such plans, from one point of view, can be more efficient, they also may prove disadvantageous because of the tendency to adhere inflexibly to a schedule.

Interviews in Ireland were drawn from a quasi-systematic sampling of people identified as Catholic and Protestant, from lower-, middle-, and upper-class groups, and in "safe" and "no-go" areas. Whenever possible, notes were made of informal and formal gatherings of people in both legal and illegal organization settings. Similar sampling plans were drawn for data collection in Mississippi.

Recording data

The unexpected riots in Houston and Watts allowed little preplanning of interview questions or systematic sampling of individuals during the actual events. In these situations a tape recorder was carried on the researchers, which allowed the recording of spontaneous reactions and responses to questions. In such situations a technical problem of unraveling the series of responses from extraneous background noises was encountered. It was critical, just as in the recording of observation notes and responses to semistructured and unstructured interviews conducted in Ireland and Mississippi, that the researcher make immediate notes in the form of a narrative in order to preserve recall.[31]

A researcher in conflict situations encounters many problems that may or may not be directly confronted by those conducting laboratory studies or a survey. It is evident, however, from the discussion that the problems are not unique in all ways. Perhaps the major difference lies in the need for sensitivity to issues such as values, objectivity, and ethics, necessitated by conflict situations.

SUMMARY

Beginning from the premise that conflict is inherent to all social relationships, an attempt is made in this book to answer the following questions about the relationship between urban life and social conflict:

1. What characteristics of urbanization, or life in urban settings, contribute to the development of conflict?
2. What factors in urban life affect the manifestation of underlying strife? What factors affect the nature of conflict resolution?
3. Under what conditions can we expect positive (or negative) consequences to accrue from urban existence?

These questions were derived from two facts: first, urbanization has been the most prominent social fact of modern times; second, the problem of social conflict has been increased in areas of high-density populations.

Beyond these facts, we have lived through many of the situations recorded throughout the text of this book. Personal experience, however, must be tempered by the knowledge and experience of others. Thus, before examining specific case histories of strife, it is important to be acquainted with the theories and data that many men have accumulated concerning the nature of urban development and human conflict.

Issues for further discussion

1. Can conflict in human life ever be eradicated?

2. What are the major social-psychological effects of urbanization?

3. Can societies that consciously aim at the eradication of inequality such as Israeli *kibbutzim* put an end to social conflict?

4. Why have both "progress" and an increased pace of social strife been associated with the growth of cities?

5. Under what conditions can historical case histories lead to sociological generalizations?

6. If an investigator directly observes (or participates in) an urban social conflict, how can one determine the validity of his opinions?

7. If a person is directly involved in an urban conflict, is it possible for him to make "value-free" observations? If so, how?

8. What are the advantages and disadvantages of first-hand observations of urban social conflict?

FOOTNOTES

1. The specific dating of the world's earliest cities is complicated by an absence of records, conceptual problems, and scarcity of archaeological remains. For a more complete discussion of the history of cities, see Robert Braidwood and Gordon Wiley, eds., *Courses Toward Urban Life,* Viking Fund Publications in Anthropology, no. 32 (New York: 1962).
2. Figures taken from Peter Hall, *The World Cities* (New York: McGraw-Hill Book Co., 1971), table 4, and Kingsley Davis, *World Urbanization, 1950–1970* (Berkeley and Los Angeles: Institute of International Studies, University of California, 1972), vol. 2, table F.
3. Davis, *World Urbanization* (1969), vol. 1, table C.
4. Population Reference Bureau, Inc., *World Population Data Sheet* (1972), and Davis, *World Urbanization,* 2:187.
5. Noel P. Gist and Sylvia F. Fava, *Urban Society* (New York: Thomas Y. Crowell Co., 1974), table 4.2, p. 111.
6. Ibid., pp. 110–111.
7. See, for example, Gordon Allport, *Becoming* (New Haven, Conn.: Yale University Press, 1955), and Abraham Maslow, *Motivation and Personality* (New York: Harper & Row, Publishers, 1954).
8. Friedrich Hegel, *The Philosophy of History,* trans. J. Sibee (New York: Dover Publications, 1956), and Karl Marx, *Das Kapital* (Chicago: C. H. Kerr and Co., 1932).
9. John Howard, *The Cutting Edge* (Philadelphia: J. B. Lippincott Co., 1974).
10. See Richard C. Wade, "The City in History—Some American Perspectives," in *Urban Life and Form,* ed. Werner L. Hirsch (New York: Holt, Rinehart and Winston, 1963).
11. F. J. Turner, "The Significance of the Frontier in American History," in "The Turner Thesis Concerning the Role of the Frontier in American History," *Problems in American Civilization,* ed. G. R. Taylor, rev. ed. (Boston: D. C. Heath & Co., 1956).
12. Richard C. Wade, *The Urban Frontier: The Rise of Cities in the West, 1790–1830* (Cambridge, Mass.: Harvard University Press, 1959), p. 1.
13. Wade, "The City in History," in Hirsch, *Urban Life and Form.*
14. Arthur M. Schlesinger, *Prelude to Independence: The Newspaper War on Britain, 1764–1776* (New York: Alfred A. Knopf, 1958), p. 6.
15. See, for example, Marilyn Gittell, *Participants and Participation* (New York: Praeger Publishers, 1968), and David Rogers, *110 Livingston Street* (New York: Random House, 1968).
16. See, for example, Richard A. Cloward and Frances Fox Piven, *The Politics of Turmoil* (New York: Pantheon Books, 1974).
17. See, for example, Bob Smith, *They Closed Their Schools: Prince Edward County, Va., 1951–1964* (Chapel Hill, N.C.: University of North Carolina Press, 1965).

18. William K. Stevens, "The Recession Increases Racial Tension in Detroit," *New York Times*, 15 May 1975, p. 27.
19. Ibid.
20. See Alfred M. Lee and Norman Humphrey, *Race Riot* (New York: The Dryden Press, 1943), pp. 37–38, and Hubert G. Locke, *The Detroit Riot of 1967* (Detroit: Wayne State University Press, 1969).
21. W. H. Werkmeister, "Theory Construction and the Problem of Objectivity," in *Symposium on Sociological Theory*, ed. Llewllyn Gross (New York: Harper & Row Publishers, 1959), p. 491; also see Rollo Handy, *Methodology of the Behavioral Sciences* (Springfield, Ill.: Charles C Thomas, Publisher, 1964), pp. 89–91.
22. Raymond L. Gold, "Roles in Sociological Field Observations," in Norman K. Denzin, ed., *Sociological Methods*, (Chicago: Aldine Publishing Co., 1970), pp. 373–374.
23. Leon Festinger et al., *When Prophesy Fails* (Minneapolis: University of Minnesota Press, 1956).
24. Gold, "Roles in Sociological Field Observations," in Denzin, *Sociological Methods*, p. 376.
25. For example, see Arthur Vidich and Joseph Bensman, *Small Town and Mass Society* (Princeton, N.J.: Princeton University Press, 1958); also see Melville Dalton, "Preconceptions and Methods in 'Men who Manage,'" in *Sociologists at Work*, ed. Philip E. Hammond (New York: Basic Books, Inc., Publishers, 1964).
26. This project was reported on by Philip Dorn, "Stalemate in Egypt," *Peace News* (London), 9 July 1965.
27. Gold, "Roles in Sociological Field Observations," in Denzin, *Sociological Methods*, p. 376.
28. Ibid., pt. 8.
29. Werkmeister, "Theory Construction," in Gross, *Symposium on Sociological Theory*, p. 505.
30. See Claire Seltiz, Maria Jahoda, Morton Deutsch, and Stuart Cook, *Research Methods in Social Relations* (New York: Holt, Rinehart and Winston, 1964).
31. Ibid., especially pp. 432–449.

SUGGESTED READINGS

For a theoretical treatment of the many consequences of conflict see Lewis Coser, *The Functions of Social Conflict* (Glencoe, Ill.: The Free Press, 1956).

Edward Gibbon, *The Decline and Fall of the Roman Empire* (New York: The Modern Library, 1932) presents the best historical account of the collapse of a major urban civilization.

Karl Marx, *Das Kapital* (Chicago: C. H. Kerr and Co., 1932) offers a classic theory concerning the impact of industrialization and its effect upon social conflict.

Contemporary novelists have portrayed the life of city dwellers in various ways, ranging from John Marquand and Louis Auchincloss's descriptions of urban upper classes to portrayals of urban lower class frustrations, such as Claude Brown's *Manchild in the Promised Land* (New York: Macmillan Publishing Co., 1965).

For a cross-cultural view of urbanization, the reader is directed to the following works: William J. and Judith Hanna, *Urban Dynamics in Black Africa* (Chicago: Aldine-Atherton Press, 1971); Nirmal Kumar, "Calcutta: A Premature Metropolis," *Scientific American* 213 (Sept. 1965): 91–142; William McCord, John Howard, Edwin Harwood, and Bernard Friedberg, *Life Styles in the Black Ghetto* (New York: W. W. Norton & Co., 1969). Leroy Stone, *Urban Development in Canada* (Ottowa: Dominion Bureau of Statistics, 1972); Roy Turner, ed., *India's Urban Future* (Berkeley and Los Angeles: University of California Press, 1962).

chapter 2

Theories of urban development

> The beginning of that which is distinctively modern in our civilization is best signalized by the growth of great cities. Nowhere has man been further removed from organic nature . . .
>
> *Louis Wirth*

New York is a metropolis of huge skyscrapers honeycombed by deafening subways. Hot dog vendors, pawnshops, and boutiques line the streets, and bums fill the Bowery, while on the East Side wealthy middle-aged ladies treat their dogs to the only three-star canine restaurant in the world. It is a city containing more Jews than Israel, more Italians than Rome, and more Irish than Dublin. In New York City a major thoroughfare caves in and people ignore it, a murder is committed and witnesses turn their backs, more than 268,000 students attend public colleges, and a large proportion of minority group members are jobless.[1]

Paris is all that is civilized: the Louvre, Notre-Dame, the Ile de la Cité, the Bois de Boulogne. It is also the city of the "red circle," where Renault workers starve and Sorbonne students tear the paving blocks from the street; the city of Hemingway, Collette, fashion shows . . . and the City of the Commune, of Napoleon's coup, of the decapitation of the Bourbon kings. It is the filth of the sewers (which any tourist may investigate on a guided tour) and the floating of fly boats on the Seine. It is the center of government and the capital of French murders.

In Calcutta, a metropolis of more than nine million people, hundreds of thousands of people sleep on the street every night, and 98 percent of the children under age four are undernourished. A fully employed man can earn as little as fifty cents a week, while thousands of cows, regarded as sacred, wander the streets unharmed and fed. When the cows grow old, they retire to "old-age homes"; no such facilities are provided for humans.[2]

Every city has a unique set of adjectives that best describe its pace, people, and physical characteristics. Yet, sociologists have long sought to determine some regularities in the more general urban form, its growth and development, and life in urban settings. The focus has been on the interaction of geophysical environment and the people of the city. However, after almost fifty years of research, few hard and fast generalizations can be relayed.

STAGES IN THE DEVELOPMENT OF CITIES

At a minimum, a review of the literature suggests that at least five stages of urbanization can be identified. Of course, it hardly needs reiteration that these stages are not inevitable or unilinear. Thriving villages strategically located on a river passage or as ports may stagnate into minor commercial outlets. Almost mysteriously, on the other hand, a village that has no natural advantages, such as Dallas, Texas, may expand into a major urban center.

The rural period

During the rural period, isolated agricultural settlements were established and households remained relatively self-sufficient. There was usually little specialization of labor, and typically, the folk society was preliterate. The primary preoccupation concerned gathering food for subsistence. Contacts with other human beings were limited to barter transactions, the purchase of vital material for the maintenance of the settlement, and occasional visitors. Social relations were confined largely to the family and to any accessible rural settlements near by. This was a period of some personal freedom, since neighbors could not always know what really went on within the family manors some distance away, and a period of privacy, since each family could keep "skeletons" well hidden. Necessarily, however, it was also a period of cooperation. In the event of attack, the rural settlements banded together in self-defense.

The village

Perhaps because of a shortage of land or other needs, isolated rural settlements often joined together to form villages. As in India, the village merged because land ownership patterns allocated each peasant scattered pieces of land (none big enough to hold a house). In other cases, such as medieval Europe, walled villages served as protection from marauding bands. Thus, village life exhibited a higher degree of specialization than a strictly rural settlement. Usually, the village contained a full-time priest, a scribe or lawyer, some civil servants, and merchants. Anonymity in a village was virtually unknown. Everyone's business and activities were known to others, and for many village residents it was a stifling environment lacking freedom, excitement, and diversity. For other village residents, however, it provided security, comfort in affliction, and a sense of continuing tradition. Whatever the advantages of village life, it remains a common pattern throughout the world for the young to flee its confines in order to seek their fortunes in the city. And the youth in America and Europe are replaced by a handful of literati or the very rich who bought a country mansion hoping for a return to the peaceful bliss of village life.

The preindustrial city

Gideon Sjoberg, in his now classic survey of cities throughout the ancient world, produced a portrait of large urban centers that sprang up from Mesopotamia to China long before the age of industrialism. These cities emerged as a food surplus developed, as well as a complex social structure, which allowed the distribution of goods on a wide basis. As Sjoberg contended:

> The city and civilization are inseparable: with the city's rise and spread, man at last emerged from the primitive state. . . . In turn, the city enabled him to construct an ever more complex and, we would like to believe, more satisfying way of life. Some scholars regard the city as second only to agriculture among the significant inventions in human history.[3]

These early urban centers, although distinctive, resembled our own modern cities in many ways. They were densely populated, heterogeneous units of people grouped around the palaces of the urban elite, and developed around 1200 B.C. with the introduction of iron and increases in agricultural production.

In their social class structure, preindustrial cities were usually feudal. The bottom echelons of the hierarchy were grievously poor and had little chance of advancing their position in the society. In economic structure, merchants proliferated throughout these ancient cities and specialized in the sale of goods. Weights and measures were not standardized, and haggling over the price of an item was standard procedure. In general, merchants were held in low esteem by the feudal aristocracies who ruled the cities. As organizers of economic life, guilds took preeminence in manufacturing, trade, services, and even robbery. A middle class then emerged, tied neither to the land nor strongly to the feudal nobility.

Politically, a small, privileged upper echelon ruled all realms of life, using workers organized in a bureaucratic structure. However, the bureaucrat was commonly a part-time worker whose appointment did not hold tenure. Individuals then could be replaced at the caprice of the feudal ruler.

Thus, in economic base, family structure, and bureaucratic form, these preindustrial cities differed substantially from the industrial urban complexes with which most of us are familiar.

While Sjoberg dealt primarily with ancient cities, it should be remembered that large urban conglomerations still exist, in essence, resembling the preindustrial city of earlier times. An African city such as Ibadan, many Indian cities, and even some Latin American urban centers have a veneer of industrialization, but basically conform to the model Sjoberg has outlined.

The industrial city

Many urban complexes today were born of industrialization, and their life centers on factories and the economic sphere. Birmingham, Belfast, Manchester, Pittsburgh, and the "Red Belt" around Paris are exemplars of such cities. These cities of necessity produced the multitude of factory workers who absorbed the interest and concern of Marx.

The metropolis: a postindustrial city

In the middle of the twentieth century, still a new form of urbanization has appeared —the metropolis. Economically, these great urban centers—Tokyo, New York, London, Paris, Berlin—were not predominantly industrial in character. In population density, heterogeneity, and dependence upon highly advanced technology, they also were unlike the village.

Metropolitan areas appear to exhibit at at least four basic characteristics: (1) they produce services (political, financial, literary, cultural) for vast numbers of people; (2) they are characterized by the city's assumption of a variety of economic activities—such as welfare, mass transit, hospitalization, education—which were formerly part of the private domain; (3) they require a large increase in the forces of social control (regular police, subway police, private police, housing authority police); and (4) spatially, the metropolitan area spreads over such vast areas that distinctions between urban and suburban life become almost meaningless. Los Angeles, of course, is a prime example of urban sprawl, but it, in turn, has become part of a vast complex extending southward to San Diego and northward to San Francisco. Similarly, the Eastern complex of Boston, New York, Philadelphia, Baltimore, and Washington spilled down the coast uninterrupted except for artificial boundaries. The Netherlands has become one great urban concentration. Belgium, between Louvain, Brussels, Ghent, and Bruges, exhibits the same characteristic. Naturally, "bedroom" suburbs persist on the periphery of these areas, but they function primarily as places of presumed rest and relaxation for a harried middle class who commonly work in the center of urban complexes.

DEFINITION: THE CITY

Given the nature and diversity of cities, their study and the examination of urbanism as a social rather than physical phenomenon has been somewhat complicated by the lack of an agreed upon definition for even the most basic terms. Ralph Thomlinson, for example, noted the use of fifteen different, if at times overlapping, criteria used by researchers to identify a city.[4] In abbreviated form, the definitions discussed by Thomlinson include an emphasis of the physical impression of a place, that is we recognize a city by its exterior aspects, or by the fact that things happen there, as in Chicago's

Loop, New York's Times Square, or London's Trifalgar Square. Cities also have been identified through the use of absolute population figures or population density usually set by a legislative body. The institutional patterns also have been used as criteria. For example, the number of industrial workers, the commercial character, government or religious functions, and the dependence on outside agricultural labor for subsistence may be used as the identifying marks of a city. A city also has been defined in terms of its historical significance (i.e., the title, "city," having been conferred insofar as its role in the past is concerned), in the attitudes and feelings of the people, and the diversity in life-styles. Of course, the city may be undefined explicitly except in its relationship to its environment (e.g., nation or culture) including a consideration of the centrality of transportation and commuting activities.

One could, no doubt, posit a legitimate argument for each definition used by social scientists in identifying a city. Agreement can be reached, however, on certain common elements that make up the urban scene. A city normally provides centralized commercial activities: transportation facilities which encourage the flow of materials and people; a relatively heterogeneous population involved in economic activities characterized by specialization; a pervasive exposure to the mass media; rule by a relatively impersonal, bureaucratic hierarchy; and the use of force by specific official groups. These elements then have been accepted as defining the urban setting in this book.

The definition we have accepted allows the exploration of the unique, as well as common, characteristics of urban settings. It is, for example, clear that the people of any large city—New York, Paris, Calcutta, or Moscow—share many common experiences. They all experience economic specialization, technological diversity, exposure to many different life-styles, the diverse influences of newspapers and radios, and the impersonality of bureaucratic rule. Yet, the residents of the various cities also have created unique life-styles within their urban environment. The life-styles vary within any given city, from the retreatism of New York's Hasidic Jews, who intentionally sought to isolate themselves; to the establishment of Bohemian enclaves, such as London's Soho, which allowed the expression of deviant, even illegal, life-styles; to the creation of associations such as "The Sons of Italy," based on tribal, ethnic, or religious loyalties that provided aid, protection, and political expression to their adherents.

STUDYING THE CITY AND LIFE THEREIN

The first systematic study of city life can be dated to the thirteenth century in the writings of the Arabic philosopher-sociologist Ibn Khaldun.[5] The immediate predecessor to the American study of urbanism, however, can be found in the writings of many German social philosophers of the nineteenth century. Formal recognition of the study of cities by American sociologists awaited the actual growth and development of urban areas in the United States as rapid industrialization and massive immigration took place. It was not until 1925, then, that the American Sociological Society gave urban sociology an independent status as a special area of study. Sociologists at the University of Chicago were among the first social scientists to rise to the challenge.

Both the American and the German interest in urban areas stemmed from a fear that the growth of cities led to intense social disorganization. German thinkers first expressed this concern.

The German School

Among the most influential German social analysts were Ferdinand Toënnies (1855–1936), Max Weber (1864–1930), and Georg Simmel (1858–1918).

Toënnies most famous work, *Gemeinschaft und Gesellschaft*,[6] spelled out the characteristics of social relationships in rural and urban settings. Gemeinschaft, associated with rural life in Toënnies view, was dominated by fellowship, kinship, or neighborliness and controlled through folkways, mores, and religion. Gesellschaft, on the other hand, was dominated by exchange and rational consideration and characterized the arbitrary will of the state and the activities of businessmen, scientists, and military officers. Gemeinschaft, Toënnies believed, was slowly giving way to the urban decisions of anonymous groups; face-to-face primary communities were declining. The essential mechanism for change in urban areas was the growth of impersonal systems of exchange of goods and services. With the rise of urban systems, according to Toënnies, law would replace custom and compulsion would become increasingly necessary.

Toënnies's main influence on the thought and work of later social scientists probably came through the work of French sociologist Emile Durkheim. Durkheim's familiarity with the work by Toënnies, Comte, Spencer, Wundt, and others enabled him to ask precise questions about the problems of preserving and transforming society.

Societal integration (solidarity) was maintained mechanically in primitive society, Durkheim wrote.[7] People were united by friendliness and kinship as they were relatively undifferentiated. Laws, in this stage of development, were repressive and served mainly to satisfy an outraged collective sentiment. As society attained greater complexity, on the other hand, a new motive arose in the establishment of law. Restitution, rather than repressive sanction, became important. The social system in the more differentiated state must be restored, after all, to a workable state. Laws then, for Durkheim, represented the most important index of solidarity, which, in turn, for him was the most important social fact.

Durkheim's monumental contribution was, no doubt, also influenced by his personal witnessing of the defeat of France in 1870, the Paris Commune, and the subsequent disintegration of French society. Not unexpectedly, he developed a theory that stressed man's need for collective representations; that is, unquestioned, if at times mythical, symbols as a means of holding society together. As a French propagandist during the First World War, he personally attempted to create the myths that would sustain France in its moment of peril.

Writing at the same time (and, ironically, grinding out propaganda for the Kaiser), German social analysts Max Weber and Georg Simmel[8] responded to their own insights that theories of urban life and urban growth and development should be included in the repertoire of any thoughtful social observer. Each, however, based on his unique philosophical position,[9] focused on different dimensions for such study.

Simmel found the proper sociological analysis of the city in the mentality (ideas, sentiments, and attitudes) of the urbanite. Because of the nature of institutions (i.e., the money economy) and the more general intensified milieu of the city, Simmel argued that urban man has been dominated by intellectuality, calculativeness, and punctuality. Further, Simmel believed that the attitude of the urbanite toward others has been characterized by formality and reserve, if not aversion. This, in turn, ensures a kind of autonomy not possible under other conditions. Thus, according to Martindale in his excellent preface to Max Weber's *The City*, ". . . Simmel thought that the great creativity of ancient Athens was due to its retention of some of the aspects of a small town in combustible tension with the stimulating intellectuality of the metropolis."[10] Hence, out of strife could be born positive contributions to society.

Max Weber, familiar with Simmel's writings and recognizing their import, explored beyond the somewhat restrictive area of study outlined by the latter. Focusing on historical and cultural variations, Weber argued that urban communities could not, and did not, emerge in all places. Moreover, reviewing the concept of the city in terms of evidence drawn from history, Weber was able to present the urban community not as unstructured congeries of activity, but as a patterning of different facets of human life, including person-to-person interaction, organizations, and institutions.[11] He was, therefore, enabled to include consideration of both the heterogeneous mentalities of different urban residents, as did Simmel, and the broader patterns of organization in the city that provided the more stable, recurrent activities for its residents. Weber focused not on a single institution, but on the order of institutions, as diverse as the relationship of the religious to the economic institution. Thus Weber's formulation of the city took into account many of the partial portraits of the city (e.g., those focusing on the economic or the political institution) current in the work of his day and continuing into the present.[12]

Influenced by Weber and Simmel, sociologists at the University of Chicago launched a series of empirical studies of the American city in the 1920s.

The Chicago School

Drawing together articles and ideas of their time in a volume entitled *The City*,[13] Robert Park, Ernest Burgess, and Roderick McKenzie laid the cornerstone of systematic theorizing about the city by American sociologists. The specific study, known as ecology, was soon associated with many outstanding sociologists at the University of Chicago.

The term *ecology* was drawn from the biological study of the relationship between plant and animal forms as they relate to each other and their environment. Ecological laws or processes were spelled out by McKenzie.[14] The processes (competition, concentration, centralization, segregation, invasion, and succession) were thought to account for the creation of the physical structure of the city.[15]

It was Robert Park's assumption that cities, as a natural phenomenon, should be studied in terms other than those used for any other social group. In the city traditional social and economic institutions broke down, to be substituted by a new organization based on occupational and vocational interests. Park realized that subsections of the city, or urban neighborhoods, because of isolation were able to maintain some unique characteristics. Much of the significance of the type of relationship between residents of a neighborhood and their more unique qualities, however, were thought to be lost when compared to life in other times and places. For Park, the economic process shaped the cultural superstructure of urban society, which was seen as all pervasive.

Burgess,[16] as his main contribution to the growing study of urban centers, focused on the descriptions of hypothesized physical expansion and differentiation of the city in space. The pattern of expansion, he thought, formed a series of concentric rings: radiating from a central business district, the first ring represents an area of transition being invaded by light manufacturing and business. In the next ring could be found the residences of workmen, ringed, in turn, by more desirable apartment buildings, single family dwellings, and the suburbs. The areas were hypothesized to differ in terms of degree of social and personal disorganization and thought to decrease as they radiated from the central business district. Preliminary to the adoption of new attitudes and behaviors appropriate to urban life, Burgess argued, a person discarded habitual modes of thinking and values. Personal conflict and social disorganization in the center of the city then were associated, since that was where new migrants initially live.

Using the basic ideas presented by Park, Burgess, and McKenzie, numerous projects destined to become classics in sociology were undertaken. Among the studies were Nels Anderson, *The Slum: An Area of Deteriora-*

tion in the Growth of the City and *The Hobo;* Harvey W. Zorbaugh, *The Gold Coast and the Slum;* Walter C. Reckless, *The Natural History of Vice Areas in Chicago;* R. S. Cavan, *Suicide;* and R. M. Thrasher, *The Gang.*

Any discussion of the ideas and work emerging from the University of Chicago is hardly complete without mention of Louis Wirth, possibly one of the most brilliant scholars of the Chicago School.

As Albert Reiss, Jr., suggests in his prefatory statement to Wirth's collected works,[17] the latter's interest in urban sociology reflected both a metasociological as well as an ethical position. That is, Wirth's basic concern was that sociologists should have an active interest and involvement in planning and influencing social life. "Urbanism as a Way of Life,"[18] for example, now a classic sociological framework for the study of urban life, was written when Louis Wirth was a consultant to the Committee on Urbanism of the (Roosevelt) National Resources Planning Board. In this article Wirth argues that the impact of the urban community was the key determinant of social organization and individual behavior for modern man. The urban community itself was characterized by huge size, great density, and heterogeneity. Like Simmel, Wirth felt that the nature of cities was typified by secularization, secondary associates, increased segmentation of roles, and poorly defined norms. Wirth also felt that because of the heterogeneity of population and the predominance of secondary rather than primary relationships, mass communication assumed an import in the lives of people in an urban society. We will, in the next chapter, review Wirth's ideas in this regard.

Wirth in reality was not so naive as to believe that urban structure affected all groups or individuals in the same way. In his own study of the Jewish ghetto,[19] for example, much attention was devoted to the study of the desirability of interaction between Jews and gentiles. On the one hand, he demonstrated that the development of a ghetto reflected a voluntary segregation of the Jewish population as a mode of defense against the encroachment of the gentile style of life. On the other hand, the segregation was shown to be forced by the politically dominant population. In this study, then, Wirth did not emphasize biotic factors as such. Inadvertently he provided a rejoinder to those who criticized the ecological school for their reification of the biological model, and the use of it as the sole explanation of the ecological structure of urban areas.[20]

Simplifying the many scholarly works from the Chicago School, it is evident that the focus of theorizing was "the city." This approach is in contrast to the work of Walter Firey who focused on cultural values and their relationship to ecological organization; William F. Ogburn, Amos Hawley, and others who focused on technology and industrialization; or William Form and Barrington Moore who used power as the central variable.[21] Power, in these studies, was viewed in terms of the organization and activities of special interest groups, or the role of decisions made at the national or regional level, in the ecological structure of the city. The use of the city as a focus has the disadvantage of not allowing for the consideration of historical-cultural differences as they relate to urban phenomenon. As our own work progresses, explication of such differences may well support the contention that the urban phenomenon is a dependent, as well as an independent, variable. Therefore, cities are different, and different consequences can be expected for the lives of the residents.

Rather than explore the geophysical aspect of the urban phenomenon, our concern will focus on the impact of urbanism on the lives of people. We are, of course, not alone in such an interest. Wirth, following the lead of Durkheim and Simmel, carefully outlined his conception of the social impact of urbanism. Unlike Wirth, however, we would speculate that urbanism as an attitude can pervade areas outside the boundaries of an officially defined city. Moreover, the specific interest of this book has been defined in the emergence of conflicts rather than consensus along with the recognition that conflict may result from a lack of consensus. Alternatively, conflict also can lead to consensus. The specific linkage of these terms can only be explored through the case histories presented in part II of this volume.

As a first step in understanding the impact of urbanism as a way of life one must examine some of the empirical research on urban man which was partially inspired by Wirth and the Chicago School.

URBANISM: AN ATTITUDE

"The city is the teacher of man," Plutarch once commented. And indeed no one who passes through the cities of today could deny this observation. In New York the antiseptic affluence of Park Avenue mixes with the garbage-strewn streets of Harlem. In Cairo, flowing galbiyas mingle with Western clothes, camels compete with buses, and hundreds of thousands of students flock to the universities. In New Delhi, jets fly overhead while untouchables sleep in the streets and snakecharmers practice their art in front of air-conditioned hotels. In Djakarta, gourmets dine on the cuisine of the Hotel Indonesia, bicycles block the streets, and military trucks patrol—while a few miles away religious instructors teach children the ancient method of reciting the Koran in classical Arabic.

The cities and all of their accompanying appurtenances—most importantly their factories and their ubiquitous televisions, newspapers, and radios—teach significant lessons. Today one might expand Plutarch's observation by noting that technology, machines in all their manifestations from a tiny transitor radio to a giant coke oven, is a portent teacher. Yet what is learned? And what is the result of such lessons? Despair or hope? Frustration or a belief in progress? Tolerance or hatred? Acceptance of the present order or revolution? Are people freer than in the past or mere automatons?

Contemporary sociologists have extended the study of the city beyond that of the traditional studies of the old Chicago School and have launched empirical investigations in a variety of countries concerning the effects of urbanization upon modern man. Most importantly, Alex Inkeles and his collaborators have given the most thoughtful consideration to the effects of modernization. Inkeles believes that certain new forces intricately involved with urbanization such as an increased level of education, exposure to the mass media, industrialization, and politicization contribute to the creation of a modern man. The term *urban man* might well substitute for Inkeles's modern man.[22]

Inkeles does not believe that the characteristics of urban man he posits are limited to particular historical periods. He sees the same configuration exhibited in Ancient Greece and Elizabethan England. We can hardly call people of these periods modern. Yet, even in these periods, cities flourished; and as most theorists agree, urbanization created a new man, imbued with attitudes and conflicts quite different from those of the traditional peasantry.

For the great majority of the world, the folk era and peasant societies remain memories of the past. In many countries, urbanization stripped the countryside of the young, the better educated, the highly skilled artisans, and those with the most ambition. Most important, as Inkeles comments, "Indeed, in the end, the idea of development requires the very transformation of the nature of man—a transformation that is both a means to the end of yet greater growth, and at the same time of the great end itself of the developmental process."[23]

Specifically, Inkeles conceives modern, urbanized men in somewhat different and more optimistic terms than the founders of either the German or Chicago schools. Whereas the latter drew a picture of urban man as disorganized, anomic, or indifferent, Inkeles's urban man is open to innovation, to change, to risk-taking, and to new ideas. Inkeles, like Daniel Lerner,[24] believes that modern, urbanized men are more capable of forming opinions about complex issues that extend beyond the confines of their immediate environment than are rural dwellers or village peasants. They are more empathic because of their experience of different life-styles. Related to this point, Inkeles contends that modern man is more "democratic," in the sense that he acknowledges and tolerates differences of opinion. Urban man, then, recognizes the dignity of others; consequently, he has changed his view about the traditional role of women and children.

Modern man, according to Inkeles, developed a sophisticated sense of time oriented to the present and future rather than the past. He learned punctuality in order to adjust to the industrial process. Partially as a consequence of this adherence to punctuality, modern man learned to plan, visualize, and organize his future. Inkeles argues that modern man abandoned fatalism, characteristic of peasant society, and assumed instead that events in this world are indeed calculable and open to human control. The modern man evinced great faith in science and technology as means of controlling nature and held to the view that all men should be rewarded for their contribution to society, rather than for the particular status to which they were born.

Case: urbanism—a transportable attitude?

For the most part, American attitudes and values regarding minority groups are interpreted by the federal judiciary and promoted through public education and the mass media. The wave of civil rights workers from urban centers in the North, who flooded into Mississippi in 1964, and the internal supporters of the movement within the state, provide an example of attempts to bring one small portion of rural America into line with the larger part of the nation. This attitude is clearly expressed in the titles of such articles as "If We Can Crack Mississippi . . . ," which appeared in the *Saturday Evening Post*,[25] and "Mississippi's Press vs. Invaders,"[26] an article in the *San Francisco Chronicle.*

The setting: separate but equal?

The white, dominant population in Mississippi before 1964 justified its treatment of the black population in terms of four central beliefs: (1) the black is innately inferior[27]; (2) a Communist plot menaces the white system[28]; (3) God sanctions white supremacy[29]; and (4) the Mississippian's personal ethics come before man-made law.[30] Black people, therefore, were the victims of white society long after their emancipation and protection under the Constitution of the United States. The inequities extended to all spheres of living.

Justice was a mockery for black people in Mississippi. The Mississippi Advisory Committee to the U.S. Commission on Civil Rights has summarized the administration of justice in Mississippi:

> From the moment a Negro adult is hailed as "boy" or "girl" by a police officer, through his arrest detention, trial . . . and eventual imprisonment, he is treated with a pernicious difference. This difference is incompatible with Christian ideals about the dignity of man and with principles of Anglo-Saxon law.[31]

Education: Blacks had achieved a much lower educational attainment than the white Mississippi population. In 1960 all blacks over the age of twenty-five had completed an average of only six years of school, or five years less than whites. While 168,000 whites had graduated from high school, only 16,000 blacks had been awarded a secondary diploma.[32]

Even after the 1954 Supreme Court decision that children of all races should have an opportunity for equal education, the white power elite in Mississippi dedicated itself to the maintenance of the system they had established. Former Governor James K.

Vardaman declared: "Education would be a positive unkindness to [the black man]. It simply renders him unfit for the work he will be forced to perform. After all, [the black man] is a lazy, lying, lustful animal which no amount of training can transform into a tolerable citizen."[33]

Housing: The 1960 census categorized 66 percent of all Negro housing in Mississippi as "dilapidated or deteriorating." In rural areas (where the majority of blacks subsisted) 71 percent of the homes had neither toilets nor bathing facilities.

Health: Proportionately, about one-third more blacks died each year than whites. In Mississippi, the chances of a black baby's death within the first year of life were twice that of a white child. The black death rate in 1960 was not as low as the 1913 white death rate.[34]

Economics: More than 7 percent of the black population could not find employment in 1960, an unemployment rate twice that for whites. Thus, black families earned an average annual income of $606, or 71 percent less than that of white families. In rural regions the average black family earned $474. During the 1950s, the income of rural blacks actually decreased as white earnings increased.[35]

Knowledge of these conditions and the impetus of various civil rights movements elsewhere led to the attempted imposition of the values of the broader society on Mississippi. In 1964 the major civil rights organizations, composed of urbanized, northern people, joined together to attack Mississippi's bastions of segregation. The umbrella federation, the Council of Federated Organizations (COFO), issued the following statement:

> . . . after three years of struggling, accompanied by extreme harassment in Mississippi, COFO has decided that only by confrontation within the state of civil rights movement and the forces maintaining the status quo can significant change in the social and legal structure be effected.[36]

The first wave of several hundred civil rights workers entered Mississippi in June of 1964, and the activity which followed throughout the "invasion" of Mississippi has been chronicled in numerous places.

In assessing the record of the civil rights workers in Mississippi, William McCord noted that: "while the record checkered, Mississippi would never be the same again."[37] Indeed some progress was made.

Justice: The FBI arrest of a few white persons and the nation's surveillance led to some optimism regarding law enforcement. Bob Moses, Director of COFO, is quoted by William Cook, *Newsweek* reporter, as saying: "The whole pattern of law enforcement of the past hundred years has been reversed."[38]

Education: A few black children were enrolled in formerly white elementary schools. Schools initiated by COFO were running without incident, and subjects such as political science and black history were included in their curriculum.

Services: In larger towns many of the libraries and parks were opened to use by black people. Twenty-three community centers, located largely in rural areas, had been established to serve needs such as information on childcare, nutrition, housing maintenance, and federal benefits programs.

Politics: Between 1962 and 1964, a total of 11,250 blacks were registered to vote. Approximately 2,150 of these were enrolled in the summer of 1964.[39] This represents a 75 percent increase, although only 6.7 percent of the black population was eligible to vote.

Although the Mississippi reformers achieved few tangible results immediately after their massive effort, the martyrdom of some of them, national publicity, and federal action eventually brought about a transformation of the state. By 1976, the state had dropped many of its more archaic legal and voting practices. Perhaps most importantly, blacks had been integrated into the ruling Democratic party and were allowed to participate in such important events as the private caucuses which choose presidential nominees. Whites still ruled the state in 1976, but new Mississippi governors felt obliged to appoint blacks such as Charles Evers as members of their honorary brigade of "Colonels."

Appropriately, someone had chalked on the wall of the COFO headquarters in 1964, "Lord, we ain't what we wanna be—we ain't what we gonna be—but thank God, we ain't what we was." The civil rights workers had indeed inspired some optimism during that summer of 1964.[40]

URBANISM: IMPACT OF THE CITY ON MIGRANTS IN DEVELOPING NATIONS

Among those deeply concerned about the fate of developing nations, two points of view have developed. Economists and sociologists such as Kingsley Davis, Daniel Lerner, and Robert Heilbroner[41] argued that urban growth is inevitable and a requisite for industrial development. Those taking this position commonly cite the necessity of grouping industry and labor in areas that already have transit facilities, electricity, and port outlets.

The second point of view is that urban growth necessarily need not precede industrialization. Indeed, rapid population shifts from small towns and rural areas into existing cities could hinder industrial development. Arthur Lewis, for example, the distinguished economist, while admitting that new industries tend to locate in areas where industries already are located, has argued that these same cities may become crowded beyond the capacity of the municipality to supply jobs, housing, transportation, or schools.[42]

Without dwelling on the merits and demerits of these arguments, it is a fact that cities in many areas of the world today are strained, festering with people who were lured by the promise of a new and better life than that which they experienced in their old home because of the opportunities provided by growing industrialism. In many cases, however, their lives have been worse than that of immigrant labor actively solicited by American capitalists in past generations.[43] The major difference possibly has been in the opportunities that have been at least partially fulfilled for the children of older migrants during times of industrial growth, and in the lack of readily visible, more successful "others" at that time, with whom comparisons could be made.

The plight of new migrants to cities of underdeveloped nations, however, is in many respects comparable to that of many new migrants from rural settings to the cities of developed nations. When they arrive in Cairo, Accra, or Mexico City, new migrants are faced with a series of shocks. The first shock is the tangible demonstration that they are neither wanted nor needed. Migrants do not always have appropriate skills, even if there were enough jobs. Paradoxically, unemployment in cities frequently exceeds even that of the most stagnant villages. In Madras, India, only 25 percent of employable people actually find work.[44] The rest scrape along at odd jobs selling shoestrings, begging, or running errands. While the unemployment rate in Indian villages remains unimaginably high to most Westerners, it sometimes does not reach the same level of deprivation as in Indian cities.

Typically, too, newly transported urbanites find the quality of housing is less than in the rural area; that is, if they manage to find any at all. In India, approximately 48 percent of all rural families crowd into one room, but in urban areas 53 percent of the families live in a single chamber. An unlucky number of Indian urbanites find no place to sleep but the streets.[45]

Further, the new urban dweller will probably suffer tremendous health deprivation. In many Indian cities, for example, the average subsistence budget is much above the real wages of the typical urbanite.[46] In addition, the Indian peasant farmers often are paid with a share of the crop.[47] Consequently, despite a greater number of hospitals and health facilities, maintaining a level of subsistence in cities is often more difficult than in rural areas.

Within this context then, what happens to the newly arrived migrant's character and values? An empirical study that we and Abdullah Lutfiyya[48] conducted in the Middle East bears directly upon this question.

In this study, 2,795 people were interviewed in desert settlements, peasant villages, and cities. They ranged from illiterate wanderers to sophisticated members of Beirut's elite. Essentially three groups of people were chosen: (1) *rural people* engaged in agricultural work; (2) *transitional people* who have recently moved to cities such as Amman and Beirut and have not been directly exposed to an industrial experience; and (3) *urbanites*, a selection of people from different social classes who lived in an urban environment and, in addition, were actively involved in industrial, professional,

Table 1. A comparison of rural, transitional, and urban man*

	Traditional rural (%) (N† = 667)	Transitional urban (%) (N=948)	Urban (%) (N=1180)
I. How often do you pray in a day?			
1. Not at all	10	10	50
2. 1–4 times	2	4	2
3. 5 times	75	35	24
4. DK–NR‡	12	51	24
II. Efficacy of science			
1. Science will be effective	37	50	49
2. Science will not be effective	60	20	39
3. DK–NR	3	30	12
III. Can man change his destiny?			
1. Yes	26	35	44
2. No	70	57	44
3. DK–NR	4	8	12
IV. What determines success?			
1. Luck is all important	21	10	1
2. Luck is a little more important than planning	28	27	35
3. Planning is more important than luck	41	35	60
4. DK–NR	10	28	4
V. What does *late* mean?			
1. 15 minutes	15	37	55
2. 16–60 minutes	51	44	37
3. Over an hour or never	19	17	8
4. DK–NR	15	2	0
VI. Percent willing to do someone else's job	81	82	65

*From McCord, W., and Abdullah Lutfiyya, "Urbanization and World View in the Middle East," in *Essays on Modernization of Underdeveloped Societies*, ed. A. R. Desai (Bombay: Thacker and Co., 1962).
†N = number interviewed.
‡DK–NR = don't know or no response.

or commercial aspects of the city. The findings are, in part, presented in Table 1.

From the data presented in Table 1, it is evident that the urban experience affected the behavior and attitudes of men in a manner predicted by Inkeles. Urban man evidences a greater belief in the efficacy of science as a means of solving problems rather than relying on traditional mechanisms like praying. The urbanite believes in controlling personal destiny and punctuality more than the transitional or rural dweller and is only slightly less willing to help a co-worker. A more revealing difference was noted in an examination of responses to "willing to help." Urbanites more often cited their own self-interest (e.g., "I would do it to please the boss and maybe get a raise") as their motive for helping someone. Thirty-four percent of the "cooperative" urbanites noted self-interest as their motive; 22 percent of transitionals and only 9 percent of rural dwellers responded in the same manner. The urbanite is, then, more autonomous and ego-centered.

For the theorist of either strife or urbanization the transitional man demands attention. These people serve as the majority of muggers in Rio de Janeiro, rioters in Bombay, and the supporters of periodic revolutionary attempts in many cities around the world.

The world of these transitional men requires attention from those who care about the plight of people, for they are the men, not of the future or the past, but of our strife-ridden present. The world of these transitional men also merits attention from those interested in looking at the effects of urban life; for their lives, though at times agonizingly bare, present some clues concerning not only the characteristics of cities and urbanism as an attitude, but also the mechanism of transforming individual misery into collective action and some of its consequences.

New vistas are open to all urban dwellers and enable them to picture themselves as participants in a variety of different and new life-styles.[49] Some data suggests that many of the transitional urbanites are willing to accept almost any strong leader who promises to fulfill their wishes. The "true believer" flourishes among this urban population, and, consequently, so do the politics of irresponsibility and passion. In India, for example, one urban district enthusiastically supported S. P. Mukerji, the leader of the Jan Singh, the most authoritarian of right wing movements.[50] When Mukerji died, the same electorate swung immediately and with equal enthusiasm to the support of a Communist candidate. In doing so, they repudiated all of the traditional values for which the Jan Singh stood.

The seemingly nonrational political behavior of new urban dwellers, no doubt, is a result of becoming socially and emotionally isolated. Former chiefs, Brahman-priests, or patrons lost influence, and new authorities, frequently in the form of charismatic political figures inciting the masses to conflict, have taken their place. Temporarily, the transitional urbanite may replace some old forms of traditional life with urban associations such as the church or brotherhoods. But as one study of Stanleyville, the Congo, illustrated, these attempts to maintain traditional values soon erode in the face of an unresponding urban structure.[51]

In addition, the average urbanite loses the metaphysical system that formerly gave meaning to life. In South America, 50 percent of urban migrants gave up their Christian beliefs. In Africa, the conflict between Western city values and traditional religion "results either in the abandonment of all belief, which is perhaps the most logical solution, or else in the adoption of the outer form of Western belief without any inner conviction."[52]

The lesson appears to be clear: the new urbanite, as Burgess suggested, is a hollow person who cannot subscribe easily to old religious, political, or social values, and finds it difficult to adapt to a new way of life. Aside from these traumas, the newly arrived urban dweller is confronted with physical discomforts and frustrated ambitions. That the urbanite might seek solace in the promise of a politician, in crime, alcohol, magic, or drugs is comprehensible.

The life-style that characterizes a large number of residents of urban areas in developing nations has its counterpart in the already advanced cities of Berlin, New York, Paris, and London. The discussion of the effect of urban settings on the lives and attitudes of those in the United States is pursued in chapter 3.

SUMMARY

The most probable antecedents to the study of urban life by Americans is found in the writings of German social analysts Ferdinand Töennies, Max Weber, and Georg Simmel, and the Frenchman, Emile Durkheim. Each of these Europeans was concerned with the nature of social relationships in emerging urbanism and the consequences to individuals and societal organization.

American students of urban life followed the lead of the European intellectuals but were most directly stimulated by the rapid growth of urban areas in the United States as industrialization encouraged waves of immigrants from other nations. Borrowing concepts from the biological study of plant and animal life as they relate to their environment, the most prominent study of urban areas came to be known as *ecology*, and associated with sociologists at the University of Chicago. Robert Park, Ernest Burgess, Roderick McKenzie, and their colleagues (the most prominent of whom was Louis Wirth) developed the basic parameters of such study. Their major concerns, consonant with their social experience, were with the rapidity of urban growth, the characteristics of various areas of the city, and the disorganizing consequences of these phenomenon for the urban resident. All of their work was restricted to urban life in the United States.

More recent empirical work done in other parts of the world, however, has borne out and explicated some of the ideas of the Chicago School. A set of particular attitudes and values, for example, has been identified and associated with the process of industrialization and urbanization by Inkeles. The case of Mississippi during the 1960s civil rights movement was presented as an example of the attempt to infuse urban attitudes and values on a more rural section of the nation.

McCord and Lutfiyya's study in the Middle East supported not only Inkeles, but, in part, the Burgess hypothesis of the stages of transformation of urban (modern) man. A look at some of the events in urban areas in underdeveloped countries, however, suggested that a reorganization of urban dwellers, if unaccompanied by significant changes in education, economic opportunities, and life circumstances, may follow rather erratic, nonrational action. That is, organization may occur under the leadership of anyone promising the good life, which previously for the new migrant has been a frustrated ambition.

In the lesson of the cities of underdeveloped nations, there is a message that may well be heeded by those in industrial nations: the newly arrived transitional peasant in the Middle East or India has a counterpart in the more industrialized cities of the world.

Issues for further discussion

1. How does the postindustrial city differ significantly from other social groupings?

2. According to scholars of the German and Chicago schools, how does urbanization affect the lives of people? Are they correct?

3. Can the attitudes associated with urbanization be transplanted to rural areas such as Mississippi?

4. What are the major changes in attitudes that migrants to cities in the "developing" sector of the world undergo?

FOOTNOTES

1. New York Police Department Public Information reports more than 1,550 homocides in 1974. City University Admissions Office reports 268,993 students in 1974. There were over 50,000 unemployed blacks in New York City in 1973, which represents 7.2 percent of the black population 16 years and over. U.S. Department of Labor, Bureau of Labor Statistics, *Employment and Earnings*, vol. 21, no. 9 (March 1975).
2. Bernard Weintraub, "Food an Obsession in Misery Ridden Calcutta," *New York Times* 8 September 1974, p. 39.
3. Gideon Sjoberg, *The Preindustrial City* (New York: The Macmillan Co., 1960), p. 1.
4. Ralph Thomlinson, "The Nature and Rise of Cities," *in Social Science and Urban Crisis*, ed. Victor B. Ficker and Herbert S. Graves (New York: The Macmillan Co., 1971).
5. See Mushin Mahdi, *Ibn Khaldun's Philosophy of History* (London: George Allen and Unwin, 1957).
6. Ferdinand Toënnies, *Community and Society*, trans. Charles P. Loomis (East Lansing, Mich.: Michigan State University Press, 1957).
7. Emile Durkheim, *The Division of Labor in Society*, trans. George Simpson (Glencoe, Ill.: The Free Press, 1947).
8. See, for example, Max Weber, *The City* (Glencoe, Ill.: The Free Press, 1958), and Georg Simmel, *The Sociology of Georg Simmel*, trans. and ed. Kurt H. Wolff (London: The Free Press of Glencoe; Collier-Macmillan, 1950).
9. See Don Martindale, *The Nature and Types of Sociological Theory* (Boston, Mass: Houghton Mifflin Co., 1960).
10. Don Martindale, "Prefatory Remarks: The Theory of the City," in Weber, *The City*, p. 34.
11. Ibid., pp. 50–56.
12. See, for example, Robert E. Dickinson, *The West European City* (London: Routledge & Kegan Paul, 1951); William F. Ogburn, "Inventions of Local Transportation and the Pattern of Cities," in *Cities and Society: The Revised Reader in Urban Sociology*, ed. Paul K. Hatt and Albert Reiss, Jr. (New York: The Free Press, 1957).
13. Robert E. Park, Ernest W. Burgess, Roderick D. McKenzie, eds., *The City* (Chicago: The University of Chicago Press, 1925).
14. Roderick McKenzie, "The Neighborhood," *American Journal of Sociology*, vol. 27 (September 1921, March 1922, May 1922).
15. For another point of view see D. W. G. Timms, *The Urban Mosaic* (London: Cambridge University Press, 1971).
16. E. W. Burgess, "The Growth of the City," in Park, Burgess, McKenzie, *The City*, pp. 47–62.
17. Louis Wirth, *On Cities and Social Life* (Chicago: University of Chicago Press, Phoenix Books, 1964).
18. Louis Wirth, "Urbanism as a Way of Life," *American Journal of Sociology* 44 (July 1938):3–24.
19. Louis Wirth, *The Ghetto* (Chicago: University of Chicago Press, 1928).
20. See, for example, Timms, *The Urban Mosaic*, p. 89.
21. Gideon Sjoberg, "Comparative Urban Sociology," in *Sociology Today*, ed. Robert Merton, Leonard Broom, Leonard S. Cotrell, Jr. (New York: Basic Books, Inc., Publishers, 1959).
22. Alex Inkeles, "The Modernization of Man," in *Modernization*, ed. Myron Weiner (New York: Basic Books, Inc., Publishers, 1966), chap. 10.
23. Ibid., p. 138.
24. Daniel Lerner, *The Passing of Traditional Societies* (New York: The Free Press, 1958).
25. James Atwater, "If We Can Crack Mississippi . . . ," *Saturday Evening Post*, 25 July 1964.
26. Claude Sitton, "Mississippi's Press vs. Invaders," *San Francisco Chronicle*, 30 June 1964.
27. See, for example, poll by William Brink and Louis Harris, *The Negro Revolution in America* (New York: Simon & Schuster, 1964), chap. 9.
28. See, Letters to the Editor, *Jackson Daily News*, 11 July 1964, and Manning Johnson, *Color, Communism and Common Sense*, American Opinion reprint series (Belmont, Mass.: Robert Welch, 1958).
29. James Silver, *Mississippi: The Closed Society* (New York: Harcourt Brace and World, 1964).
30. William McCord, *Mississippi: The Long Hot Summer* (New York: W. W. Norton and Co., 1965), p. 133.
31. Silver, *Mississippi: The Closed Society*, pp. 101–102.
32. "The General Condition of the Mississippi Negro," mimeographed (Jackson, Miss.: Council of Federated Organizations, 1964).
33. Silver, *Mississippi: The Closed Society*, p. 19.
34. McCord, *Mississippi: The Long Hot Summer*, p. 41.
35. See, "COFO's Proposed Community Center,"

mimeographed (Jackson, Miss.: Council of Federated Organizations, 1964).
36. Council of Federated Organizations, press release, mimeographed (April 1964).
37. McCord, *Mississippi: The Long Hot Summer.* Also see Peter Weiss, "Nightmare in Mississippi," *The Progressive* (Sept. 1964), and Christopher Jencks, "Mississippi: From Conversion to Coercion," *The New Republic* (22 August 1964).
38. *Newsweek,* 24 August 1964, p. 20.
39. Southern Regional Council Survey, 1964.
40. McCord, *Mississippi: The Long Hot Summer,* especially chap. 6, "The Quiet Revolt: Mississippi Negroes."
41. Kingsley Davis, "Urbanization in India," in *India's Urban Future,* ed. Roy Turner (Berkeley and Los Angeles: University of California Press, 1952); Daniel Lerner, *Traditional Societies;* and Robert Heilbroner, *The Great Ascent* (New York: Harper & Row, 1963).
42. Arthur Lewis, "Mexico Since Cardenas," *Social Research* (Spring 1959), p. 26.
43. Harrison Selig, *India: The Most Dangerous Decade* (Princeton, N.J.: Princeton University Press, 1965).
44. Ibid.
45. Statistical Office of the United Nations, Department of Economic and Social Affairs, *Statistical Yearbook: 1972,* no. 24 (1973).
46. Selig, *India: The Most Dangerous Decade.*
47. Keuval Krishan Dewitt, *Indian Economics* (New Dehli: Premiem Publishing Co., 1966).
48. William McCord and Abdullah Lutfiyya, "Urbanization and World View in the Middle East," in *Essays on Modernization of Underdeveloped Societies,* ed. A. R. Desai (Bombay, India: Thacker and Co., 1967).
49. Colin Turnbull, *The Lonely African* (New York: Simon & Schuster, 1962).
50. Selig, *India: The Most Dangerous Decade.*
51. Nelly Xydias, *Social Implications of Industrialization and Organization in Africa South of the Sahara* (Paris: Unesco, 1956).
52. Turnbull, *Lonely African,* p. 59.

SUGGESTED READINGS

Louis Wirth, "Urbanism as a Way of Life," *American Journal of Sociology* 44(July 1938): 3–24, and Philip Hauser, "On the Impact of Urbanism on Social Organization, Human Nature and the Political Order," *Confluence* 7 (Spring 1958):27–30, provide two of the best descriptions of urbanism and its impact.

Gideon Sjoberg, *The Preindustrial City* (New York: The Macmillan Co., 1960), and *Scientific American,* "The Earliest Cities," part I of, *Cities and Their Origin, Growth and Human Impact* (San Francisco: W. H. Freeman and Co. Publishers, 1973) present excellent portrayals of preindustrial cities.

Colin Turnbull, *The Lonely African* (New York: Simon & Schuster, 1962), depicts the transition of Africans from rural to urban settings. Once in the city the new migrant is commonly caught up in a web of despair. Some excellent source materials include Ruth Bussey, *The Flight from Rural Poverty: How Nations Cope* (Lexington, Mass.: D. C. Heath & Co., 1973); Arnold Rose, *Migrants in Europe* (Minneapolis: University of Minnesota Press, 1969); and Andrei Simié, *The Peasant Urbanites* (New York: Seminar Press, 1973).

chapter 3

Urban life in the United States

The city is to the nation what the white church spire
is to the village—the visible symbol of aspiration and faith,
the white plume saying that way is up.

E. B. White

This mantrap of gigantic dimensions devouring manhood . . .
is as good an example of barbarism as exists.

Frank Lloyd Wright

Throughout American history the city has been characterized as both paradise and hell. It has symbolized charm, sophistication, achievement, and learning. Yet, simultaneously, many Americans have regarded the city as a true "den of iniquity," a rude place marred by crime and degradation. The dual character of the city in America has been well summarized by Thomas Wolfe:

> The city has a million faces, and . . . no man ever knows just what another means when he tells about the city he sees. For the city that he sees is just the city that he brings with him, that he has within his heart . . . made out of sense but shaped and colored and unalterable from all that he has felt and thought and dreamed about before.[1]

For good or evil, the city in American life has served as the cradle of both conflict and innovation. Boston spawned the American Revolution, Brooklynites headed the abolitionist movement, San Francisco launched America on its "consciousness expanding" experiments. Political decisions emanate from Washington (affected, but not directed, by the political hustings); New York dictates our choice in clothes, books, the mass media, and finances; Boston, with some legitimacy, still considers itself the "Athens of America"; and Los Angeles heralds the fads in everything from Eastern religions to hula-hoops.

Rural people may decry the city's influence and agree with Crowley, the nineteenth century poet, that "God the first garden made, and the first city Cain." Nonetheless, they sway their tastes to the cities' fashions and have migrated to metropolitan areas with unprecedented alacrity.

Urbanized Americans, in turn, may well agree with Alexander Klein's judgment "that the only real advantage of living in New York is that all of its residents ascend to heaven directly after their deaths, having served their full term in purgatory right on Manhattan Island."[2] Yet, a taste for variety, an interest in higher culture, or the crude demands of economic necessity force most Americans to live in metropolitan areas and to forego their dreams of a rural utopia.

After all, as Philip M. Hauser wrote: "the modern city stands as a dramatic example of man's ability to shape his physical and social world."[3] Many of the current problems, for example, smog, inadequate supply of clean water and housing, as well as traffic congestion, are considered soluble by those who have set out to salvage or plan city life.[4] Indeed, urban planners, health officials, and other interested professionals tell us that these problems not only can, but must be solved if life in urban areas is to continue. All of this bespeaks an optimism in man's capacity to control his environment.

Paradoxically, urban residents and urban culture are the products of forces that are not easily controlled; nor are these forces even fully understood. In general, for example, it is known that geographic, economic, social, and political forces, as well as the individual decisions of persons and families, contribute to migratory patterns. However, the precise balance of factors underlying population shifts from rural to urban, and within urban areas, is yet to be learned. For the moment, let us set aside causal factors associated with changes in the population distribution and examine some facts about twentieth century population changes.

THE GROWTH OF AMERICAN CITIES

The phenomenal growth of urban areas around the world, reported in chapter 1, was evidenced in all of the metropolitan areas in the United States. (Urban growth has long outstripped overall population increases in the United States.) Only 5 percent of the total American population was urban in 1790.[5] In 1950 approximately 64 percent of Americans were urban dwellers; and by the 1970s more than three-fourths of the American people were living in urban areas,[6] thus demonstrating a steady, rapid growth of standard metropolitan areas. In fact, the rapidity of urban sprawl has concerned many urban dwellers, causing them to try to stem or control the growth rate of their own area. On 21 March 1974 the residents of St. Petersburg, Florida, adopted an ordinance requiring that the last 25,000 people who had settled there move out.[7] The ordinance was rescinded two weeks later but indicates the almost hysterical nature of the reaction to the problem of urban growth. Most other areas have adopted somewhat less drastic measures than that proposed by the residents of St. Petersburg, but they have all, in essence, moved in the direction of restricting population growth. Boca Raton, Florida; Marin County, California; Palo Alto, California; Southhampton, Long Island; San Jose, California; and Loudoun County, Virginia (a suburb of Washington, D.C.) all have imposed some restriction on further building.[8] Contrary to popular belief, few of the attempts to alter growth of urban areas have resulted from an exhaustion of space. In fact, urban population density has declined from 6,580 people per square mile in 1920 to 4,230 in the 1970s.[9] The ostensible reasons given for controlling the rate of growth in these areas immediately adjacent to the central city core have included inadequacy of services (e.g., water supply, schools) and other strained public facilities.

The desire to restrict growth, then, is a result of urban sprawl, as large numbers of persons shift from the center to the periphery of urban areas. The rapid growth of these peripheral areas has been most pronounced since 1920[10] and represents the second important population shift in urban development. Whereas industrialization, the expansion of markets, and great advances in agricultural technology account for the initial centralization of the population in cities, subsequent dispersal of people into areas outside of the central city may be explained by such factors as the widespread use of the automobile and the paving of highways, improved public transportation, transmittal of electric power over great distances, and improvement in means of communication (i.e., telephones, radio, television, and the press), as well as the presumed values associated with suburban existence.

Census bureau surveys for the first third of the 1970s suggest a trend that reverses the tremendous urban area gains to this point. Rural growth in areas such as the Ozark Plateau between St. Louis and Dallas, the Upper Great Lakes region, the Rocky Mountains, and the southern Appalachian coal fields has been almost double that of metropolitan areas during the same period. Whereas the latter gained 2.9 percent population between April 1970 and July 1973, the nonmetropolitan areas listed gained 4.2 percent.[11] Nonmetropolitan areas listed refer to those with no population centers of at least 50,000 people.

Calvin L. Beal, a demographer in the Economic Research Service of the Department of Agriculture, has attributed the turnaround of migration patterns to a number of factors including "a decentralization of manufacturing, the growth of recreation and retirement areas beyond the traditional 'sun belt,' earlier retirement, [and] a narrowing of the gap in rural-urban life styles."[12] What is suggested by this interpretation, then, is the urbanization of formally rural areas, and not a return to rural life.

A selective migration has occurred from the central city. In general, it has been white, middle-class families who fled to the suburbs, leaving much of the central city as a center of poverty, personal disorganization, and social strife. The earlier migrants have been continually replaced by poor, relatively uneducated black minority migrants, who in turn commonly find that even when they obtain a degree of success, they must continue to live in the central city because of suburban bigotry.[13] These are the transitional men of industrially advanced areas.

Many cities have attempted to lure middle- and upper-income persons through the creation of selected rebuilt areas such as East Greenwich Village in New York, the area surrounding Forest Park in St. Louis, the John Hancock rehabilitation area in Boston, and Chicago's Hyde Park. Phoenix, Arizona, on the other hand, evolved a unique solution to the problem:

> . . . after developers built tract developments on unincorporated city land out on the desert expanse, the city offered services and the new residents voted to be annexed.[14]

This plan of incorporation of what would otherwise be suburban areas has helped the city maintain its tax dollars and white population. Other cities such as Los Angeles and Oklahoma City have also used this plan; however, different areas of these three cities remain segregated as ghetto and high crime areas.[15] People who are similar in economic status or ethnicity continue to concentrate.

Some recent evidence indicates that the proportion of black persons who have moved into the suburbs of Hartford, New York, Pittsburgh, Detroit, St. Louis, and other major cities has increased considerably between 1960 and 1970. However, the total numbers and characteristics of the migrants did not serve to alleviate the problem of selective migration. Overwhelmingly, the new black migrant to the suburbs also has been selectively middle class in terms of income, education, and home ownership. Thus, those minority group members who have moved from the central city have left behind a large number who are relatively poor and disadvantaged.[16]

Between 1960 and 1966 the black population of all central cities amounted to 88 percent of the total black population growth in the nation.[17] Between 1960 and 1970 the black population in metropolitan areas grew from 12.8 million to 16.7 million people. In both the central city and its immediately surrounding area, these figures represented an average annual growth of 2.8 percent.[18] Much greater concentrations of black over white populations have occurred in the largest cities in the United States, and it is expected that, if the trend continues, cities such as Baltimore, Cleveland, St. Louis, Detroit, Philadelphia, Chicago, and Richmond will have a black population of over 50 percent by 1984. In 1974, Washington, D.C., and Newark already totaled well over a 66 percent black population[19] Each increasingly black central city is, in turn, surrounded by a vast suburban area of richer groups, which together constitute new metropolitan areas.

THE CENTRAL CITY

The central cities of the United States, surrounded by relatively affluent satellite suburbs, exhibit a variety of characteristics as a consequence of the population shifts just described.

- There has been a decrease in the proportion of middle- to lower-class residents and a greater demand for social services on the part of the disadvantaged population left in the urban core.[20]
- As employed people have left the central cities, increasing numbers of impoverished people have entered. As a result, three problems endemic to central cities–family disorganization, dependence on welfare, and crime–have largely been identified with the new minority population in the public mind. Black female-headed families have increased from 18 percent of all black families in 1950 to 33 percent in 1973; recipients of aid from welfare programs totaled approximately 25 percent of the total black population in 1974; and, in absolute numbers, blacks accounted for more murder, rape, and robbery arrests in 1972 than whites–although blacks constituted a minority of the population.[21]

Such statistics ignore two facts: (1) blacks have entered the middle class in greater numbers than ever before; and (2) American cities have always had malignant influences on new migrant groups. Yet, these facts have contributed to the fears of the middle class remaining in American cities of being overcome by a wave of poverty-stricken, violent migrants.

- There has been an increase in formal controls, such as the police force. In addition, numerous security officer positions have been created in the transit system, schools, business offices, and residential buildings in urban areas. New York City, for example, maintains a school security force of over nine hundred people.[22]
- Many public schools have fallen into decay because of fragmentation of the educational facilities into private schools (attended by children of the rich) and parochial schools (attended by children of different religious faiths), thus forcing the public schools to be populated only by children of the poor.[23]
- There has been an alteration, if not disorganization, of traditional family patterns because of economic and social conditions of the urban core.[24]
- Many theologians believe that the growth of urbanization entails the death of organized religion. Harvey Cox, in his influential book *The Secular City*, summarized his inquiry into the state of the modern world with the flat assertion: "The rise of urban civilization and the collapse of traditional religion are the two main hallmarks of our era and are closely related movements."[25] As Cox viewed the change which has come over modern man, "The world looks less and less to religious rules and ritual for its morality or its meanings."[26] Cox contended that the growth in anonymity and mobility that accompany urbanization cut off people from traditional sources of meaning but offer new horizons and may eventually provide greater freedom and a new religious viewpoint.[27]
- Political institutions in the city have changed drastically to fit new situations. Old affiliations carry little weight. What counts is the degree to which a particular political machine or organization can satisfy (at least superficially) the material hopes of its constituents.[28] Political power tends to coalesce temporarily in individuals–Daley in Chicago, Lindsay in New York, Powell in Harlem–who promise to usher in a new era. Inevitably, these persons must fail to satisfy *all* factions. They pass from the scene only to be replaced by new figures who, in turn, represent a variety of class, caste, religious, or ethnic claims. The all-pervasive mass media provide an important mode of providing status and credulity.

In the face of these changes there remains

a continuing vigor of cultural institutions—the opera, ballet, arts, theatre, and "high scholarship"—which characterizes urban centers. Despite the deterioration in other aspects of life, cultural life continues to be a dominant characteristic in the largest cities of the United States and Europe. In fact, urban domination of national cultural life continued in spite of deliberate and vigorous efforts on the part of governments, such as in France, to decentralize culture to the provinces.

Of course, even the abbreviated portrait of the central city must be placed in the context of the general society, which experienced a generally improved state during the 1960s. As we have already indicated, central cities in America actually became less dense between 1960 and 1970, yet municipal employees in the same period increased by 33 percent. The dropout rate from the remaining public schools went down from 24 percent to 16 percent between 1960 and 1970.[29]

In view of this picture of central cities, it is hardly surprising that their problems appear to be almost incomprehensible. For the social analyst dealing with urban social conditions, the rapidity of change and the complex nature of the problems obscures easy answers. To the politicians who tried to curb the riots of the 1960s, the law and order reformers of Philadelphia, and the mayors who try to deal with striking workers, the cities are so torn with conflict and problems that they appear to be ungovernable.

Strife in the mid-1970s has not been overtly strident. Much of the concern in most American urban areas has been with the allocation of local, state, and federal funds, and the overall balancing of municipal budgets.[30] Regardless of the specific decisions made and the relative quiescence, if one accepts the basic assumption and definition of strife presented in chapter 1, the overt manifestations of feelings of discontent and inequity are a potential aspect of all social relationships.

These are some of the facts that help to create the urban milieu. In turn, it is the urban milieu that fashions the experiences of those who live in it. It is to this problem that we next direct attention.

THE URBAN MILIEU: LOUIS WIRTH

Urban areas are not merely a conglomeration of physical facts: skyscrapers, neon lights, or muggers lurking in parks, subways, and buses. Beyond the often appalling urban reality lies a mental and moral outlook that can be considered urbane. In fact, this outlook stretches well beyond the geographical boundaries of metropolitan areas. Relayed through the mass media, the attitudes and emotions associated with urbanity have been extended throughout all areas of most highly industralized countries.

Louis Wirth was among America's most thorough scholars to examine the basis, nature, and impact of the urban milieu. First, argued Wirth, "the bonds of kinship, of neighborliness and sentiment arising out of living together for generations under a common folk tradition are likely to be absent."[31] Instead, direct competition for occupations, desirable living quarters, and educational opportunities replace the customary folk pattern. Formal control mechanisms such as police, courts, and a proliferation of rules replace the bonds of solidarity that once held the community together.

Second, the very fact that a large number of people live in urban centers makes it impossible for people to know each other in any depth. Contacts between people become segmented and secondary, rather than primary. Thus, people are not only anonymous, but human relations, superficial and atomized.

Third, the fact that urbanites meet each other in highly segmental specialized roles means that they are dependent on more people and organized groups for the satisfaction of their needs. This increases the probability of superficial, rather than intimate, relationships.

Fourth, Wirth predicted that the lack of direct interpersonal communication between individuals increases the importance of two forms of communication: on the one hand, impersonal mass media are used to convey much information to the masses; on the other hand, urbanites are forced to articulate individual interests through the process of delegation. Since the individual counts for little, a dependency on power brokers, ward-healers, elected officials, and bureaucrats occurs.

Fifth, thought Wirth, typical urbanites have little ability in the confusion of city life to determine what is in their best interest. Thus, the urbanite has become prone to the suggestions of mass agencies: " . . . individuals who are thus detached from the organized bodies which integrate society comprise the fluid masses that make collective behavior in the urban community so unpredictable and hence so problematical."[32]

Sixth, corporations dominate city life because they are able to bring together the great number of specializations necessary to keep an advanced, rationalized organization functioning.

Seventh, with corporations and the large number of people in the cities, bureaucracy becomes pervasive. Human beings are subjected to highly rationalized, role-specific decisions which anonymously affect their lives. Students in universities become computer numbers and people are subjected to universalistic standards. The size of the reigning bureaucracy itself grows to gigantic proportions.

Eighth, the physical closeness of people who have few sentimental ties, the competition and mutual exploitation, the predominance of anonymity, wrote Wirth, inevitably gives rise to individual loneliness.

Ninth, to compensate for the negative aspects of urban living, Wirth and his associates in Chicago believed that the individual gains a degree of emancipation from the personal and emotional controls of more intimate groups. In spite of this, there is a price to pay for living in the city. As Wirth observed:

> He [the urbanite] loses the spontaneous self expression, the morale, and the sense of participation that comes with living in an integrated society. This constitutes essentially the state of anomie, or the social void to which Durkheim alludes in attempting to account for the various forms of social disorganization in technological society.[33]

In summary, Wirth's analysis indicates that the urban milieu is a result of the density of population and the predominance of industry and commerce. With the development of large scale bureaucracies and the disappearance of folk controls, life in the city can be characterized as competitive, anonymous, superficial, and lonely. Further, though people are afforded the possibility of more individual freedom, at the same time they are more dependent upon, and susceptible to, the mass media.

Essentially, according to Wirth, urban centers provide a setting for an atomized, alienated existence. Much data exists to support such a conclusion: inference, for example, can be based on the plethora of statistics regarding crime, drug addiction, mental disorders, and familial disorganization. Such a conclusion also can be supported by data derived from public opinion polls. As Walter Lippmann observed in his 1916 book, *Deft and Mastery:* "We live in great cities without knowing our neighbors, the loyalties cemented by very little direct contact . . . this impersonal quality is intolerable."[34]

SOME EFFECTS OF THE URBAN MILIEU: SOCIAL AND PERSONAL DISORGANIZATION

By any criteria, urbanites in America exhibit numerous symptoms of social malaise.

Crime

An obvious form of social disorder, crime, has long plagued American cities and resulted in a great deal of concern among urbanites. Surveys of ten major American cities under the Urban Observatory Program in 1971, for example, reported that "law and order, police services, and courts appeared to be an important issue," of the highest priority.[35]

By any standard, America has been a highly criminal nation; and its already high rate of crime soared upward as the nation became urbanized. Even in the short period between 1960 and 1974 the number of violent crimes increased from 287,000 to 970,000.[36] Crime rates for violent crimes run directly inverse to population density. In 1973, for example, 1,003 violent crimes were committed per 100,000 population in cities of 250,000 or more. In cities of 50,000 to 99,999 people, the rates per 100,000 population were 372. For cities under 10,000, the crime rate was 199.[37]

Thus, one aspect of the urban milieu is enormously inflated violence, which brings with it a siege mentality: triple-locked doors, neighborhood vigilante groups, and the abandonment of public schools by those who can afford to "protect" their children in parochial and private schools.

Mental disorders

Except at the extremes, mental health is a difficult concept to define. A simple, yet useful definition is provided by Levy and Visotsky:

> A mentally healthy person has a sense of participation in the life process. He has a sense of personal worth. He has a sense of dignity, of knowing who he is; and he does not have to contend continually with the problem of justifying his existence to himself.[38]

Americans living in urban centers struggle to survive in the face of fear and competition in a rapidly paced impersonal setting. This perhaps partially explains the rates of mental disorder associated with urban living.[39] In a recent national probability sample of over six thousand American adults, Srole and his associates[40] found that a large proportion of residents in urban areas have superior mental health to those living in smaller communities. In his analysis of the data he suggests that the relevant research question may be what kinds of people are drawn to various kinds of communities; rather than inquiring as to the effect of urban life.

The relationship between urban living and mental disorders is such that rates of mental illness increase as one approaches the center of the city.[41] Many people in the center of the city are single, unemployed, or marginally employed. These are, then, persons who are less successful in the competition. It is interesting to note that patients in mental hospitals can be similarly characterized.[42]

It is difficult to determine from existing data whether living in the environment of an urban center actually causes mental illness, or whether mentally disordered people tend to fall into residential patterns, placing them in the more deteriorated areas of the central city.[43] Moreover, major cities draw a disproportionate number of talented eccentrics and ambitious people into their confines. Thus, selective migration of certain types of people and their relative success may help to account for the differential rate of those who fall mentally ill.

Another, earlier survey of the mental health of persons in urban centers had been conducted by Srole and his associates.[44] Researchers in this instance gathered statistics on the mental health of the midtown Manhattan area of New York City. Perhaps the most striking finding of this survey was that only a small proportion of midtown Manhattanites were judged to be emotionally well.

As Table 2 indicates, more than 23 percent of midtown Manhattanites were identified as seriously impaired in their emotional well-being, and only one in five midtowners were viewed by the team psychiatrists as mentally healthy. A majority of midtown Manhattanites (58.1 percent) apparently were able to function in their work or other activities but exhibited some symptoms of mental disorder.

Table 2. Home survey sample (age 20–59) respondents distribution on symptom-formation* (N† = 1,660)

Symptom-formation	Percent
Well	18.5
Mild symptom formation	36.3
Moderate symptom formation	21.8
Marked symptom formation	13.2
Severe symptom formation	7.5
Incapacitated	2.7

*From Leo Srole, et al., *Mental Health in the Metropolis* (New York: McGraw-Hill Book Co., 1962), p. 138.
†N = number interviewed.

Foreshadowing his own later findings, however, even in this earlier work Srole found that the degree of success in an occupation, at least as indicated by social class, modified the overall conclusion. When contrasted, the mental health ratings for the highest and lowest socioeconomic strata within the midtown area show that 67.5 percent of the highest social stratum were judged to be well or only mildly disturbed, whereas 29.6 percent of the lowest social class were so categorized. Obversely, 32.5 percent of the highest social class and 70.4 percent of the lowest social class were moderately or more severely impaired. Regardless of the causation, this population contributes to the general milieu of the central city.

In any estimate of mental disorder, black people in America, as one of the most recent and numerous migrants to urban areas, deserve special attention. Work conducted by Seymour Parker and Robert J. Kleiner on the problem of mental illness among black persons in contemporary cities provides information in this regard.[45] From a survey of black persons in Philadelphia, Parker and Kleiner concluded the following:

- Lower-class urban blacks had strikingly high rates of mental disorder.
- Black migrants from the rural South had lower rates of mental disorder than their urban counterparts.
- Black persons who set either very high or very low achievement goals had the greatest proportion of mental disorders.
- In general, urban blacks who stood at the highest level of economic achievement and had fought their way to the top or those who were at the bottom of the economic ladder and had fallen from a more privileged status were most likely to be mentally ill.

Within the black urban population, then, it appeared that both winning and losing the rat race correlated highly with major mental disorders. Frank Lloyd Wright's judgment on city life (presented in the introduction to this chapter) appears to appropriately summarize the destiny of an unfortunately large number of urban residents.

Alcoholism

Like mental disorder, alcoholism also has been found to correlate with residence in large urban centers.[46] Further, the number of deaths from alcoholism increases strikingly as one moves toward the center of a major American city. In New York, for example, deaths from alcoholism ranged from 17 per 100,000 population in midtown Manhattan to 6 per 100,000 in the outer boroughs.[47] Reasonably, part of this difference could be attributed to the existence of skid row or bowery areas in most American cities where certain types of deviant alcoholics congregate.[48]

However, it appears that urbanism generally can be associated with an increase in alcoholism. Users of alcohol have increased from approximately 50 percent of the population in 1850 to approximately 70 percent in 1970.[49] Deaths from alcoholic disorders increased in the short span between 1950 and 1963 from 5.5 to 8.7 per 100,000 population.[50]

The relation between alcoholism and urbanization can perhaps be attributed partially to the general pressures of urban centers and also to the decline of family controls over the use of alcohol. In the nineteenth century, strict family observances controlled the use of alcohol. "Wild, destructive behavior" associated with alcoholism was to be found only in unattached men.[51] In the twentieth century, not only have familial controls over drinking decreased, but as urbanization has proceeded women have joined the ranks of men as alcoholics.[52]

Drug addiction

The use of heroin, cocaine, and opium has been associated in the public mind with the influence of city life. This stereotype was totally inaccurate until the early twentieth century[53] but has become increasingly true between 1950 and 1970. Drug control was mentioned second only to law and order by a majority of respondents as a top priority concern in the ten cities surveyed by the Urban Observatory Program.[54] Since the end of World War II, heroin addiction has emerged as a unique problem of American urban centers. The best estimates made in the 1960s indicated that nearly half of all known addicts live in New York City and that another quarter live in Los Angeles or Chicago.[55] Generally, contemporary heroin addiction tends to have concentrated in urban slum areas.[56]

Suicide

Suicide is the ultimate form of self-destructive behavior of individuals who seek to cope with the depersonalized urban milieu. Emile Durkheim, in his nineteenth century treatise on suicide, provided one of the earliest, most comprehensive understandings of this drastic mode of behavior. In general he concluded that "the social suicide rate of any population is explicable only in reference to the consequence of varying degrees of social cohesion, not the attributes of the individuals who make up the population.[57]

We are enabled with this type of explanation to understand more clearly reports of suicides in different parts of an urban area. Ronald W. Maris, for example, reported that in Chicago two areas had high suicide rates.[58] One region, labeled the Gold Coast (Rogers Park, Uptown, Lakeview, Lincoln Park, New North Side, and Hyde Park), contained a population of relatively high social class and high levels of educational attainment compared to those in other areas of Chicago. The second region, labeled Skid Row (Lower West Side, Pullman, and McKinley Park), was reported to be populated by many persons age 65 and older, blue-collar workers, and those of low educational attainment, as well as many foreign-born residents. The immediate precipitates to suicide in these two sections of Chicago were no doubt different. That is, the population of the Gold Coast, it may be speculated, in line with Durkheim's more extended discussion, was vulnerable to abrupt economic change (such as the Depression of the 1930s) and anomie (characteristic of a rapidly changing city life oriented to the future, rather than the past). Residents of the Skid Row section of Chicago, on the other hand, were probably most vulnerable to excessive individuation and apathy common to modern industrial society. Both instances suggest that social cohesion has been attenuated in these urban areas, resulting in despair and a loss of meaning in life.

As a United Nations study suggests, urban life and a high rate of suicide go hand in hand around the world. Thus, the five nations with the highest rate of suicide all are relatively urbanized, technologically advanced, industrialized nations. The five with the lowest recorded rate are relatively rural, nonurbanized nations.[59]

The relationship between urbanization and suicide rates admittedly has not been found to be a perfect one. Sri Lanka (formerly called Ceylon), for example, is an agricultural nation; yet it has a relatively high suicide rate of 12.2 per 100,000 popu-

Table 3. Suicide rates per 100,000 population*

Highest	
Hungary	29.6
Austria	23.1
Czechoslovakia	21.5
Sweden	20.1
Germany	20.0
Lowest	
Jordan	0.1
Philippines	0.5
Ecuador	0.6
Nicaragua	1.2
Mexico	1.6

*Adopted from *Demographic Yearbook* (New York: United Nations, 1967), table 24.

lation. In contrast, Canada is an urbanized nation with a suicide rate of only 8.6 per 100,000.[60] Other factors such as age, sex, and religiosity obviously interact with urbanization as causative elements. Yet, it would be rash to deny that many of the same characteristics of urban life associated with alcoholism and dope addiction possibly play a part in setting the state for suicide.

Suicide rates in the United States have fluctuated widely since the turn of the century. The suicide rate in America climbed from 10 per 100,000 population in 1901 to a peak of 17 in 1930 as the Great Depression struck America. With the advent of World War II the rate dropped, as it does during times of war. By 1973, however, the rate again rose to 17.7 per 100,000 for American men and 6.5 per 100,000 for American women.[61]

In spite of Durkheim's early work, suicide has been widely recognized as a social, rather than a personal, idiosyncratic problem only recently. The recognition was forced largely through the efforts of the Los Angeles Suicide Prevention Center and the National Institute of Mental Health Centers for the Study of Suicide Prevention. Both of these organizations have been instrumental in setting up prevention centers in most urban areas.[62]

Family disorganization

The disorganization of the family also has been one persistent theme in the study of urban problems. Indeed, family life has been altered in the urban setting. In turn, the changes have affected the socialization experience and life-style for participants. This has proven distasteful to many who recall a different, more traditional, family life.[63]

There can be little doubt that the family system in America faces some change and the magnitude of the problem has grown simultaneously with urbanization. Between 1945 and 1973, for example, the marriage rate per 1,000 population declined from 16 to 11.[64] During the same period, the birth rate dropped even more strikingly from 26 to approximately 15 per 1,000 population. Children, after all, cannot be seen to be an economic asset in the city where physical living space has always been at a premium.[65] Moreover, there are many one-parent, female-headed families in urban areas.

Divorce rates have risen as America has become urbanized. In 1880 the divorce rate was 55.6 per 1,000 marriages. By 1920 the rate was 133.3, and it rose to 231.7 by 1950. In 1973 the divorce rate was about 455 per 1,000 marriages.[66]

Such statistics are dramatic evidence that the traditional American family has undergone alteration. Of course, no one has attributed the changes solely to urbanization, but there can be little doubt that industrialization and urbanization together have exerted severe strains upon the family system. Among the more important effects of urbanization are the following:

1. *The compartmentalization of work and family life:* In an agricultural environment, every member of the family had a specific economic job to perform. In an industrialized society, however, work and the family have been dissociated. Father leaves

the house to work in a factory or business geographically and psychologically separated from the children. Increasingly mothers also have disappeared from the home to participate in work that usually is meaningless to the husband (except for the paycheck she brings home). Approximately 43.8 percent of all women of working age labored outside the home in the mid-1970s. In 1900 the comparable figure was 20.4 percent.[67] This change altered an important bond that held the family together in the past. It also made it possible for women to thrive economically outside the purview of their husbands.

2. *Urban public services:* Governmental agencies have taken over many of the functions of the family. Education, for example, is conducted formally outside of the home in an urban school. Many cities also provide day-care centers where a working mother may leave her preschool children. Each of these developments has stripped the family of one more function and placed it in the hands of relatively impersonal urban agencies.

Many other public service agencies may be seen as having altered the nature of family functions. Family planning agencies, where legal, provide information about contraception; welfare agencies and social security provide income for families in trouble or old age.

3. *Mobility:* Approximately forty million Americans change their home addresses at least once each year. The average American moves about fourteen times in his lifetime.[68] The requirements of a postindustrial urban society for a mobile labor force made this transition inevitable. One consequence, however, is that the American family is forced to survive as a relatively isolated unit with no particular roots or heritage in any geographical region. In the face of such a high degree of change, many families find it increasingly difficult to ensure a stable socialization period and few, if any, attempt to maintain a sense of history or kinship.[69]

4. *Companionship:* The anonymity of city life and its lack of intimate social bonds added another pressure to family life. The nuclear family became the most important, sometimes the sole, source of intimate friendship, conviviality, and companionship. Involved in different occupational worlds and different interests, however, it has become easier for man and wife to grow apart from one another. This development has occurred concomitantly with the demand placed upon the family to serve as the primary source of social support.

As Ernest Burgess reminded us some decades ago, changes in the form and function of American families represent only relative, rather than absolute, alteration.[70] There has always been a diversity of family life in America: the Hopi Indians were primarily maternal; the Amish, patriarchal; the Italian immigrant, semipatriarchal; the oriental, extended; the apartment dweller, equalitarian; and the suburban family, matricentric. However, it cannot be denied that the family, whether rural or urban, is the first and most important social group to be encountered by most individuals. Bonds between members are encompassing and emotionally charged, extending for the first twenty years of an individual's lifetime, and frequently even longer. It is hardly surprising, then, that under these conditions change of any sort in the family may be viewed as threatening to the stability of personality and society.

The shift of emphasis to companionship marriage would appear to be a healthy sign for industrialized, urban society. The particular family form that provides the fulfillment of such needs can counteract the numerous secondary, impersonal, segmental relationships experienced by individuals. Knowledge of the extent to which the family is, in fact, successful in providing diffuse, emotionally gratifying bonds can serve as a basis of predicting its probable persistence. As some of the more rebellious youths of the 1960s found in their experiment with alternative family forms,[71] relationships not too dissimilar to those of the "ideal urban family" developed. The substitution of different titles, or even different persons, in these new families apparently did not signify a dissolution of the family. Like generals, the family is so encrusted with tradition and emotion it is not likely to die a natural death; our family system may merely fade into new forms, no doubt creating much pain for some individuals in the process.

The inference that can be drawn from our description of the personal and social disorganization in urban areas is consistent with that described by Wirth, as well as Durkheim and Simmel. More recent attitude polls taken of New York City residents also would tend to support this rather negative position. In a representative sample poll of New Yorkers, 53 percent of those questioned believed that they would be better off living any place but New York, 57 percent of the respondents believed that any other environment would be healthier, and fully 85 percent of the respondents thought that big cities, generally, were the worst place to raise children. To add insult to injury, *native* New Yorkers disliked the city as much as those who had migrated from smaller towns or rural areas.[72]

This description, however, is surely only one aspect of life in the city. Obviously all people do not withdraw from the stresses and strains imposed by urban conditions. Most people experience street crimes, extreme alcoholism, dope addiction, and suicide only as news items brought into the home via the mass media. The impact of such information no doubt includes the creation of fear and increased suspiciousness of others; however, many persons constantly exposed to this type of information only develop an attitude of indifference to the plight of others, as work and personal needs dictate the continuation of activities as usual.

Most urban residents created their own world of associates: involvement with family (albeit in modified form), special interest groups, religious organizations, ethnic neighborhoods, and political associations, which provide relief from the anomie and atomism described. To balance the picture let us focus on how these factors operate to ameliorate some of the disorganizing facets of urban life.

BUFFERS: EMERGENT ORGANIZATIONS IN URBAN SETTINGS

The complex of new social relationships found in urban areas must be included in any portrait of the urban environment. To ignore them would be to provide a gross oversimplification and erroneous picture, serving only to hinder an understanding of social strife in urban areas. Urbanization and industrialization have created many new groups that help individuals cope with urban life, thus providing the boundaries of identification that exaggerate similarities within and differences without. Moreover, these same groups also serve as basic units in conflict situations.

Family and friends

As already discussed, a close-knit, supportive family provides the most effective buffer to stressful urban conditions. The family also serves its members as a refractor of perceptions of their community, the larger city, and life therein. Evidence indicates that in spite of the high rates of geographic and social mobility in industrial society, extended families continue to play an important role in maintaining primary relationships for many people. Evidence provided by researchers such as Sussman, Axelrod, Litwak, and Geer,[73] for example, does not demonstrate the desire of family members to live in the same dwelling; it does, however, clearly support the continued existence of a pattern of mutual aid between parents, grown offspring, and siblings, as well as frequent visits and communication, which contradict those who decry the complete disappearance of extended family ties.

Evidence also indicates that an important factor in determining the specific city of migrant destination is the prior location of relatives.[74] For many individuals, kin provide a buffer for the newly arrived, at least until they have established their independent associations with other institutions. The degree to which new arrivals are dependent on kin for support and aid is in large part determined by their resources (such as skills and finances) and familiarity with the language and customs of the new locale. Continued relationships between family members, then, is not uniform for all types of families. In highly industrialized societies such as Great Britain and the United States, family relationships have been found to be most important for the lowest and working classes, and for upper-upper class families. Family ties are least important to middle-class and professional families. The support and aid function of the bonds that hold extended families together in the lower and working class is obvious; whereas trust funds and other mutually-owned pieces of family wealth provide part of the explanation for family involvement by the upper-upper class persons.[75] The relative lack of involvement with extended family in the middle and professional groups, on the other hand, may simply be attributable to their greater geographic mobility. For this population, possibly, neighbors and friends provide some of the reciprocal services that would otherwise have been the function of the extended kin. These relationships, however, tend to be restricted to the female member of the families with children rather than entire family groups.

Family and friends apparently continue to provide one source of personal involvement for many urban residents. These relationships, in turn, possibly serve as a mode of integrating many individuals into "communities" within the urban setting. Perceived or actual crisis situations, like threatened territorial infringement, commonly serve as the triggering mechanisms for manifest community (or neighborhood) identification and cooperative action. This is evidenced in the many school district squabbles and neighborhood associations formed to resist change. Ninety-four families in Brooklyn's Northside, for example, united and resisted industrial and city demands that they move, even as their homes were being torn down to allow the expansion of a local paper box machinery factory.[76]

Suzanne Keller has noted that many characteristics of the industrial-urban complex moved against the development and perpetuation of tightly knit communities. These characteristics included the presence of multiple sources of information and opinion, highly developed transportation systems, improved social services, and economic security, as well as increased differentiated interests and desires and rhythms of work and leisure.[77]

Although it is true that many associations formed around a particular crisis disappear with the resolution of the specific problem, contrary to the conclusion drawn by Keller, we feel that some of the characteristics she noted as detrimental to the formation of a sense of community may, in fact, contribute to the emergence of other forms of organization in urban settings. For example, just as Kerr and Siegel[78] found that differentiated rhythms of work and leisure experienced by those in industries such as mining, maritime, and longshore were associated with the formation of tightly knit militant groups, similarly large numbers of workers isolated from others in urban areas also have formed strong unions. Of course, we realize that the bureaucratic, large scale nature of business in urban areas as well as occupational specialization served as contributing factors to the development of unions. Nonetheless, labor unions, once formed, have proven to be a formidable, important unit in the operation of urban society. Moreover, unions have served not only to forward the economic interests of their urban workers, but also have served as centers of political loyalty. The AFL-CIO, for example, has founded the single most powerful lobby for the aid of congressional candidates.

Further, Keller is probably correct in assuming that exposure to multiple sources of information and opinion serve to prevent the development of communities. In reality, however, few persons voluntarily prolong their exposure to contradictory ideas. It is easy to switch a dial or buy literature congruent with one's predilections. We tend, also, to prefer association with others who share our attitudes.[79] It might be suggested that urban areas are only *potentially* conducive to introducing people to diverse ideas through the mass media and conversation between acquaintances. The potential may or may not be realized. We, however, will set a conditional specification about urban social relations. Serving as a setting for bringing together people who might otherwise not have identified or associated with one another, we suggest that the basis of interaction has altered, not attenuated, in cities. The battles between groups of parents and educators, landlords and tenants, workers and management, and ethnic groups over the past few decades attest to the possible cohesiveness between people in an otherwise mass society.

Ethnic ties

Many social scientists have observed the fact that communities based on nationality ties were formed early in many of the major American city centers, as new immigrants came to seek their fortunes in the land of opportunity. Waves of Europeans, gentiles, Jews, Orientals, blacks, American Indians, and Puerto Ricans poured into American cities. Little Italy, Chinatown, Jewish communities, and settlements representing most of the world's people remain identifiable in many American cities long after the initial period of immigration, and provide one mode of organizing "we" from "they."

With few exceptions, each wave of immigration brought poor, relatively unskilled people into the city. The formation of the early ethnic enclaves eased the strain of the newly arrived. There they found food similar to that of their homeland, others who spoke the same language, and services familiar to them. For the immigrant until the early decades of the twentieth century, work and housing were usually obtained through the help of relatives, friends, or political machines. At times, the task of assisting new immigrants was assumed by groups of earlier, established immigrants. Thus, aid was provided by earlier arrived Jews from Germany for eastern Jewish immigrants; the patron system for Italian immigrants; compadrazgo for Mexican immigrants; and the churches for Irish, Puerto Rican, and Japanese immigrants.

The extent to which a particular group was able to help their own people depended on at least two conditions: (1) the economic and social conditions of the area to which they arrived and (2) the pattern of social organization the immigrants brought with them.

The relevance of economic success and internal organization of a particular group of persons to their eventual adjustment within cities is evident in the case of the many different groups of American Indians. A small enclave of Caughnawaga Indians (commonly known as Christian Mohawks), for example, can be found in Brooklyn's North Gowanus area. The emergence and relative success of this small community of approximately 800 people, compared to Indians in other cities, has been attributed to the economic success of the male members of the group in their role as steelworkers on high-rise projects.[80] The economic and social adjustment of Mohawks to urban life has been related to their ability to fulfill a dangerous and necessary task for the city. On the other hand, the nature of the work assumed by these people is also congruent to the family organization and attitudes they brought with them. As Murray L. Wax has written: "Work on the high iron fitted well with the warrior ethos of the Iroquois. Much of the work is performed by small gangs and egalitarian cooperation." In addition, the matrilineal structure of the family allowed the men to migrate in search of work. Once established, the Indian worker has been afforded the opportunity to commute seasonally, or even weekly, to the tribal reserve in Quebec.[81]

In contrast, Robert White, in describing the urban experience of the Sioux Indians in Rapid City, South Dakota, noted the personal and socially disorganizing effects of job insecurity and the breakdown of peer relationships in an environment perceived as hostile and indifferent.[82] Wax has noted that many of the Sioux in Rapid City live in a style characterized by "excessive drinking, physical violence, frequent travel, sexual exploits and violations of the law."[83] Such descriptions, of course, are not restricted only to the least successful Indian migrant. Similar descriptions have been provided for most immigrant and migrant groups at some time or another. The instance of the Indian, however, signifies the importance of the development of economically viable community and the role of economic success in aiding the adjustment of these individuals.

Such examples remind us of the conditions perpetuating the lines drawn between people of middle-class America and those defined as outsiders; that is, those of lower-class standing, a racial caste, or otherwise visibly different. Ironically, although the strength of the ethnic enclave in many instances initially played a positive part in providing a buffer for individual immigrants, such communities have continued to perpetuate themselves and, at times, exaggerate differences between themselves and others.

Politics

The study of urban politics is the study of power, and municipal governance has been commonly associated with a monolithic concept of power.[84] In all large American cities, however, where the population is economically diversified or identified in terms of ethnicity or religious affiliation, interest groups have formed in order to voice their opinion on decisions that affect them.

The organization of pressure groups may be around voluntary associations such as the League of Women Voters, the PTA, the NAACP, labor unions, or the church. The political impact of these groups may be felt especially where large numbers of a given interest group cluster coterminously with political boundaries. The effectiveness of their voice depends on a number of factors: the skill of their leadership, voter participation, the role of the mass media, and the extent to which the control over the economic institution is by local decision makers. Federal or state government may, in fact, control the ability of local government to act.[85]

Religion

Another group relevant to our understanding of life in the city also should be mentioned. Religious cults, at times new and different to most Americans, emerged seeking to replace formerly dominant religions. The Hare Krishna, with shaven heads, filmy, colorful, flowing costumes, and music strange to the Western ear appeared in the 1960s in Los Angeles, Detroit, New York, and other major cities. They were a supposed derivative of an ancient Hindu cult and drew their converts mainly from white, middle-class, college-aged rebels.

The Hare Krishna provided one example of the possibility in urban areas for the blossoming of exotic, counter-cultural beliefs. The city served as a fertile ground for many a "true believer"—the fanatics of any persuasion who found prototypic fascist, socialist, anarchist, vegetarian, conservative, or liberal organizations. Exactly in pace with the proliferation of such groups, the opportunity for the tolerance of further growth in divergent groups grows. Alternatively, the emergence of a large number of groups with different ideologies and lifestyles at the same time increases the areas of possible social conflict.

The metropolis—suburbia

Most suburbanites set out in search of a sense of community. Following the discussion presented in this chapter, however, it is clear that the concept of community needs to be reassessed by urbanites and suburban residents alike. Old benchmarks for the concept are inappropriate and necessarily relegated to the realm of nostalgia.

If one uses the preliterate or peasant village as a point of reference, the term *community* means a situation where each member's life was bound up with the collective experiences of his group. Work, residence, and social intercourse with family and friends took place within the confines of a small territory. Political power was usually vested in one party, undisputed by those internal to the group and free from external interference, except for times of war.[86]

Few, if any, communities of the twentieth century can be economically independent. Social isolation and self-contained existence is possible. Further, friends are scattered over large, but accessible, areas, and major service and cultural institutions (e.g., higher education and museums) are usually found in the city centers, while many other facilities tend to be located in the periphery. Perhaps, then, economic independence and the concomitant social isolation of a particular group may not be the only base for the establishment of a community. The flourishing voluntary organizations, from PTAs to country clubs, found in the suburbs can be used to support a notion of community spirit, but it is hardly comparable to life in a peasant village or congruent with analyses that would differentiate such organization with that found in urban centers. In describing suburban communities, Robert Wood has written:

> Americans use political boundaries in place of economic interdependence as the catalyst to create some of the important social and symbolic conditions of grassroots life. . . . as the urban exodus goes on, new communities appear, using the legal powers of local self-government and the variety of classes and vocations which industrialization has spawned to fashion islands of small town life.[87]

Communities based on the premise described by Wood, we contend, are not unlike those that emerged in many of the central cities during the 1960s. In fact, as *Crestwood Heights, Organization Man, Worker's Suburbia,* and a variety of other studies of suburban life have noted, the very quality of the suburbanite's life basically is not different from that of the urbanite. Suburban areas appear to be more "child-centered." Yet, the political views of suburban migrants has not changed, and their personal relationships are frequently as superficial and segmented as in the city. Perhaps the only discernible effect of suburbia upon the nature of ex-urbanites is that the focus of social strife changes. In a variety of disputes affecting metropolitan areas—school desegregation, housing discrimination, law and order—the suburbanites have organized *against* the inner city.[88] Thus, while metropolitan areas sprawl over the map, a new set of dimensions (reflecting economic realities) divide most suburbs from their adjoining central cities, just as village and rural areas once stood against the encroachment of growing cities.

The fragility of the form of community that has developed both in urban and suburban areas is underlined by the fact that a large number of families move each year as the array of economic alternatives broadens. Under such conditions long-lasting bonds of affection and sentiment can hardly be established between peoples even in suburban areas. Disappointing as it may be for those preferring to return to the nostalgia of the good old days (if they ever existed), there is little likelihood that the United States or other industrialized nations can return to the type of folk society thought to have characterized the small town.

SUMMARY: THE AMERICAN CITY

Throughout American history, urban areas have been the center of innovation and social conflict. As America entered the twentieth century, cities became the center of life for most Americans. Metropolitan areas—central cities surrounded by satellite suburbs—emerged as geographical settings in which Americans, willingly or not, led their lives.

As a result of this change, most Americans acculturated themselves to an "urbane" life-style: a way of life emphasizing privacy, mobility, and anonymity. From a positive point of view, this new environment offered the opportunity of greater freedom by exposing people to a wide variety of different beliefs and requiring a high degree of tolerance for diverse opinions.

Simultaneously, the growth of cities has entailed a concentration of America's lower class in increasingly deteriorated central cities, an expansion in public services (particularly those directed to controlling a potentially rebellious population),[89] an extension of education, and the rise of electronic media as a dominating factor in people's lives.

In an urban milieu, many of the old institutions of American life faced steady erosion. The family system underwent drastic alterations, organized religion suffered a decline, and traditional political allegiances were shaken. On a personal and social level, American cities exhibited extremely high rates of crime, alcoholism, mental disorder, drug addiction, and suicide. Compared to their rural ancestors, Americans suffered from an extraordinary degree of social malaise.

New social groups emerged in urban areas to buffer the individual from the more deleterious effects of city life and aid in adjustment. Ethnic enclaves and unions were created. Urbanites experimented with new forms of family life, new political organizations, and new religions. Meanwhile, city officials attempted to quell urban tensions by multiplying the forces of public safety, dispensing more funds for education and welfare, recognizing the power of unions, and creating new political coalitions. The essential purpose of these actions was to give some expression to the more intense private and public conflicts experienced by urbanites, and to find new ways of mediating the strife peculiarly endemic to life in a metropolis.

The most dramatic, far-reaching effects of urbanization have encompassed three areas of social conflict.

An intensification of social conflict

Both in the past and today, cities have been noted as the centers for violent social conflict and extremely high rates of crime. Simultaneously, they have served as the progenitors of reform movements, riots, revolts, and revolutions. The people who come to cities are, of course, selectively chosen. Generally, urbanites represent the more ambitious, most independent segment of any country's population. They arrive with high expectations. They may be exposed to a variety of influences from the mass media and the different life-styles around them. To advance their particular interests, buffer groups ranging from gangs to political parties have emerged. These groups, in turn, have clashed in a series of unceasing conflicts.

Changes in the nature of social conflict

In cities, totally new arenas for conflict are opened. People have fought over language differences (as in Bombay), ethnic divisions (as in Watts), class distinctions (as in revolutionary Petrograd), and political beliefs (as in East Side New York). Some issues are muted in a city environment. Few conflicts arise, for example, over religious disagreements, which become somewhat irrelevant in the secular city. Other issues inflate beyond the comprehension of most villagers or farmers. In 1974, for example, Jews in New York protested the hearing of the Palestine Liberation Front at the United Nations, requiring the city to dispatch squadrons of police, coast guard cutters, and helicopters to protect the Arab delegation; students in Paris ripped up paving blocks and fought bitterly with police over the number of seats provided at the Sorbonne; South-end Bostonians beat up blacks who participated in the desegregation of schools, which resulted from court decisions. Ulster Protestants killed Catholics in Belfast, and Catholics fought back, because of severe political and economic divisions that cut across religious lines. The precipitating issues are as diverse as the urban landscape: a black woman sitting in the front of a bus (United States), the theft of a hair from the beard of a prophet (New Delhi), or an arrest for drunken driving (Los Angeles). Whatever the source, urban conflicts—particularly in those congested areas where class, territorial, and ethnic lines frequently coalesce—sprout in all of their manifestations.

The invention of new ways of resolving social conflict

Cities not only change the nature and pace of human conflict. By necessity, they also provide new means for mediating conflicts. The law, for example, is a characteristically urban invention. Police forces (which now function so prominently in America's cities) are a relatively modern invention of the more stable citizens of London who feared for their lives in the midst of urban chaos.[90] Cities also created political parties, formal organizations aimed at reforming the system, and a variety of groups that hoped to rehabilitate the victims of city life. Thus, the city is mother to such diverse groups as the Democratic party and Alcoholics Anonymous, the Women's Liberation Movement and the Police Benevolent League, the AFL-CIO and the Union League Club.

The breakdown of traditional ties, the growth of new urban interests, the influence of mass media and the exposure to alternative life-styles led to the creation of these novel forms of expressing and resolving social conflict. In the next chapter we will outline some other thoughts by social scientists and philosophers on the origins, manifestations, and resolutions of conflict in the unsettling, chaotic scene of urban life.

Issues for further discussion

1. What has been the consequence of population shifts in American central cities in recent years?

2. Is there a core of "urbane" attitudes created by the process of urbanization? If so, what forces lead to this new frame of mind?

3. Does urbanization lead to higher rates of crime and mental illness? Why?

4. How does urbanization affect family life?

5. What is the influence of urbanization upon political affairs in America?

6. Is there a relationship between religious beliefs and urbanization? Why?

7. What are the primary functions of buffer groups in urban areas?

8. In what ways has urbanization changed the form, nature, and intensity of social conflict?

FOOTNOTES

1. Thomas Wolfe, *The Web and the Rock* (New York: Alfred A. Knopf, 1939), p. 223.
2. Alexander Klein, *The Empire City: A Treasury of New York* (New York: Rinehart & Co., 1955), chap. 21.

3. Philip M. Hauser, "The Changing Population Pattern of the Modern City," in *Cities and Society,* ed. Paul K. Hatt and Albert Reiss, Jr. (New York: Basic Books, Inc., Publishers, 1957).
4. Gorden Mitchell, *Sick Cities* (New York: The Macmillan Co., 1963), or William A. Caldwell, *How to Save Urban America* (New York: New American Library, 1973).
5. Richard B. Andrews, *Urban Growth and Development* (New York: Simmons-Boardman, 1962).
6. Kingsley Davis, *World Urbanization: 1950–1970,* vol. 1 (Berkeley and Los Angeles: Institute of International Studies, University of California, 1969).
7. Gladwin Hill, "Nation's Cities Fighting to Stem Growth," *New York Times,* 28 July 1974, p. 1.
8. Ibid.
9. Ibid.
10. Hauser, "Changing Population," in Hatt and Reiss, *Cities and Society.*
11. Roy Reed, "Rural Areas' Population Gains Now Outpacing Urban Region," *New York Times,* 18 May 1975, pp. 1, 32B.
12. Ibid., p. 32B.
13. See, for example, Eileen Shanahan, "Study Finds Poor Blacks in Cities, Whites Outside," *New York Times,* 30 August 1974, p. 14.
14. Michael T. Kaufman, "In Era of Urban Decline One City Rises: Phoenix," *New York Times,* 5 April 1975, p. 1.
15. Ibid.
16. Harod X. Connolly, "Black Movements into Suburbs: Suburbs Doubling their Black Population During 1960s," *Urban Affairs Quarterly* 9 (Sept. 1973):1. Also see Ernest Holsendolph, "Survey finds Decline in Black Population in Capital with a Sharp Rise in Suburbs," *New York Times,* 20 May 1975, p. 20.
17. The President's Commission on Civil Disorder, "The Future of the Slums," in *Social Problems: Pesistent Challenges,* ed. Edward C. McDonagh and Jon E. Simpson (New York: Holt, Rinehart and Winston, 1968).
18. U.S. Department of Commerce, Bureau of the Census, *Statistical Abstracts* (1975), p. 70.
19. Ibid.
20. Richard A. Cloward and Francis Fox Piven, *The Politics of Turmoil* (New York: Random House, 1970).
21. See Ben J. Wattenberg, *The Real America* (New York: Doubleday & Co., 1974).
22. Leonard Buder, "Retired Top Policeman Will Head School Security," *New York Times,* 12 September 1974.
23. Michael T. Kaufman, "Bitter Local School Dispute Reflects Citywide Concerns," *New York Times,* 1 April 1974, pp. 33, 35.
24. For example, see John Edwards, *The Family and Social Change* (New York: Alfred A. Knopf, 1969), and Richard Sennett, *Families Against the City* (Cambridge, Mass.: Harvard University Press, 1970).
25. Harvey Cox, *The Secular City* (New York: The Macmillan Co., 1968), p. 1.
26. Ibid., p. 3.
27. For a view of the state of religious organizations in urban areas see "Religious Orders are Increasingly Hanging Out the For Sale Sign," *New York Times,* 29 September 1974, p. 14.
28. See, for example, Constance Green, *The Rise of Urban America* (New York: Harper & Row, Publishers, 1965).
29. Wattenberg, *Real America,* p. 114.
30. William K. Stevens, "The Recession Increases Racial Tension in Detroit," *New York Times,* 15 May 1975, p. 27.
31. Louis Wirth, *On Cities and Social Life* (Chicago: University of Chicago Press, 1964).
32. Ibid.
33. Ibid.
34. Walter Lippmann, *Deft and Mastery* (New York: M. Kennerly, 1916).
35. York Willbern and Lawrence A Williams, "An Urban Observation Report," *Nation's Cities* (Aug. 1971), pp. 10–25.
36. U.S. Department of Commerce, *Statistical Abstracts* (1975), p. 159.
37. Ibid., p. 152.
38. Leo Levy and Harold M. Visotsky, "The Quality of Urban Life: An Analysis from the Perspective of Mental Health," in *The Quality of Urban Life,* ed. Henry J. Schmandt and Warner Bloomberg, Jr. (Beverly Hills, Calif.: Sage Publications, 1969), p. 259.
39. See, for example, Robert E. L. Faris and H. Waren Dunham, *Mental Disorders in Urban Areas* (Chicago: University of Chicago Press, 1939), and Berton Kaplan, *Psychiatric Disorder and the Urban Environment: Report of the Cornell Social Science Seminar* (New York: Behavioral Publications, 1971).
40. Leo Srole, "Urbanization and Mental Health: Some Reformulations," *American Scientist* 60 (Sept./Oct. 1972):576–583. The test of mental health consisted of self-report on various degrees of psychosomatic symptoms.
41. See, for example, August Hollingshead and Fredrick Redlich, *Social Class and Mental Illness* (New York: John Wiley & Sons, 1956),

and Leo Levy and Louis Rowitz, *The Ecology of Mental Disorder* (New York: Behavioral Science Publications, 1973).
42. S. Kirson Weinberg, *Deviant Behavior and Social Control* (Dubuque, Iowa: William C. Brown Co., 1974).
43. Levy and Visotsky, *Urban Life*, p. 266.
44. Leo Srole et al., *Mental Health in the Metropolis* (New York: McGraw-Hill Book Co., 1962), pp. 138, 230. Mental health, in this instance, was defined by an examination of responses to semi-structured interviews of a representative sample of Manhattanites. The assessment was made through independent ratings by two psychiatrists.
45. Seymour Parker and Robert J. Kleiner, *Mental Illness in the Urban Negro Community* (New York: The Free Press, 1966).
46. Robert Strauss, "Alcohol and Alcoholism," in *Contemporary Social Problems*, ed. Robert Merton and Robert Nisbet (New York: Harcourt Brace Jovanovich, 1971).
47. Ibid., p. 113.
48. See, for example Samuel E. Wallace, *Skid Row as a Way of Life* (Totowa, N.J.: Bedminster Press, 1965).
49. Strauss, *Alcohol and Alcoholism*, p. 235.
50. Metropolitan Life Insurance Co., *Statistical Bulletin* 48 (April 1967): 4.
51. Strauss, *Alcohol and Alcoholism*, p. 234.
52. D. Cahalan and I. H. Cisin, "American Drinking Practices," *Quarterly Journal of Studies on Alcohol*, vol. 29 (March 1968).
53. William McCord, "We Ask the Wrong Questions About Crime," *New York Times*, 21 November 1965.
54. Willbern and Williams, "Urban Observation Report."
55. See John A. O'Donnell and John C. Ball, eds., *Narcotic Addiction* (New York: Harper & Row, Publishers, 1966), pp. 6–10.
56. John A. Clausen, "Drug Use," in Merton and Nisbet, *Contemporary Social Problems*.
57. Emile Durkheim, *Suicide* (New York: The Free Press, 1951).
58. Ronald W. Maris, *Social Forces in Urban Suicide* (Homewood, Ill.: The Dorsey Press, 1969).
59. *Demographic Yearbook* (New York: United Nations, 1967), table 24.
60. Ibid.
61. U.S. Department of Commerce, Bureau of the Census, *Statistical Abstracts* (1975), p. 61.
62. Maris, *Social Forces in Urban Suicide*.
63. See, for example, Charles W. Hobart, "Commitment, Value Conflict and the Future of the American Family," *Marriage and Family Living* (Nov. 1965), and John N. Edwards, "The Future of the Family Revisited," *Journal of Marriage and the Family* (Aug. 1967).
64. Wattenberg, *Real America*, p. 357.
65. The same phenomenon has been noted by William J. Goode in regard to urban migrants in African cities. See *World Revolution and Family Patterns* (New York: The Free Press, 1963).
66. Wattenberg, *Real America*.
67. U. S. Census (1970).
68. See Vance Packard, *A Nation of Strangers* (New York: Doubleday & Co., 1972), and Michael Knight, "For the Corporate Wives, Help in Adjusting to Moves," *New York Times*, 27 February 1975, p. 37.
69. Ibid.
70. Ernest Burgess, "The Family in a Changing Society," in Hatt and Reiss, *Cities and Society*, p. 482.
71. See Herbert A. Otto, *The Family in Search of a Future* (New York: Appleton-Century-Crofts, 1970).
72. Srole, *Mental Health in the Metropolis*, p. 99.
73. See Robert M. Marsh, *Comparative Sociology* (New York: Harcourt, Brace and World, 1967), pp. 72–82.
74. See, for example, Stanley Feldstein and Lawrence Costello, eds., *The Ordeal of Assimilation* (Garden City, N.Y.: Anchor Press, 1974).
75. Robert Marsh, *Comparative Sociology*.
76. Grace Lichtenstein, "Neighborhoods: New Northside," *New York Times*, 20 August 1974, p. 37.
77. Suzanne Keller, *The Urban Neighborhood* (New York: Random House, 1968).
78. Clark Kerr and A. Siegel, "The Interindustry Propensity to Strike—An International Comparison," in *Industrial Conflict*, ed. Arthur Kornhauser, et al. (New York: McGraw-Hill Book Co., 1954).
79. See, for example, Milton Rokeach, *Beliefs, Attitudes and Values* (San Francisco: Jossey-Bass, Inc., Publishers, 1968).
80. Murray L. Wax, *American Indians* (Englewood Cliffs, N.J.: Prentice-Hall, 1971).
81. Ibid.
82. Robert White, "The Urban Adjustment of the Sioux Indians in Rapid City, South Dakota," mimeographed progress report, cited in Wax, *American Indians*.
83. Wax, *American Indians*, p. 168.
84. See Scott Geer, *The Urbane View: Life and Politics in Metropolitan America* (New York: Oxford University Press, 1972) for a com-

prehensive view. Also see Michael Aiken and Paul Mott, *The Structure of Community Power* (New York: Random House, 1970).

85. See, for example, Arthur Vidich and Joseph Bensman, *Small Town and Mass Society* (Princeton, N.J.: Princeton University Press, 1958).
86. Robert Wood, *Suburbia: Its People and Their Politics* (Boston: Houghton Mifflin Co., 1958).
87. Ibid.
88. Witness, for example, the continuing fight of Clayton against incorporation with Saint Louis; the resistance of Evanston to become part of Chicago; the continuing fight of Shaker Heights to be part of Cleveland; and Grosse Point continuing to hold out against the enlargement of the Detroit tax base.
89. See Cloward and Piven, *Politics of Turmoil.*
90. See Donald J. Newman, *Introduction to Criminal Justice* (Philadelphia: J. B. Lippincott, 1975).

SUGGESTED READINGS

For a general introduction to the growth and development of cities in America read Michael Lewis, *Urban America: Institutions and Experience* (New York: John Wiley & Sons, 1973), and Daniel Bell, *The Coming of Post Industrial Society* (New York: Basic Books, Inc., Publishers, 1973).

The history of American cities is clearly presented in two books by Constance McLaughlin Green, *The Rise of Urban America* (New York: Harper & Row, Publishers, 1965), and Raymond A. Mohl and Neil Bitten, *Urban America in Historical Perspective* (New York: Weybright and Tally, 1970).

For more information regarding deviance in urban settings see Jerome K. Myers and Lee L. Bean, *A Decade Later: A Follow-up of "Social Class and Mental Illness,"* (New York: John Wiley & Sons, 1973), and Berton Kaplan, *Psychiatric Disorder and the Urban Environment: Report of the Cornell Social Science Seminar* (New York: Behavioral Publications, 1971). Also see Marshall Clinard, "The Relation of Urbanization and Urbanism to Criminal Behavior," in *Contributions to Urban Sociology,* ed. Ernest Burgess and Don Bogue (Chicago: University of Chicago Press, 1964), and Marvin Wolfgang, "Urban Crime," in *The Metropolitan Enigma,* vol. 2, ed. James Q. Wilson (Washington, D.C.: United States Chamber of Commerce, 1967).

There have been numerous case histories and sociological studies of ethnic enclaves in cities. Classic is the study of Boston's Italian population by William Foote Whyte, *Street Corner Society: The Social Structure of an Italian Slum* (Chicago: University of Chicago Press, 1943). Some years later the Italian community was restudied by Herbert Gans, *The Urban Villagers: Group and Class in the Life of Italian Americans* (New York: The Free Press, 1962). For a general review of this topic see Judith Kramer, *The American Minority Community* (New York: Thomas Y. Crowell Co., 1970).

chapter 4

Strife and urbanization

The city is the place where people first had to deal with the stranger who is not an enemy. . . . They . . . have not succeeded.

Kobo Abé

As Cicero first observed, "war is the nature of man." In all of its forms—from tribal battles through court intrigues to contemporary riots—conflict has been the midwife of change, progress, and social devastation. The birth of cities has drastically changed the nature and costs of this internecine battle. Simultaneously, urbanization has been accompanied by a growth in civilization—the creative product of a gentle, leisured, independent group of people—and by the effluence of the more brutish side of human nature. If Freud were alive, he might retitle his famous work, *Civilization and Its Discontents,* as *Urbanization and Its Discontents.*

The growth of postindustrial cities has entailed many ironies. As creativity in medicine, technology, politics, and the broad range of the arts has increased, people have been freed from the limitations of village life and the agonies of subsistence existence. At the same time they have engulfed themselves in conflicts unprecedented throughout history: the merciless, if technically perfect, extermination of six million Jews; the destruction of cities such as Hiroshima, Rotterdam, and Berlin; the rise of urban demagogues—Hitler, Mussolini, Nkrumah—who are gobbled up in the very conflagration they ignite; and the creation of apparently unending urban conflicts between American blacks and whites, Irish Catholics and Protestants, and French reactionaries and urban masses.

The analysis of the nature, roots, and implications of conflict is ingrained in the writings of many of the greatest thinkers during the various periods of recorded history.[1] The many inquiries regarding human strife have been based on the following assumptions:

- Man is a competitive being, insatiably seeking power, property, prestige, or as Freud commented, the fulfillment of the "immortal, infantile wish to be great."
- Change is inherent in the very nature of society, and for some theorists, in the universe itself.
- Strife, at times, is controlled by the desires of those with the power to constrain others and does not necessarily serve a general good of the social group.

Our subject matter, then, includes some rather grim topics: What can be gained? Who has the greatest control over others? What are the forces at work to change the balance of power? These were some of the central questions for such social philosophers as Polybius and Epictetus, Hobbes and Voltaire, Marx and Freud. Each man, of course, provided his unique response.

It would require volumes to record all of the varieties of conflict theories that have been developed. Contemporary students of the relation of urbanization and social conflict, however, should have at least some familiarity with the major outlines of the arguments presented. Let us touch first on the ancient ideas of conflict.

THE ROOTS OF CONFLICT THEORY: ANCIENT

Heraclitus (544–584 B.C.) was perhaps the most influential of the early conflict theorists. He viewed all things, animate or inanimate, as in a constant state of flux and contradiction. Such a situation, then, is conducive to strife. In fact, Heraclitus felt that conflict was the essence of human society. The justice of a particular cause could be established only in the outcome of the conflict.

Other Sophists followed Heraclitus's insight. Georgias (485–380 B.C.) first recognized the utility of propaganda, religion, and other illusions as mechanisms for keeping men under control. Callicles (481?–411 B.C.), however, went further, and condemned law and morality as tools used by a majority of weak men to keep the innately strong minority from fully asserting its will. Sophists such as Callicles, Critias, and Thrasymachus believed that only fools could believe in doctrines asserting that might was not right.

Epicurus (342?–270 B.C.) added a metaphysical framework to the gloomy views of his predecessors. He was among the first to conceive of the universe as composed of tiny atoms in a constant state of movement. Man, like all material things, was also in a state of constant change. At his worst, man was a raging beast condemned forever to struggle with nature and with fellow humans. At his best, civilized man could only withdraw from society; curbing his appetites and abstaining—as far as possible—from engagement in human strife.

Polybius (205–125 B.C.) codified some of the previous conflict theorists. Polybius believed that man as an individual was an impotent, defenseless animal. Man, therefore, grouped himself with others into herds that inevitably destroyed weaker members of the species. If the herd survived, a supreme leader arose who temporarily dominated the inferior humans. With the death of the monarch, however, humans again strove to establish a legitimate kingship to keep conflict within the group at a minimum. At this point in history the idea of justice is presumed to have been invented whereby the king was enabled to enforce his will with the consent of the majority. A variety of other forms of polities may succeed the kingship pattern—aristocracy, tyranny, democracy. In Polybius's view, democracy was least stable since people would be unrestrained in their struggle for influence and power. A reversion to some other form of monarch would then occur.[2] Roman poets adopting Polybius's views sang the praises of Roman expansion. Philosophical schools, particularly the Epicureans, followed the popular view that strife lay at the base of all experience.

Perhaps the greatest flowering of conflict theory occurred during the lifetime of the Emperor Marcus Aurelius (A.D. 121–180). By all accounts, he was a gentle man, more of a poet than a fighter, the epitome of a Stoic. Nonetheless, as the inheritor of a crumbling empire, he found himself continually in battle. At times, it is said, he composed his philosophical diary in his tent on a battlefield before leading his warriors into eventually losing battles. His central maxims concerning the gloomy nature of human life perhaps can be a motto for the school of thought emphasizing conflict: "As for life," he once wrote, "it is a battle and a sojourning in a strange land . . . the fame that comes after is oblivion." He offered little hope for man's efforts: "All is change, all is ephemeral."[3] For Marcus Aurelius, there were few options open to the reasonable man: he should accept change in his fortunes with graceful dignity; he should accept defeat and victory with equal tranquility; and he should treat all men as his brothers—for all end in death.

With the destruction of Rome and its final conquest by the barbarians, the focus on conflict in social theory receded, partially because the fate of conflict theories has always been linked to the destiny of great cities. Further, this change also was based upon experience: the Romans themselves had become the victims of strife, rather than the conquerors. As the medieval period descended upon Western civilization, theories of social conflict appeared to be inconsistent with the dominance of a pervasive church.

Beginning in the fourteenth century, however, the medieval synthesis cracked under the impact of social and economic changes: urbanization, the Reformation, industrialization, and the emergence of new social classes. As Western society entered a new epoch of economic change, political innovation, reform, and revolution, new theories again emphasizing conflict emerged to explain social phenomena. Jean Bodin, Adam Ferguson, David Hume, and Thomas Hobbes all treated conflict as a necessary, inevitable part of human life. If life was "nasty, brutish, and short," and all men were engaged in conflict, as Hobbes believed, then new theories were needed both to explain the phenomenon and to establish the philosophical basis for some sort of political order.[4]

THE ENLIGHTENMENT

The Enlightenment period, in particular, spawned a series of doctrines concerning the nature of man and society. Most of the major Enlightenment figures (all of them urban men) agreed on certain essentials: that reason, epitomized by science, offered hope for mankind; that progress could be made if man applied reason to the understanding of society; and that all men act upon a calculus of pleasure and pain. The philosophers of this period, however, diverged widely on other essential points.

The contrast between Voltaire and Rousseau best serves to illustrate these divergencies. In fact, issues that disturbed Voltaire and Rousseau continue to divide social theorists today.

On the one hand, Voltaire represented an elitist, rationalist school of thought which continues to be influential. For Voltaire, humans are flawed, but potentially rational, animals. They seek their goals of pleasure and, if left unbridled, would simply be beasts of prey. Yet, the connections that hold people together could be maintained with the application of reason to the solution of social problems: if man allowed freedom of thought to others and submitted himself to the controls of civilization.[5]

The concept of civilization in Voltaire's writings is unclear. He excluded most forms of organized religion as mere superstition; yet he included the strict political controls of the Prussian state. Possibly, by civilization, Voltaire meant a society where an aristocracy of talent ruled by force, moderated by tolerance for the masses.

Rousseau, in contrast, believed that humans essentially are motivated by egoistic concerns.[6] He did not believe, however, that man's selfishness emerged from his innate nature, rather this nature was a consequence of civilization. Man, in his pristine state, was a noble savage. Thus, thought Rousseau, an essential task was the removal of the restraints of civilization, thus allowing man to return to his natural state. He believed that men could form a social contract that would allow each person to exercise individual will without violating the rights of others. This utopia was to have been achieved when humankind established societies based on rule by the general will.

The general will was defined by Rousseau as an almost mystical consensus concerning the welfare of a community. It was not to have been reflected in a majority vote, which could easily be mistaken. Unfortunately, Rousseau neglected to formulate any precise mechanisms by which the general will could exert its beneficent influence over a community.

Despite some vagueness in his writings, Rousseau's influence continues unabated today. Romantic idealists, including some members of the New Left like Theodore Roszak, Charles Reich, and Erich Fromm,[7] wish for a return to the state of noble innocence. They glorify, as did Rousseau, the supremacy of unsophisticated emotion. Rousseau and his contemporary followers disdain the corruption supposedly inherent in civilized urban life. The noble savage who lived in a city would inevitably lose purity, altruism, and innocence.

While Voltaire and Rousseau each proclaimed his doctrines in the urban environment of Geneva and its suburb, Verney, the society around them was about to explode into violence neither anticipated. Class conflict and food riots in the cities prompted an urban revolt. The French Revolution unleashed a fury of raging emotion that Napoleon spread across Europe. As dynasties fell and new nations emerged, few would ignore the pervasive effect of human strife. First among the inheritors of the Enlightenment tradition was Hegel (1770–1831), who produced a theory of history that drastically influenced such diverse men as Karl Marx and Benito Mussolini. In the disarray following the French Revolution, it was Hegel who tried to answer the central question of the day: How can society restore order and authority to a world torn by revolution?

HEGEL: A CONSERVATIVE RESPONSE TO THE PROBLEM OF STRIFE

The personal history of Hegel is that of a rather colorless figure. He began his career as a provincial gymnasium teacher in Germany, briefly edited a newspaper, and then spent many years as a retiring, although acclaimed, professor at the University of Berlin.[8]

Bertrand Russell called Hegel "the dictator of German philosophy."[9] His competitors, particularly Schopenhauer and Nietzsche, hated him; but they clearly incorporated the premises of Hegelianism into their own thoughts. Men as diverse as Hitler, Bakunin (a leader of the Russian Revolution), and Josiah Royce (the American idealist) claimed kinship with Hegelian thought. Most important to our discussion, Hegel left a strong imprint on the work of Karl Marx. This influential man accepted the romantic atmosphere of his time; he adopted the belief that human society was full of conflict, but, nonetheless, believed that history was guided by a mystical zeitgeist or "world spirit."

Few claim complete understanding of Hegel's thought, but one can begin an exploration of his position concerning human life by first examining his beliefs concerning the process of human logic.

Hegel's first contribution was to challenge Aristotelian, commonsense logic, that is, that A equals A, or that a dog is a dog. This type of reasoning, said Hegel, gives no clue to the reality of A (or the dog). As a first step toward comprehension, one must add predicates to the original thesis: thus a "dog is a four-legged animal," an equivalent to saying that A is B. A predicate (like four-legged) is simply an abstraction from a greater whole (two-legged, ten-legged). To say this means that the concept A necessarily includes an entirely different concept, that is, B. Therefore, one has presented a *thesis:* that dogs have four legs; and an *antithesis:* that dogs are members of a family of many-legged animals. The original concept, then, is negated by another concept, which is implicitly part of it.

Hegel's basic point was made on the basis of the analysis just given: that is, every concept includes its own negation. Consequently, any conception that approaches truth must be a *synthesis* between a thesis and its antithesis. This mode of thought is essentially the *dialectical process.* It is a way of looking at thought, life, and society. It demonstrates that the reality of a being includes separate, yet conflicting, elements.

If one takes the broadest view of reality, therefore, the inherent contradiction of all things to each other and their ultimate unity must be recognized. Man, for example, cannot be understood from this point of view without relating him to dogs or centipedes. The very process of comparison leads one to the "higher" view, where the separateness of things is dissolved and replaced by an endless chain of relations. For Hegel, the entire universe was one vast chamber in which every event has a repercussion and a relation to every other event.

Following this line of reasoning, Hegel believed that history itself must be rational. On the surface, history appears to be a melange of battles, conflicts, or contradictions. Yet, history also can be viewed as the unfolding of a series of ever new syntheses. He postulated an underlying historical process—a unifying world spirit—which molds together all of the petty disputes of mankind into a rational whole.

Hegel's influence is undeniable. In some interpretations of his work, such as Mussolini's advocacy of fascism, it ended as a justification of the most tyrannical authority. Although the world was full of conflict and contradiction, it was Mussolini's view that order could, eventually, be imposed.

Indeed, through the work of his students, Hegel's work influenced much of contemporary thought. Oswald Spengler and Pitirim Sorokin, for example, both forecast the fall of Western civilization partially because of the influence of the urban "megapolis" and its secularizing effects.[10] And, of course, the work of Karl Marx has vast influence throughout the modern world.

MARX: A REVOLUTIONARY RESPONSE TO STRIFE

Karl Marx (1818–1883) possibly has done more to revolutionize contemporary societies than any other social philosopher of the nineteenth century. Marxism has influenced millions of people the world over.

Why does Marxism have such influence? Perhaps the answer to this question can be sought in the particular combination of problems Marx addressed, and the manner in which he provided solutions to these issues. First, Marxist theory is the most comprehensive explanation of the conflicts created by the advent of urbanization and industrialization. Second, Marxist explanation was presumably scientific. That is, it attempted to explain conflict by laws that allowed prediction of future events. For example, Marx, on the basis of his theory, predicted recurrent and increasingly severe economic crises to which capitalism would be subject, the oligarchic stage through which capitalism will pass, and the dependency of capitalism on colonies or neocolonies. Further, Marx wrote optimistically: to change people's lives, men must only grasp the meaning of basic laws. Thus, Marxism offered a hope that man's problems in living with other men could be solved. Third, Marxism was based upon an ethical heritage. It drew upon the Judaic-Christian traditions in its condemnation of exploitation, the degradation of the human spirit, and the alienation of man from his own labor. Essentially, Marx sought justice.

Marx offered his version of history: social life is essentially class conflict. He observed extraordinary poverty which, paradoxically, was coupled with the greatest riches ever produced. Industrialism had not only released gigantic productive forces; it also made certain groups of people appear poorer than ever. Marx and his colleague, Friedrich Engels, were appalled by these contradictions.

Perhaps the first and finest book on the combined effects of industrialism and urbanization was Engels' classic description of Manchester, then the manufacturing center of the world.[11] The work was a product of Engels' father's attempt to curb his son's radical tendencies by sending him to Manchester. Instead of concentrating on learning to operate his father's business, Engels observed the extreme, brutal forms of class exploitation existing in Manchester at the time. His description of the city is a manifesto of the degradation of English cities. Both Engels and Marx took inspiration from Hegel but postulated that material conditions rather than thought were the prime movers of historical events.

In *Das Kapital*,[12] Marx confronted the question of how the system of capitalism arose. He argued that it was not an accidental product of history, but rather an inevitable development from contradictions inherent in the preceding feudal era. Capitalism began, Marx stated, when the feudal structure of society—the serf-lord relationship—began to break down and the bourgeois class grew. The bourgeoisie possessed independent capital and stood in a position intermediate to the lords and the serfs. The prime characteristics of this class included (1) possession of capital not needed for sheer subsistence; (2) access to capital through a process of "primitive accumulation" (robbery, piracy, the gradual appropriation of land); and (3) utility to feudal lords as moneylenders, sources of capital for exploration and other ventures. Thus, ironically, the bourgeoisie were required by the feudal lords for the continuance of their system; yet, they represented an antithesis to the form of society based solely on land ownership.

During the seventeenth and eighteenth centuries the bourgeoisie increased their potential power by the invention of the concept of public credit, the national debt, and joint stock companies. In addition, they attacked urban guilds and destroyed a competing group, the small yeoman. This was accomplished through land enclosure. Through such techniques the bourgeoisie grew in economic power, finally forcing landless laborers into cities. Thus, a helpless class of unemployed labor was formed that could be hired for a pittance.

During the eighteenth and nineteenth centuries the bourgeoisie gained control of the means of production and, in so doing, controlled society itself. As the economic structure of society underwent change, so too did the political, intellectual, and religious institutions. Political power passed from the aristocracy to the parliamentary dominance of the bourgeoisie; the intellectual order was changed from a glorification of feudal rights and duties to a demand for bourgeois rights; religiously, the Catholic church was replaced by a Protestantism that emphasized individual freedom and the accumulation of wealth.

The bourgeoisie had triumphed. They built a civilization based on industrial capitalism, which in turn created great wealth and cities. But this giant simultaneously created suffering. Was this to have been the permanent condition of human existence? No, Marx emphatically answered in *Das Kapital*. Within any society lie the seeds of its own destruction. Capitalism, according to Marx, is doomed for several reasons:

First, there is inevitable conflict within capitalism between the realities of economic production and the ideological superstructure of private property. Industrial production requires close coordination. Yet, during severe depressions when the economic machinery collapses, members of the bourgeoisie are unable to cooperate with one another.

Second, capitalism depends upon labor. Consequently, it creates a class to run the machines and help produce profit. This class, however, is subjected to conditions that unify it: simultaneously, then, an intense antagonism is created to the system itself. Marx succinctly summarizes this by suggesting that the bourgeoisie acts as its own gravedigger. Capitalism is doomed to fall from its own inner conflicts.

In order to clarify the nature of the dialectical process as applied to this situation, Marx addressed himself to two seemingly irrelevant, rather obtuse issues: value and profit. Regarding value, Marx posed the question: how do commodities achieve a given level of value in a capitalist system?

Obviously the "use" value to individuals is important and lies at the heart of supply and demand. People may desire cars or diamonds and therefore create a market for them. This is not, however, the real determinant of value. People also may desire bread and meat, but without money they cannot satisfy the use value of these crucial items. The only common denominator between bread, diamonds, and automobiles is their exchange value. Exchange value, in turn, is determined by a number of factors: the cost of discovering the commodity, manufacturing it, and most importantly, the cost of labor. Thus, exchange value is essentially determined by certain fixed costs (like land) and certain variable costs (such as the average amount o skilled labor required to produce the particular item). Yet, it also is clear that a capitalist sells a particular commodity for a profit; in other words, the exchange value of the item is higher than the actual cost put in by the capitalist for labor and other costs. Thus, Marx was faced with a second question: how does the capitalist reap his profit?

After considering many alternatives, Marx concluded that the answer to the profit question could be found only in a close investigation of the expenses of a capitalist. Essentially, Marx argued that capitalists had two basic expenses: first, in the marketplace they must buy the necessary land, raw materials, and machinery to produce their product. For these items, they pay *exactly* the value that these items will produce for them. In others words, if capitalists consistently sold their land or pieces of machinery for less than they could produce, they would have only two options: sell all of their goods and go bankrupt, or create a monopoly. Obviously, Marx argued, contemporary capitalists rejected the first option and opted for monopolization.

Capitalists found, however, that monopoly was possible in some situations but not in others. Thus, the majority of capitalists turned to another way of earning profit: paying laborers less than the value they inject into a product. In this instance, capitalists go to the marketplace for labor (ranging from ditchdiggers to biochemists) and buy the laborers' value. If particular skills are in short supply, the workers will gain a high salary. If the skills are common, the workers must take what they can get in the labor contract. It is, therefore, to the capitalists' advantage to always maintain a supply of unused labor and keep down the price of labor skills. It is at this point that capitalists make a profit. If labor is paid less than the value produced, in effect, then, they create surplus value.

This point in Marxist theory has been challenged as inadequate on several grounds:

Some opponents have argued that trade unions have negated the advantage of the capitalists' control over the means of production. This, however, is true during times of inflation when labor is scarce; it is not true during times of depression when there are long lines of unemployed and unions lose their bargaining power.

Others have contended that governmental interference with the system has favored workers. Surplus value, however, could be transferred from colonies or underdeveloped countries to provide incentives to keep the proletariat in advanced nations quiet. This amelioration, however, would end as soon as the dominance of capitalist nations over such regions as Asia, Africa, and South America was broken.[13]

Contemporary Marxists, such as the late Paul Baran, are primarily concerned with the situation of underdeveloped countries.[14] As their basic proposition, they assume that capitalist nations have consistently exploited Asia, Africa, and Latin America by withdrawing capital, raw materials, and profits from these regions. The first step in development is to cut the ties between capitalist nations and developing countries. Within the latter, Baran draws a distinction between the actual economic surplus and the potential surplus that could be produced. The actual surplus is much less than the potential surplus for several reasons: excessive consumption by the rich, the economic loss entailed in such enterprises as advertising and armament, and the losses entailed by constant, widespread unemployment. Consequently, underdeveloped nations must expropriate their own rich and establish a comprehensive plan of rational planning.

Assuming that these prerequisites can be fulfilled, a new world society could emerge. Marx himself was cautious in delineating the nature of that society, since he firmly believed that people would form a future unknown to any of us. He did, however, foresee stages in the evolution of the predicted utopia.

The first task after the revolution of the proletariat would be to expropriate the former expropriators, that is, to take back the means of production and return them to their rightful owners (the people who create value in society through their own labor). Temporarily, this process would entail a dictatorship of the proletariat.

During the period of transition between the rule of the proletariat and the final utopian stages of society, the state would wither. The only function of the state, in Marx's view, was as an instrument of control by one class over another. Of course, once control over the means of production had passed to the people, the raison d'être of the state would evaporate.

In the final stages of society, the way would be paved for an end to alienation. Each individual would be his own boss, contribute according to his abilities, and receive according to his needs. The creative potentialities of individuals—once removed from class restraints—would blossom. At that point, conflict and chaos would disappear.

It should be clear why, even today, Marx's ideas are revered throughout the world. He promised an end to suffering and strife and offered humankind the chance of total fulfillment. Although Marx illuminated the impact of class conflict on human history, he could not foresee the forms of divisiveness urbanization produced. It remained the task of illustrious thinkers like Max Weber and George Simmel to explicitly recognize the potential for new forms of conflict and conflict resolution produced by urban existence.

GEORGE SIMMEL: CONFLICT AND THE CITY

It would be delightful to draw a direct line of kinship between Hegel, Marx, and George Simmel since they all made significant, often complementary contributions to theories concerning urban conflict. All were German intellectuals, some of their lives overlapped, and they moved in roughly similar intellectual circles. Strangely enough, however, they rarely, if ever, acknowledged the work of the other. Each independently groped toward an understanding of human strife.

Although for the most part overlooked by American social scientists until Kurt Wolff and Lewis Coser reformulated his thought some years later, Simmel can now be regarded as one of the major, if not foremost, modern exponents of sociological theory emphasizing conflict.[15] His writings ranged broadly over the entire field of sociology, but a consistent theme ran throughout: concern with social conflict and, at times, a glorification of its effects on human existence. Simmel welcomed the coming of World War I: "This is what is so wonderful about this time; history we are now experiencing . . . the most basic formula of a highly developed culture . . . may be suggested by designating it as a crisis constantly held back . . . . Insofar as [the war] has any effect at all on these fundamental inner forms of culture . . . it can merely inaugurate a scene or an act of this endless drama."[16] As the war progressed and Germany lost, however, Simmel refused even to read the daily newspapers.

From very abbreviated records, Simmel's life appears to have been remarkably unruffled by either the tides of history or his own problems. He constructed his own, original, often penetrating theory of society as basically a conflict between individuals.

Like Sigmund Freud, Simmel viewed the individual as caught in inescapable conflict with his own society: "The individual strives to be rounded out in himself, not merely to help to round out society. He strives to develop his full capacities, irrespective of the shifts among them that the interest of society may ask of him. This conflict between the whole . . . and the part . . . is insoluble."[17]

Whether in dealing with dyads, triads, or entire nations, Simmel was concerned with the various paths or maneuvers one side could use to secure the advantage of another. In *Divide et Impera,* he outlined specific methods by which one group could overcome the opposition of another: "It is a technique employed by many rulers: he protects the stronger of two, both of whom are actually interested in his own downfall, until he has ruined the weaker; then he changes fronts and advances against the one now left in isolation, and subjugates him."[18]

Throughout his work, Simmel devoted himself to such themes as domination, the effects of "leveling," the uses of secrecy in fooling an adversary, and the penalties of being a stranger in a social situation. In the fashion of a disinterested Machiavelli, Simmel threw out numerous suggestions as to how opponents in social strife might win their particular battles.

While he has contributed to formal sociology in a number of important ways, Simmel's major insight was his view concerning the way urban life changed social strife. In his seminal essay "The Metropolis and Mental Life," Simmel contended that "the deepest problem of modern life derives from the claim of the individual to preserve the autonomy and individuality of his existence in the face of social forces."[19]

Among many factors Simmel attributed to the growing urbanization and industrialization of society were such elements as these:

1. An increased specialization of tasks.
2. Relationships marked by exchange processes: a person's worth is evaluated in terms of economic productivity.
3. Anonymity demanded because of the large number of contacts persons must have with others.
4. Subjection to a variety of diverse and new influences resulting in an "intensification of nervous stimulation." (Simmel suggested that individuals respond to this situation by developing a sophisticated attitude or a blasé stance; a willingness to accept all things without judging them.)
5. Each individual's life becomes increasingly subjected to an external, impersonal time schedule simply because of the complexity of metropolitan existence.
6. Individuals develop a changed demeanor, a facade of reserve. The multiplicity of contacts in urban areas necessitates this reserve. Unlike small towns, we do not truly know the people with whom we come into contact, and have every right to distrust them. Further, as Simmel observed:

   > If I do not deceive myself, the inner aspect of this outer reserve is not only indifference, but more often than we are aware, it is a slight aversion, mutual strangeness and repulsion, which will break into hatred and fight at the moment of closer contact.[20]

7. This element of reserve tinged with aversion to others also results in another metropolitan phenomenon: "it grants to the individual a kind and an amount of personal freedom which has no analogy whatsoever under other conditions."[21]

Most importantly Simmel concluded that characteristics of cities had totally changed the nature of strife: "It is decisive that city life has transformed the struggle with nature for livelihood into an interhuman struggle for gain, which here is not granted by nature but by other men."[22] As insightful as Simmel's conclusion was, a gap remains in the understanding of just how conflict has been altered in its urban setting. For example, an individual does not fight other individuals singlehandedly. As we have discussed in chapter 3, new lines have been drawn and redrawn, dividing and reorganizing people. Unfortunately, many contemporary social scientists have not recognized the importance of understanding the relationship between social conflict and the unique conditions and pace of urbanization. Until recently, only a few isolated scholars had picked up portions of work such as Simmel's. Indeed, with the advent of the twentieth century, sociological interest moved away from the study of conflict and, instead, concentrated on the conclave issue: how is societal order maintained?

FUNCTIONALISM: ORDER AND STABILITY

"Functionalist" thinkers, members of a school of thought dominating sociology through the 1950s and part of the 1960s, were primarily concerned with how modern society maintained stability and order.

Max Weber, for example, one of the most famous thinkers associated with functionalism, challenged prevailing Marxist doctrine by arguing that the influence of ideas was as important as the change in modes of production in the creation of capitalism.[23] His most important contribution was probably in the development of a theory of bureaucracy. He contended that increasingly rationalized roles would come to govern human life with impartiality and a definite system of rights and obligations. Further, Weber argued that the efficiency of bureaucratic systems would soon dominate all aspects of human life—from the army to university campuses. Although he regretted some of the effects of bureaucracy, Weber argued that the increasing rationalization of society was the wave of the future.

Emile Durkheim, another scholar who served as a "father" to functionalism, devoted his attention to the role of "collective representations" (myths or ideas) created by man as a means of holding society together.[24] He regarded deviance, such as suicide, as a phenomenon that occurred primarily when the cohesive ideas of society broke down. Both Weber and Durkheim, then, indirectly recognized the new conditions created by secularized, urban life.

More contemporaneously, Talcott Parsons, the most influential of American sociologists of the functionalist tradition, came to maturity just after the holocaust of World War I. He lived through the depression and experienced World War II. Although described as having lived a cloistered life behind the walls of Harvard, Parsons' work bears witness to the sensitivities of a man who wanted above all to repair the intense divisiveness entailed by the major events of his time. Parsons, as well as other functionalists, contended that society was always attempting to maintain "equilibrium."[25] Conflict, for Parsons, represented a dysfunctional aspect of society, and he believed that society always adjusted itself to resolve it.

Throughout his work, Parsons took as his basic model the interaction of two individuals (or groups). When the interaction between the parties was stable, Parsons argued, they shared the same values and expectations facilitating conformity to each other's expectations. Following Freud, Parsons postulated that humans learn their values early in life. Since this was viewed as a primary determinant of the stability of a system, it was important to understand how one individual internalized the values and expectations of other individuals. Effective socialization, then, was seen to be a critical element in the development of a stable society.

As Gerhard Lenski has pointed out, the world view of the functionalists was based on a concept of systems inherited from the natural scientist.[26] They assumed that society was made of a complex of interdependent parts, and the good of all is served by the proper functioning of all parts. Lenski, like other social scientists who have emphasized conflict, questioned this position and pointed out that factions, classes, and groups whose interests are in fundamental opposition to the functioning of a particular society could not be ignored. In fact, he suggested that the struggle of these factions rather than socialization or stability of social systems should be the central focus of social scientific inquiry.

Despite the contentions of men such as Lenski, the views of Weber, Durkheim, Parsons, and other functionalists dominated American sociology until the 1960s; in Europe, functionalists jostled with Marxists for dominance. In the early 1960s, however, a group of German and American thinkers resurrected and explicated the theory of human strife.

SOME CONTEMPORARY THEORIES OF SOCIAL STRIFE

Ralf Dahrendorf, Lewis Coser, Alvin Gouldner, Louis Kriesberg, and a variety of other sociologists have taken issue with the functionalist position so long dominant. The 1960s marked a period marred with ethnic revolt in America, stirrings of freedom in Eastern Europe, the failure of promising revolutions in the Third World, and imperialistic adventures by all of the world's great powers. A basic revision in social theory emphasizing equilibrium was the order of the day.[27]

Support for the requisite change in orientation derived from many sources. Konrad Lorenz and Robert Ardrey, biologically oriented investigators of the sources of disorder raised questions concerning the aggressive component of human nature.[28] Liberal social philosophers such as Reinhold Niebuhr, Arthur Schlesinger, and John Kenneth Galbraith[29] took another look at the notions of "conventional wisdom" concerning society. Their work raised fundamentally different questions from those posed by the functionalists. Like many other intellectuals in Western society they could be labeled "neo-Hegelians," "neo-Marxist," and "neo-Freudian" in that they thoughtfully absorbed the ideas of their predecessors.

Ralf Dahrendorf, an inheritor of the Marxist tradition, was among the first to challenge the functionalist school of thought by arguing that sociologists had been concerned for the past fifty years with the issue, "what holds societies together?" rather than with the question, "what drives society on?"[30] He emphasized that modern, industrialized, urban societies actually increased differences in power, prestige, and wealth. Therefore, following this logic, the proper subject matter for sociological study could only be an examination of the changes within society, the nature of ubiquitous social conflict wrought by these changes, and the factors that contribute to social change. As William Chambliss pointed out, those who followed Dahrendorf's view would be concerned with such issues as the effect of social class discrimination (not its "inevitability"), the relative contributions of different social classes (that is, is the president of a corporation *really* more important to the firm than the men who work for him), and the importance of the economic structure as a determinant of culture.[31]

Lewis Coser was at the forefront of the renewed interest in the study of conflict by first reviving interest in the work of Simmel and then explicating the effects of social conflict.[32] In summary, he suggested that:

- Conflict, under some conditions, may be beneficial to a group in uniting heretofore opposing factions against an outside threat. Alternatively, overt conflict between members of a society may be minimized, suggested Coser, when groups are not continually involved in struggles with outsiders, since attention can be paid to developing specific conflict-reducing mechanisms. Scandinavia, for example, has been virtually free of devastating wars for many years. Thus, the Scandinavian nations have been able to develop such institutions as the Ombudsman, a clearing house for complaints of the citizenry against the government.

- Conflict also may reestablish relations that were previously threatened. In combat, for example, white and black soldiers share a sense of unity usually lacking in the training period.
- Conflict establishes clear boundaries between different groups and, therefore, gives credence to beliefs in legitimacy and authority.

Coser also specified some of the conditions associated with more or less intense conflict. He observed that conflict within closely knit groups was commonly more intense than in more loosely defined groups. The family, therefore, can be expected to have more intense conflict than social classes in American society.

However, the more diverse the conflict existing for members of a group, the less is the intensity of the ensuing conflict. A student, for example, may be involved in conflicts with professors, parents, friends, and lover. Because of the multiple involvements, any one of the relationships is given less attention than if it were to be the sole focus of attention.

The deliberate use of conflict by politicians as a means of seeking their own ends also is recognized by Coser. Thus, among his basic postulates, Coser contends that all social groups search for a common enemy in the belief that conflict with some outside group increases internal cohesion. Of course, an end to conflict may, in fact, result in greater unity between the former antagonists. For example, World War II resulted in a new unity between the allies and the vanquished powers by creating a new framework of cooperation. Those who surrendered needed the help of the victors, and the conquerors, in turn, required a strong Japan and West Germany for strategic reasons. Drawing largely upon Simmel, then, Coser vastly expanded the horizons of those who contemplated human strife.

A number of social scientists have empirically advanced knowledge of the various sources and effects of conflict within the past decade. One of the finest summaries of these analyses is provided in the work of Louis Kriesberg, *The Sociology of Social Conflict*.[33] Kriesberg systematically has gathered evidence on the emergence of social conflicts, the process of their escalation and de-escalation, as well as some of the consequences of conflict.

From our review concerning the study of conflict, we conclude that conflict has been an enduring and recurrent theme throughout Western thought; beginning with the broad generalizations of the Greeks, through the romantic idealism of Hegel, to the empirical propositions of current social scientists. The directions taken by modern society underscore the relevance and import of such analysis. As interest in social conflict re-emerged, sociologists simultaneously, if independently, devoted their attention to urbanization.

DISCUSSION: THE NEW FACE OF THE CITY AND SOCIAL CONFLICT

As theories of social conflict have regained some prominence in contemporary social science, sociologists cannot help but attend to the problems of the impact of urbanization upon strife. Clearly, revolutionary movements in the Third World, the spread of violence in industrialized cities, and the emergence of urban-based reform movements have invoked a concern about the relation of social conflict and the new face of urbanism.

Actually, during the past half century, only two major characteristics of the world's urbanization processes have changed:

First, the pace of urbanization in developing nations is much faster than in the past.

The masses of new urbanites flocking to Cairo, Calcutta, and Djakarta vastly exceed in absolute numbers the transitional groups that journeyed to Berlin, New York, or Chicago a century ago. Unlike the earlier era of development, the process of industrialization has not kept steady pace with urbanization. Today, more than ever, we are faced with a massive migration to overflowing cities, and we can offer little hope that economic advances will satisfy the needs of the new, teeming urban masses.[34]

Second, the industrialized regions appear to be undergoing a process of metropolitanization. Wherever they can, as we have noted, a majority of the middle class have exited from the cities to find new residences in suburbs which increasingly ring urban centers. While suburbanites have fled, presumably in search of a less crowded, more comfortable life for themselves and their children, they have found themselves enmeshed in a greater metropolitan area more closely resembling the big city than a village. The great string of cities and towns lining the East and West coasts of America are united in economic and transportation systems and in a common exposure to the mass media. Consequently, life-styles, political attitudes, and even regional accents have become increasingly homogeneous. It is perhaps wise to substitute the word "metropolitanite," since both urbanites and suburbanites exhibit many of the same characteristics. Both attempt to form bonds with others identified as similar. Both shun and fight off those defined as threatening to their own self-interest. This is not surprising in view of the pervasiveness of the urban milieu over most of the territory of highly industrialized nations.

As Simmel, Weber, Wirth, and Inkeles have pointed out, the most important traits that distinguish the metropolitanite from his rural counterpart include changes in social ties, growth in anomie, increased impersonality and bureaucracy, and a general growth in freedom. It is our opinion that each of these characteristics vitally affects the nature of social conflict and deserves reiteration with that focus.

Changes in the nature of social ties

A tribesman trekking from the bush to Accra or Ibadan and a corporation man ordered by his company to move from Detroit to Los Angeles suffer the same general fate: a severance of ties with family, familiar friends, and environment. Newcomers to the city are confronted with a new and different land topography, with few, if any, familiar landmarks. They are faced with a maze of alleys, streets, and buildings, bombarded with noise and pushing crowds, and all with little social support. The loss of contact with familiar people and places may, in fact, be a welcome development for many people who were once forced to endure the crushing conformities of a small town, and the lifelong quarrels that often plague village life. Relatives, friends, or other buffer groups may cushion the transition to urbanism. As we have discussed, newly arrived immigrants to the large cities of America—New York, Chicago, or San Francisco—established communities based on national origin or religious belief. And even two or more generations after the massive flood of immigration into the United States, one still finds remnants of an Italian neighborhood, Chinatown, or Jewish area.

Similarly, in Ghana, 67 percent of migrants originally resided with some relative, and in Nigeria the influx of Ibos into the walled cities of the North was, in one sense, facilitated by their forced crowding into *sabon garis*.[35] There they found other Ibos and could maintain their customary social life.

Aside from the social support provided for all new immigrants by the more established residents of these areas, other consequences have accrued from the establishment of specific boundaries. One such consequence, germane to our discussion of social conflict, has been the definition of segments of urban territory in terms of "belonging" to a specific group, thus drawing the lines of battle when issues such as school districting, the use of recreational facilities, and housing are brought to the fore.

Anomie

Another consequence of urban development is the sheer diversity of life-styles in the city, which drastically challenges the traditional, unquestioned set of values pervading an agrarian society. The old values and religions seldom survive in the melange of urban life. Individuals are faced with gaps in the normative system. The direction a particular individual takes depends on many factors such as social class position, early socialization, and the escape hatches offered.

On a collective level, transitional people are most vulnerable to anomic conditions and are open to almost any political or religious movement promising some hope and meaning in their lives. The importance of mass media in anomic situations cannot be overlooked. The mass media can play a critical role in shaping urban society by providing credulity and status to persons who might otherwise be unheard and unrecognized; by providing a definition of social reality to many who would not ordinarily see beyond their immediate confines; and by helping to fill gaps in matters concerning rights and obligations.

At the same time the anomic nature of urban life opens the door to phenomena such as an increase in dissatisfactions, anarchic riots led by some self-styled savior, or even a massive rebellion, it also offers the possibility for creating reform movements: social innovations unthinkable in a village environment (see chapter 5).

Innovation

Many facets of urbanism—anonymity, physical mobility, and social isolation—allow greater freedom to many individuals. Urbanism, at least in developing countries, correlates strongly with a lack of fatalism and a belief that one *can* and *should* plan one's own destiny. This feeling of greater freedom, of course, can be exercised in antisocial behavior. Alternatively, greater creativity also can be expected from persons in urban, rather than rural, areas, particularly those people who are marginal or transitional and forced to act independently.

The fact that the city offers many escape channels and alternatives allows individuals and groups to establish different life-styles. The tendency for innovations to emerge from an urban atmosphere and its correlates—industrialization, education, and sophistication—lends credence to Alex Inkeles's position that a distinctively "modern" person is produced in urban environments.

Depending on one's ideology, this enhancement of freedom and innovation may be either welcomed or condemned. As demonstrated in chapters 5 and 7, it can constitute a threat to the traditional elite—as in Tokugawa Japan or Protestants in Ulster—when the elite rebuff prior innovative efforts and may be displaced by a reform movement, revolt, or revolution. The conditions that govern how and which innovative tendencies (growing out of the discontent and freedom of urbanism) resolve themselves into a particular manifestation of conflict await our further analysis.

The growth in bureaucracy

Another result of urbanization is a proliferation of bureaucracy in all realms of life. As Max Weber first noted, bureaucracy emerged as a mode of coping efficiently with large scale problems. With the development of the massive, impersonal, directive tool, however, the public with which it frequently has to deal also had to effect more efficient modes of obtaining a hearing. Thus, workers organized to deal with management, parents organized to deal with schools, and tenants organized to deal with conglomerates or management firms. In all instances conflicts have ensued.

With masses of people crowded together and the breakdown of informal social controls, the city must devise impersonal regulations to govern the behavior of the urban dweller. Thus, formal mechanisms of social control such as police forces and a bureaucratized court system appear in urban centers.

The reliance on police and militia for controlling the population often results in such frontal confrontations as Houston's police riot. The growth of bureaucracy further allows for the mediation of conflict such as those associated with disputes concerning schools and labor. Bureaucracy, however, also can serve to confuse those enmeshed in its workings and to hide the real forces in conflict. A company manager or a school superintendent could easily shift blame to a board or committee for his own failure to satisfy the parties in the conflict.

Impersonality

One characteristic of bureaucratic systems that is particularly heightened when intertwined with city existence is impersonality. Most human relationships within an urban environment are segmented, totally impersonal, and often limited to a few minutes of contact. People are reacted to in their specific roles—butcher, taxi driver, policeman, judge—not as individual human beings with unique needs, desires, and characteristics. The impersonality of urban life has consequences for social conflict:

Impersonality allows the competitiveness of city life to continue almost unchecked. Space, for example, is scarce in most major cities, and people must struggle to find shelter. Opponents in the "game" can be treated with total impersonality—cheated, lied to, or circumvented in some other way—since they are obstacles, rather than specific people and potential friends.

At an extreme, impersonality defines the "enemy" as nonhuman. In conflicts for territory, jobs, or other urban privileges, there is an extremely strong tendency (just as in actual war) to divide the world between "we" (the relatively small group of people with whom one has personal relations) and "they"—the "spics," 'kikes," "niggers," "dagos"—who are regarded as subhuman or nonhuman threats to one's own interests.

Defining one's enemies as nonhuman, or reacting to them impersonally, then, can lead to their ruthless destruction during times of conflict. If the opponent in a business conflict or a gang fight, the victim in a welfare line or a mugging, is merely an object, rather than a fellow human being, it is easy to treat that person with detachment, disdain, or brutal hostility. The novel *Death Wish* colorfully summarizes the attitudes of many urbanites who would violently destroy their defined enemy with great dispatch if illegal means were more readily available.[36]

SUMMARY

Conflict is the essence of human life. Society exists only as an unstable mechanism for reducing or resolving the strife inherent in the human condition. Social philosophers have long recognized this fact. Ancient thinkers such as Heraclitus and Polybius first delineated the nature of social conflict. Enlightenment figures such as Voltaire and Rousseau debated the ways in which human combative instincts could be channeled and controlled. Romantic idealists like Hegel invented theories of history that portrayed human conflict as culminating in eventual order. Marx and Engels continued this line of thought by examining the nature and consequences of class conflict upon all aspects of human life. More recent sociologists, particularly George Simmel and Max Weber, outlined the specific impact of urban life upon the nature of human conflict. Functionalists, like Durkheim and Parsons, were appalled at the disorder of the first half of the twentieth century and attempted to develop theories to explain how social order could be maintained. Contemporary writers ranging from Lewis Coser to Ralf Dahrendorf have examined some of the necessary, even beneficial effects of conflict on society.

Simultaneously, other social scientists have devoted themselves to the intimate relationship between social conflict and new forms of urbanization.[37] They have noted that developing areas of the world are experiencing immense increases in the pace of urbanization. Further, they have concluded that the cities burgeoning in Asia, the Middle East, and Africa are growing at a rate far exceeding the capability of these continents to support the new cities.

In the already industrialized world, urbanization has extended to the point where distinctions between cities, suburbs, and towns have melded into metropolitanism. The huge metropolitan areas of America, Western Europe, Japan, and Russia are characterized by a basic change in the nature of social relationships, an increase in anomie, a greater tolerance for all forms of innovation, a spread in bureaucracy, and greater impersonality.

These developments in urban life have a profound impact upon the form and nature of human conflict so brilliantly described in the past by men ranging from Polybius to Marx to Freud. Our task in the remainder of this book is to extend an understanding of the gigantic metropolitan areas where humans try to civilize their existence by reforming or revolutionizing urban conditions.

Issues for further discussion

1. In what ways, if any, did theorists about social conflict in ancient Rome or Greece differ from contemporary scholars? Why?

2. How did the Enlightenment period influence theories of social conflict?

3. Why do theories of social conflict almost always emerge from urban settings?

4. What, if anything, is wrong about Marx's prediction that the urban capitalist society would collapse because of its own inner contradictions? Why?

5. How did Simmel view the connection between urbanization and social conflict? Was he correct?

6. What are the major divergences between "functionalist" and "conflict" theorists in sociology? Can they be reconciled?

7. Does "anomie" grow hand-in-hand with urbanization?

FOOTNOTES

1. See Don Martindale, *The Nature and Types of Sociological Theory* (Boston: Houghton Mifflin, 1960) for a more comprehensive discussion of the varieties of conflict theory. Also see Lewis Coser and Bernard Rosenberg, eds., *Sociological Theory* (New York: The Macmillan Co., 1969), and William J. Chambliss, ed., *Sociological Readings in the Conflict Perspective* (Reading, Mass.: Addison-Wesley, 1972) for an overview of some of the major theorists discussed in this section.
2. Polybius, *The Histories,* trans. W. R. Paton, Loeb Classical Library (Cambridge, Mass.: Harvard University Press, 1954–55).
3. Marcus Aurelius, "Meditations," in *Stoic and Epicurean Philosophers,* ed. Whitney Oates (New York: Random House, 1940).
4. See Chambliss, *Sociological Readings.*
5. Carl Becker, *The Heavenly City of the 18th Century Philosophers* (New Haven, Conn.: Yale University Press, 1932).
6. Jean J. Rousseau, *The Social Contract,* originally published in 1762.
7. Theodore Roszak, *The Making of a Counter Culture* (Garden City, N.Y.: Doubleday & Co., 1969); Charles A. Reich, *The Greening of America* (New York: Random House, 1970); and Erich Fromm, *The Sane Society* (New York: Rinehart and Co., 1955).
8. See G. W. F. Hegel, *The Philosophy of Right,* trans. S. W. Dyde (London: George Bell, 1896), and G. W. F. Hegel, *The Philosophy of History,* trans. J. Sibee (New York: Dover Publications, 1956).
9. Bertrand Russell, *The History of Western Philosophy* (New York: Alfred A. Knopf, 1945).
10. See Pitirim Sorokin, *The Reconstruction of Humanity* (Boston: Beacon Press, 1948), especially chap. 11.
11. Friedrich Engels, *The Conditions of the Working Class,* trans. and ed. W. O. Henderson and W. H. Chaloner (Oxford: B. Blackwell, 1956).
12. Karl Marx, *Das Kapital* (London: J. M. Dent and Sons, 1939–40).

13. See, for example, Frederick Hyack, *The Road to Serfdom* (Chicago: University of Chicago Press, 1944), and Russell Kirk, *A Program for Conservatives* (Chicago: Henry Regnery Co., 1962).
14. Paul A. Baran, *The Political Economy of Growth* (New York: Monthly Review Press, 1957).
15. Kurt H. Wolff, trans. and ed., *The Sociology of Georg Simmel* (London: The Free Press of Glencoe; Collier–Macmillan International, 1950).
16. Ibid., p. 51.
17. Ibid., p. 59.
18. Ibid., p. 169.
19. Ibid., p. 409.
20. Ibid., p. 415.
21. Ibid., p. 416.
22. Ibid., p. 420.
23. Max Weber, *The Protestant Ethic and the Spirit of Capitalism,* trans. Talcott Parsons (New York: Charles Scribner's Sons, 1958).
24. See Emile Durkheim, *De la Division du Travail Social* (Paris: F. Alcan, 1897). For a commentary, see Harry Alpert, *Emile Durkheim and His Sociology* (New York: Columbia University Press, 1939).
25. See Talcott Parsons, *The Structure of Social Action* (New York: The Free Press, 1949).
26. Gerhard Lenski, *Power and Privilege* (New York: McGraw-Hill Book Co., 1966).
27. See Alvin Gouldner, *The Coming Crisis of Western Sociology* (New York: Basic Books, Inc., Publishers, 1970); Pierre van den Berghe, "Dialectic and Functionalism," *American Sociological Review* 28 (Oct. 1963):5; and Andre Duner Frank, "Functionalism, Dialectic and Synthetics," *Science and Society* (Spring 1966).
28. Konrad Lorenz, *On Aggression* (London: Methuen & Co., 1966), and Robert Ardrey, *The Social Contract* (New York: Atheneum Publishers, 1970).
29. Reinhold Niebuhr, *Reflections on the End of An Era* (New York: Charles Scribner's Sons, 1951); Arthur Schlesinger, *The Vital Center* (Boston: Houghton Mifflin, 1949); and John K. Galbraith, *The New Industrial State* (New York: The New American Library, 1967).
30. See Ralf Dahrendorf, "Toward A Theory of Social Conflict," *Journal of Peace and Conflict Resolution* 20 (1958).
31. See Chambliss, *Sociological Readings.*
32. Lewis Coser, *Functions of Social Conflict* (Glencoe, Ill.: The Free Press, 1956).
33. Louis Kriesberg, *The Sociology of Social Conflict* (Englewood Cliffs, N.J.: Prentice-Hall, 1973).
34. See W. W. Rostow, *The Stages of Economic Growth* (London: Cambridge University Press, 1960), and William McCord, *The Springtime of Freedom* (New York: Oxford University Press, 1965).
35. Robert Kelly, "Urbanization in Nigeria and Brazil," unpublished paper (New York: Graduate Center, City University of New York, 1973), and Hugh Smythe and Mabel Smythe, *The New Nigerian Elite* (Stanford, Calif.: Stanford University Press, 1960).
36. Brian Garfield, *Death Wish* (Greenwich, Conn.: Fawcett Publications, 1972).
37. See, for example, Martin Oppenheimer, "Para-Military Activities in Urban Areas," in *Riots and Rebellions,* ed. Louis H. Masotti and Don Bowen (Beverly Hills, Calif.: Sage Publications, 1968), and Anthony Oberschall, *Social Conflict and Social Movements* (Englewood Cliffs, N.J.: Prentice-Hall, 1973).

SUGGESTED READINGS

In portraying the social conflict which has wracked the world, no social scientist has surpassed such works as:

André Malraux, *Man's Fate,* trans. Haakon M. Chevalier (New York: H. Smith and H. Haas, 1935). Malraux relates the story of an abortive uprising in China against the ascent to power of Chiang Kai-Shek.

John Reed, *Ten Days that Shook the World,* foreword by V. I. Lenin, edited with introduction and notes by Bertram D. Wolfe (New York: Modern Library, 1960). This is a portrayal of the Russian Revolution by the only American buried in the Kremlin.

Charles Dickens, *A Tale of Two Cities* (New York: The Modern Library, 1935). This is a classic rendering of the French Revolution. One also may wish to include other works by Dickens that describe the horrors of life in nineteenth century England during the process of industrialization and urbanization.

The memoirs of Lincoln Steffens in *The Autobiography of Lincoln Steffens* (New York: Harcourt, Brace and Co., 1931) and *The Letters of Lincoln Steffens,* edited with introductory notes by Ella Winter and Granville Hicks (New York: Harcourt, Brace and Co., 1938), relay the story of America's most distinguished muckraker who first exposed the corruption inherent in urban political machines.

Joachim Fest, *Hitler* (New York: Harcourt Brace Jovanovich, 1973) brilliantly analyzes how one man took advantage of Germany's defeat in World War I, its inflationary process, and its urban conflict to unleash the scourge of Nazism.

Richard Collier, *Duce* (New York: Viking Press, 1971) demonstrates how the haphazard march on Rome delivered Italy's major city and eventually the entire nation into the hands of Fascism.

part II

URBAN STRIFE

selected cases

chapter 5

Urban reform movements

No other age has gone so far in the belief that the spirit of modernity might be widely shared, and that all men might participate in the goods and responsibilities of a modern civilization.

Charles Frankel

Reform movements are characteristic of urban modern society, emerging from the tolerance developed when urban people experience, directly and indirectly, different ways of life. Based on the premise that the scarce commodities (power, wealth, or prestige) can be redistributed in ways that avoid bloodshed, they are democratic in nature, for they require the involvement of the masses for the achievement of their program.

Reform is usually effected through means considered by the majority of the society to be within the bounds of legitimate behavior. The reformer and the opponent normally agree, at least superficially, on many of the basic values of the system. However, conflict may occur between those in power fighting to maintain that power and those desiring what they define as a fair share of society's rewards.

The three cases of reform presented in this chapter are the Meiji reformation, women's liberation, and educational reform. We chose these examples because they represent different, salient aspects of urban reform movements. Further, they differ in the scope of change desired. The first case presented in this chapter took place in Japan during the latter part of the nineteenth century. Although Japan was largely rural and feudal at that time, the reformation originated in a highly urbane group. The reformers, who called themselves the Meiji, attempted to change all major institutions of society, and did so nonviolently.

The second case, women's liberation, involved an effort to alter the status of a particular group. The women's lib movement of the 1970s is a direct product of American urbanization. Increased education and ongoing participation in the work force that occurred with industrialization and urbanization forced the demand for equalization on other fronts: political power, positions for women desiring work, and equal opportunity to compete in all spheres of the economy.

Urban educational reform, represented in the case of the City University of New York, was an attempt to alter a specific institution, as a part of a larger effort to effect an equalization of opportunity for all in urban areas. Education in American society is thought to lead to possible economic rewards and prestigious occupations. The battle over schooling is perhaps the most intense issue plaguing American cities in the 1970s.

The development of each of these three cases is traced according to the outline presented at the conclusion of chapter 1: (1)

the historical or conditioning factors; (2) the immediate precipitates; (3) the action; and (4) some of the consequences.

Case 1
The Meiji reformation (1868)

The Meiji reformation in Japan touched almost every aspect of Japanese life including the military, economic, political, familial, and educational institutions. Although Japan was primarily agricultural at the time of the initiation of the reforms, we consider this movement as having been essentially urban in nature. The movement began in Tokyo which, though preindustrial, was the largest city in the world. Further, the movement was spearheaded by urban leaders who effectively transformed a feudal society into a major military power within a period of less than fifty years.

To understand the nature and magnitude of the changes the Meiji reformers brought about, it is necessary to know something of Japan preceding their rule.

THE SETTING: TOKUGAWA JAPAN[1]

Before 1868, Japan was largely a feudal, agricultural society consciously secluded from the outside world. Yet, the country was passing through an unplanned evolution which eventually culminated in the fall of the Tokugawa shogunate that had ruled for several centuries. Hardly realizing their effects, the Tokugawans gradually had initiated changes over the years that eventually served to undermine their own rule.

Tokyo: the growth of a city

First, the Tokugawans maintained a firm policy of requiring rulers of feudal domains to make annual trips to Tokyo (Edo). This policy not only required the daimyo (lords) to relinquish partial control over their estates, but also to maintain residences in the city. The manifest purpose of the policy enforced by the Tokugawa shogunate was the centralization of feudal lords under their rule. They were successful in this effort, and by the eighteenth century Tokyo was the largest city in the world. Of course, some of the consequences of this enforced centralization of people were not anticipated. For example, the concentration of leaders unified the Japanese people. It also provided an opportunity for many persons to change traditional patterns of life and afforded them exposure to foreign ways.

The emergence of a middle class

Cultivation of the land had long been regarded by the Japanese as the most honorable mode of earning a living. However, many people were forced, because of scarce land or the irrelevance of their skills, into other choices. The samurai (traditional, but outmoded, warriors) could either remain in the agricultural hinterland as farm managers for their feudal lords, or migrate to the new city and attempt new occupations. Unlike the lords of the major territories, the samurai were unable to tax producers of goods; hence their income rose more slowly than their expected standard of living.[2] A few samurai tried their hand as merchants or entrepreneurs.

Gradually, after the introduction of money, a commercial economy flourished; a strong merchant class emerged by the end of the eighteenth century, and the samurai experienced a relative decline in their lifestyle.[3] Further, as Dore has noted:

> The discrepancy between the pretensions of the Samurai and their economic status was matched by another discrepancy between the high moral ideals of their mission in society and the aimless routine lives the majority of them were forced to live. Bravery and loyalty to the death were no longer called for in a world of pompous processions and formal guard duty.[4]

The development of bureaucracy

The establismment of the huge concentration of people in Tokyo necessitated the development of new ways of maintaining order. Thus, an elaborate bureaucratic structure emerged. This proved to be another source of problems that helped to undermine the Tokugawan rule. Many of the displaced samurai found new positions in the fast-growing bureaucracy. Spurred by the influence of Confucianism,[5] these samurai quickly adapted to bureaucratic rule and evolved into a group of well-educated administrators, teachers, and intellectuals in key posts. The sweeping changes in education, demanded by the bureaucratic system, required literacy of its employees and resulted in an overall literacy rate of 45 percent among men and 10 percent among women in Japan by 1868.[6] One aspect of the education obtained in Tokugawan schools was particularly important to the changes that were to take place. A political vocabulary, while not particularly subtle or refined, allowed the samurai not only "to understand and describe the workings of his own society, but also to conceive of alternative forms of organization."[7]

Education

The urban culture nourished a respect for learning, even European learning. Although all things Western officially were forbidden fruit (even to the point that foreign sailors shipwrecked on Japan's shores faced possible execution), Japanese bureaucrats had mastered the essentials of Western technology. The Tokugawa regime was compelled to gradually allow the influx of Western ideas. A small, but eventually influential, group of scholars grew learned in Western medicine, technology, and gunnery. These "Dutch scholars" who drew their name and education from a small Dutch colony allowed to exist in Nagasaki were destined to become important members of the Meiji reformation. The early development of these studies has been attributed to

> the energy of individual ronin or low ranking samurai motivated by intellectual curiosity, by a humanitarian desire to improve medical knowledge, by a patriotic concern for the military danger which faced the nation, by a simple enthusiasm for the exotic world beyond the seas, or, according to one cynical observer, by the desire to make a name for themselves quickly in a branch of study which required the mastery of only 26 letters.[8]

Economically, administratively, and educationally the basis had been laid to tear away the veil of feudalism.

PRECIPITANT TO REFORM: OUTSIDERS FORCE THE IMPENDING CHANGES

While the feudal facade remained outwardly unchanged for many years, the preconditions for reform in Japan had been laid. An important factor that can be noted as a more immediate precipitate of change was the intervention of a third force—invaders.

Russians, Englishmen, and Portuguese repeatedly had tried to persuade the Tokugawa regime to open Japanese ports to foreign trade. They failed in the face of obdurate opposition from the majority of the old feudal class. In 1853, the Americans took a different tack: a direct invasion of Japan by a formidable naval squadron. The Americans limited their interests primarily to opening coaling stations and ports for the replenishment of stores; but, unlike other Western powers, they were prepared to force the issue. After demanding the establishment of trade relations with Tokyo, Admiral Perry withdrew his fleet to Okinawa for the winter. He required an answer by the beginning of the new year.

The new and ambitious samurai in Tokyo, and for the first time, the Tokugawans, recognized Japan's military impotence against the black, huge barrels of the American ships. Conservatives in the Tokugawa regime, however, continued to argue against foreign incursions. Faced with the ultimatum by Perry, the Tokugawans sought the advice of the emperor and their presumed allies, the landholding daimyo. These conservative factions, however, had never actually observed the power of the American fleet and each counseled continued isolationism.

In February of 1854, when the American fleet threatened Tokyo harbor, the Tokugawans had no choice but to announce the opening of several ports. In so doing, they humbled themselves to both the emperor and the existing elite, the daimyo. The inability of the central government to protect the nation was held up for ridicule. As Edwin Reischauer has noted:

> The Tokugawa regime was obviously floundering, not because the machinery of government had broken down, but because Edo (Tokyo) had lost the confidence of the nation. Ruling in theory as the military arm of the Emperor's government, it had shown itself unable to fulfill its basic duty of defending the nation, and it had acted counter to a specific imperial order.[9]

The newly urbanized samurai were particularly disgusted by this show of ineptitude by the Tokugawans and began their move to take over the governing of Japan.

REFORM: THE MEIJI

The Meiji leaders fortuitously possessed a power base the central government had never brought under its control: Satsuma and Chosho. These two domains were the largest in Japan and had remained relatively autonomous. The samurai also possessed some independent incomes, and even those who remained in their provinces were able to arm themselves with modern weapons. The aspiring rulers, then, had both the will and the means to launch an active program of reform. The Tokugawa government was unable to curb their dissent.

The declared aim of the new group was to restore the imperial regime, which dated back a thousand years. In reality, they wished not only to conquer the central government, but to launch a program of modernization that would protect Japan from incursions such as Perry's. Further, if successful, they also could effect changes that would enhance and consolidate their own position in society. In the name of the emperor (Meiji) a small group of samurai (cum administrator, scholar, and entrepreneur) successfully brought about reforms that allowed them great power, even within the court.

Disarming the opposition

Ironically, however, in the reforms that followed 1868 the majority of samurai in the outer provinces who had provided support during the earliest part of the political maneuvering suffered a loss greater than any other group in Japan. The leaders of the reform movement were careful to preserve the prestige of the emperor and the daimyo while systematically stripping away their power through a redistribution of land. The samurai who remained in the provinces were the most deprived, for they received the least compensation. Indeed, the most serious revolt against the reform regime came when the newly formed Meiji government ordered all samurai to hand in their swords in a symbolic gesture of their obedience to the new government. Understandably, this generated intense hostility. A modernized army sent from Tokyo quickly disarmed the traditionalists.

Once having taken over the government, the Meiji reformers used a variety of subtle maneuvers to maintain, solidify, and finally extend their reforms. Their primary task was to dispose of the remnants of feudalism and to secure the allegiance of the nobility to the new central regime, thus eliminating the single most important conservative group. In 1869, one year after gaining control of the government, the Meiji reformers convinced the feudal lords to relinquish their land in return for a lifetime salary and temporary appointments as governors of their former territories. In one bold stroke the Meiji reformers deprived the feudal landlords of the substance of their power without completely undermining their status.

Establishing a military

Next, the central government introduced universal military service. This measure, though undercutting their own status as privileged warriors, gave the new government a huge conscript army modeled after the French and German examples. No revolt by a dissatisfied noble in the provinces could match the power of this modernized army. Even the Eta (a formerly untouchable caste) were declared equal and used in the army.

In pensioning off the old government leaders and many of the former leaders who might otherwise arise as opposition, the newly emerged Meiji leaders assumed a heavy financial burden. On the other hand, by building a strong central government unthreatened by the remaining nobility or by an army loyal to the old government, the new government was able to bring about change with little bloodshed or hostility. Further, the groundwork for individual land ownership and subsequent taxation (which would help pay for the changes) was laid.

The majority of samurai, of course, lost their former status as warriors. However, superior literacy and administrative training opened more posts to them in the government bureaucracy, the military officer corps, and the burgeoning industrial system of Japan. Only one group remained against the Meiji reformers—the most conservative members of the samurai who still lived in the rural provinces. In 1877, these die-hard warriors fought one decisive battle against the newly raised conscript army. The efficacy of the new army in disposing of the minor uprising convinced even the most traditional conservative that a new day had dawned.

Institutional changes

During the decade of the 1870s the reformers quietly buried the myths about foreign barbarians and sent the very best Japanese students abroad to learn skills such as seamanship from the English, medicine and miliary tactics from the Germans, law from the French, and business techniques from the Americans. They chose their teachers carefully and had the advantage of building their society along the lines of the most modern societies abroad. They carried with them, however, many of the prejudices of the past, thus blending the old and the new.[10]

In spite of a lack of carefully detailed plans the Meiji reformers quickly brought about vast changes, unmatched in history.

- In 1868, Japan totally lacked an industrial base. It possessed only tiny amounts of land that could be cultivated and virtually no mineral resources. Despite these unpropitious circumstances, Japan underwent an economic transformation, building 4,600 industrial concerns by 1896. In the decade between 1878 and 1887 the total national product almost doubled.[11]
- Food production until 1868 was unable to support Japan's population. After the Meiji reforms, Japan achieved a food surplus with the introduction of fertilizer, the expanded use of rice, and the use of new methods of irrigation. The population burgeoned; yet Japan actually became a major exporter of food.[12]
- Japan previously had secluded itself from foreign contacts and sedulously tried to repulse the efforts of foreigners, particularly Western "barbarians," from achieving any foothold in its territory. After 1868, however, the Meiji regime opened the door to profitable trade opportunities. More important, perhaps, the Meiji rulers chose the political, economic, educational, and military techniques they felt would benefit their nation. With a pragmatism unblemished by allegiance to any ideological model, the Meiji adopted the most modern practices from nations as diverse as England, France, Germany, and America.[13]
- With the introduction of compulsory education, the Meiji regime achieved almost universal literacy by 1900. Moreover, they established a variety of institutions of higher education and systematically sent their brightest young men to Europe or America to absorb the most modern ideas in all fields.[14]

· The military expanded its influence and was transformed from a small group of sword-wielding feudalists into a mass conscript army equipped with efficient weapons.[15] The army budget swelled from one million yen in 1868 to 107 million yen by 1908.[16] This massive injection of money into the military not only allowed Japan to defend itself but also to embark on imperialist ventures in Korea, Okinawa, Formosa, and China. The success of the military culminated in the defeat of Russia in the Russo-Japanese War (1905). These adventures worked to Japan's advantage in two ways: first, they provided resources and opened markets that previously were closed. Second, nationalism, cultivated by the Meiji regime, and supported by its external victories, provided the people with a psychological framework of identification with the nation's goals, thus diverting attention from some of the rigors of economic growth.

· The central government assumed paramount importance as the initial stimulant to economic growth. As Reischauer has noted:

> It had to provide sound currency, adequate banking institutions, a modernized tax and budgetary system, and political stability.[17]

Fully 50 percent of all investments in industrial concerns initially came from the government treasury; further, the government provided the railroads, irrigation canals, and roads necessary for development. The rulers established model industries, demonstrated their efficiency, and then sold them to private investors.[18] The financial benefits soon were concentrated in the hands of a small group of private businessmen, some of whom were later to develop into the financial magnates called the "zaibutsu." Only a few of these men were descendants of the earliest urban merchants. Reischauer reported that:

> Some of the new businessmen came from the aggressive rural entrepreneurs who had appeared in the latter part of the Tokugawa period. . . . The bulk of the new business community, however, came from the samurai class. Such men took advantage of their greater educational attainments and their connections with samurai in government to forge ahead in the business world.[19]

· The money for the economic growth came essentially from the peasant class.[20] The Meiji rulers consistently followed a pattern of extricating extra taxes from the peasants. After abolishing feudal estates with relative ease, since many of the old landowners already were living in Japan's cities and had been pensioned by the reform government, the Meiji gave land to individual peasants. Production soared. A land tax imposed in 1873 gave the central government a fixed charge on the value of peasant land amounting to approximately 25 percent of the yield. Consequently, by 1875, revenue from the land tax accounted for 85 percent of government income.[21] Thus, while production and government revenue soared, the peasant's level of consumption was held down to a pre-1868 level.[22] Paul Baran has noted the immense significance of this measure: "It is . . . no exaggeration to say that the main source of primary accumulation of capital in Japan was the village which, in the course of its entire modern history, played for Japanese capitalism the role of an internal colony."[23]

· Unlike Western nations or Russia, Japan used two methods of undertaking its massive program of industrialization. First, the Meiji concentrated on "labor-intensive" industries. This emphasized light, cottage industries and utilized Japan's labor force. Since human energy could replace expensive machinery in the production process, capital could be conserved. Simultaneously, the talents of unemployed men could be tapped. In 1878, for example, 81 percent of all production in the textile industry came from light and cottage industry.[24] As late as 1957, 30 percent of Japan's labor force worked in their own home with their families, as compared to only 0.2 percent in Britain.[25] Familialism was extended in another direction. The factory in Japan long assumed an extremely paternalistic stance toward employees. An employee was expected to remain loyal to the firm for his entire life. In return the company provided a guaranteed job, wide social security benefits, social functions, and even arranged marriages for the worker's children.[26]

While modernizing Japan in so many sectors, the Meiji rulers also strove to reinforce many traditional customs. The emperor was elevated to a higher status than before, and ritual indicating symbolic obedience was prescribed.

While modernizing education through the introduction of courses useful to industrialization, the reformers also compelled students to attend courses in Japanese "morals." The classes were consciously devised forms of propaganda that instilled the traditional virtues of respect for the emperor, obedience to parents, and self-discipline.[27] Legally, the government made the individual responsible to family and village of origin; children were required to support aged relatives; and the courts declared that the head of each family was to be held legally accountable for the actions of any of its members. The Meiji, in following this course of action, attempted to cement the bonds between the individual, family, community, traditional values, factory, and the emperor, all of which the Meiji controlled.

The result of the changes was to transform Japanese society from one in which ascribed status determined one's prestige and function to a highly rationalized system in which talent, manifested largely in educational success, became a key to advancement. By the early twentieth century Japan emerged a much more egalitarian society than England.[28]

In 1880 a few leaders attempted to introduce a parliamentary democracy based on the English model. This particular reform, however, failed. Several opposition parties were formed against the government when the emperor allowed a constitutional assembly to convene. The resulting government, however, was based on a highly limited franchise, subordinate to the will of the emperor. The ruling group protected the emperor's privileges; but since it controlled him, it was, in effect, also defending its own position.[29]

By the 1890s the reformers opened the door slightly to a constitutional representative government. The meager gesture, however, limited the franchise to 450,000[30] people and served as a way of winning diplomatic representation. In 1894, Japan was able to convince other nations that it belonged in a world of free nations.[31] Disadvantageous treaties and tariff practices were canceled. By the turn of the century, Japan put the stamp of military victory upon its status with the defeat of the Tsar's power.

DISCUSSION: A SUCCESSFUL REFORM

In a tantalizing footnote, Edwin Reischauer, the foremost American historian of Japan, suggested that a period of feudalism may be prerequisite for economic and political development. "Since only Europe and Japan developed fully feudal societies," he has commented, "it may be reasonable to assume that feudalism, or more probably its aftermath, has something to do with the development of attitudes and institutions conducive to success in modernization."[32] He does not develop this point further. It is perhaps equally germane in the study of industrialization and modernization to examine the growth of urbanism, national consolidation, and the development of a frustrated secondary elite.

The enormous success of the Meiji reformers cannot, of course, be entirely attributed to their political situation or their diverse talents. More factors apparently accounted for their success: first, the Tokugawa regime, before its collapse, laid the seeds for change. To some degree, Japan already had experienced a commercial revolution. Money, for example, had circulated since 1690; a merchant class receptive to modernization had evolved before 1868; and urban concentrations, with a pool of workers, had already grown.[33] Receptive to new ideas and already occupying many key positions in the urban social structure, a small group of potential leaders awaited the wresting of power from the old regime. Inadvertently, the Tokugawans, through their own ineptness, gave them their chance.

Second, through a variety of moves, the reformers, once in power, changed the agricultural, economic, educational, and social structures of Japan with hardly a drop of blood. Independent of mass support[34] for their reforms, the Meiji initiated changes that stripped the power, *but not the status,* of existing elites. They successfully retired their enemies by increasing the prestige of the emperor and depriving the feudal nobility of their land, while awarding them pensions and positions within their own formerly held territories.

Thus, the Meiji reformers assured national pride through success in agricultural achievements, industrial growth, military power, and a conscious effort to maintain a morality akin to feudal ties between people. Thus, the Japanese were able to modernize quickly and with few growth pains.

Unlike Western nations, Japan modernized without creating high rates of social disorganization that characterized the great ascent of capitalist or socialist societies. Essentially, this was because there was no further massive push into urbanization: between 1868 and 1940 the sum of those living off the land declined by only 12 percent. Rates of crime, alcoholism, and other symptoms of urban social disorder did not skyrocket as they had in Europe and America. Suicide rates remained high, but stable, during the reformation. This was due, perhaps to the original culture of the nation rather than the effects of reform.[35]

The great reforms brought about under the Meiji regime have been summarized by Edwin Reischauer.

> The changes which [the Meiji] brought to Japan proved to be indeed revolutionary, but . . . unlike the nineteenth century revolutions of Europe, had not welled up from below. In Japan . . . a small group from the lower fringes of the old ruling class, armed with a native "revolutionary" political concept, had been able to sweep away the old central government, and take over the nation almost intact.[36]

Fourth, the importance of this secondary elite cannot be overemphasized, for their successful efforts at reform did not stem from their economic power (as Marxists would predict), but rather from their strategic location in the political system of the old regime. As Robert Bellah has cogently observed:

> Only one class was in a position to lead the nation in breaking new ground: the Samurai class. From the nature of its situation, its locus of strength was the polity, not the economy. I am insistent on this point because the tendency to regard economic developments as "basic" and political developments as "superstructure" is by no means confined to Marxist circles but permeates most current thinking on such matters.[37]

The Meiji succeeded in their endeavor because they held a base of power that allowed them economic, bureaucratic, and military supremacy, as well as an intellectual quality that gave them a broader view of the world's history and an innovative conception of their own destiny.

Case 2
The feminist movement

The American reform movement of the 1960s and 1970s known as "women's liberation" has been directed at altering the behavior and attitudes of women, as well as equalizing their power and prestige relative to men in the society. Unlike the indisputably successful Meiji reform, no one knows the final outcome of the women's movement. Since women's lib is clearly an urban-based, urban-oriented movement, and urbanization is the wave of the future, one might reasonably anticipate a spread of its influence.

THE SETTING
Early feminism

The most recent feminist movement is part of a long and sporadic history in the fight for equality between the sexes. Well ahead of their time, writers like Rousseau, John Stuart Mill, and Mary Wollstonecraft in her *A Vindication of the Rights of Women* announced in 1792 that it was time to effect a revolution in female manners. Women, according to Wollstonecraft, should obtain better education, an increase in pay, and more than menial jobs.[38] A revolution at that time, however, was not imminent. Women did not have the vote and they possessed very little economic power (except their own labor). Thus, they did not form the secondary elite such as the samurai in Japan, who could use their economic leverage to achieve liberation. It was not until the nineteenth century, under the leadership of outspoken opponents of Negro slavery in America like Sarah and Angelina Grimke (who were not allowed to express their opinions in the meetings), that the position of women and their right to even speak on social issues was openly questioned.

Finding themselves in a position similar to that of the Grimke sisters, two other abolitionists, Lucretia Mott and Elizabeth Cady decided to take positive action on their own behalf. In July of 1848 these two women organized and chaired a "Woman's Rights Convention" in Seneca Falls, New York. Attended by approximately 300 men and women, this convention marked the official beginning of the suffragette movement. As well as urging the right to vote, the 1848 convention members also called for the right of women to gain control of their property, their earnings, guardianship of their children, and rights to divorce. Of foremost import, of course, is the fact that the 1848 convention marked the first public affirmation of a common problem by a group of women. From 1848 until the beginning of the Civil War, meetings were held almost every year in different cities around the country.[39]

A survey of the literature of the history of the feminist movement indicates that it lost momentum after the 1920 passage of female suffrage. A few feeble attempts were made to obtain equity: for example, in 1868, the National Labor Union Convention demanded for the first time that equal pay be granted to all government employees. In 1923 this demand became a legal requirement.[40] For the most part, however, between 1920 and 1960 a truly active reform movement on behalf of, or by women, can hardly be said to have existed. The question posed is, why did the women's liberation movement only come to the fore in the 1960s?

Sugar and spice

One part of the explanation for the emergence of the women's liberation movement of the 1960s might be sought in the personal histories of women during the last few decades. Let us explore the nature of the female role as it has been experienced by many individual women in American society.

The most important reason for the women's reform movement lies, of course, in the industrialization and urbanization of the nation. These factors allowed women greater mobility, more anonymity, independent incomes, and freedom from the traditional constraints of village life.[41] More than 32 million American women hold fulltime jobs, which means that four of every ten workers are female. An additional 32 percent of all women work fulltime part of the year, and 20 percent work parttime for part of the year.[42] It should not come as a surprise that women finally demanded a social and political status to match their economic position. If, in contrast, women had remained on farms isolated from city life, they would have lacked both the economic power and exposure to urban life-styles that led to their demands for liberation.

The urban female in American society, then, like males, can be described as fulfilling an increasing number of multiple roles. She may, for example, be someone's daughter, friend, or student; then wife, schoolteacher, and writer. Still later, the same woman may be described as a mother and a grandmother. Each of these groups of different positions are consonant with a generalized cultural definition of "woman." Yet, detailed descriptions of the actual or expected behaviors of these same women may indicate incongruencies between roles that are played simultaneously.

The most common description of female attributes by social scientists, for example, has been an expressive, or socioemotionally based role, in contrast to descriptions of males as instrumental (or task-oriented).[43] Indeed, the portrait of the idealized American female as expressive is consistent with the much romanticized version of the "sugar and spice" sweetheart, wife, and mother version of women.

While the simple distinctions between being a loving, emotionally supportive wife versus the undertaking of physically demanding or goal-oriented tasks may create conflict in many women, we do not believe, however, that it is the most important element in their attempts to reform the system. Such a notion would grossly oversimplify the image of men and women in contemporary America.

In the first place, American women in diverse parts of the socioeconomic structure carry out their lives differently. In general, women of the upperclass are free to devote themselves to home, husbands, and various voluntary and leisure activities; in the middleclass the tasks of the household are commonly divided, with the husband tending the children while the wife may be working. Disproportionately, in the lowerclass the woman must assume the task of wage earner, housewife, and mother simultaneously.[44] Thus, men and women in America appear to have integrated both aspects of task and socioemotional behavior as appropriate to their respective sex roles. As persons move through their life cycle, transformations in sex role activities occur; therefore, at different points in a woman's life cycle we can expect either socioemotional or task behavior to be more prominent. Neither sex, however, appears to have a monopoly on one set of traits throughout his or her lifetime.

The assumption of simultaneous roles by a given individual can, of course, provide a basis for role conflict and personal anxieties and tensions. This is true to the extent that a particular pattern of behavior associated with multiple positions involves associations with different groups, each demanding contradictory behavior. Anxiety also can be expected under the condition that mechanisms or escape hatches have not been provided by the various social groups for latent identities maintained by a given individual.

The type of anxiety that may be experienced is simply exemplified by a mother returning to college after a time spent in housewifery. She may, on occasion, find that her children are at home when she is required to be at school. Under the condition that there are few facilities available to aid her with the care of her children, and to the extent that she is subject to disapproval from members of the class (or the instructor) for bringing the children to school, the woman will obviously feel some degree of conflict.

Another anxiety or tension-producing situation is exemplified by the older woman who decides to return to work or college after her children are in school. She is likely to find that her co-workers (or classmates) are much younger and in different phases of their life cycle. Her co-workers or fellow students, then, will have different interests and concerns that serve to isolate the older worker or student in such a way that the social support usually derived from peer group association in these situations is lacking.

For any given individual the preceding examples of role conflict are most appropriately examined as a problem in time and energy allocation, or a mismatch between roles within a rather rigidly defined age-graded society.

Resolution of the strain can be predicted on the basis of information about the individual's commitments to respective self-identities and groups, or the rewards anticipated as a result of having made a specific choice. The resolution, however, remains distant from that of effecting a social movement. Perhaps individual role conflict and the anxieties and tensions accompanying the change from one status to another might best be viewed as a precursor to the emergence of a reform movement. Some psychological stress experienced by women is a result of social changes that already have occurred in an urban society. From this point of view the women's liberation movement is a mode of resolving the incongruities, an attempt to bring into balance such factors as power, prestige, and opportunities with altered activities that have taken place because of historical, social, and technological developments.

The two most obvious social changes that have affected females during the past few decades have been initiated by industrialization and urbanization: increased education and participation in the labor force. A third change in the lives of most women during the twentieth century has been the pattern of roles they are able to assume. Each of these factors bears on the emergence of the feminist movement of the twentieth century.

Education and work

Educational opportunities, especially in higher education, that permit participation in more prestigious positions in the society are very recent in American society. Thomas Woody, in his authoritative history of female education, reports:

> [Women's] higher education is a development of the last seventy-five years. From the days of our primitive ancestors women have generally occupied a sheltered place and have not, therefore, received a higher cultural and professional training such as would enable them to deal with large affairs, remote from the fireside.[45]

Even within the short period between 1960 and 1972, however, the proportion of women in higher education increased steadily, bringing them into line with the proportion of American males in college. In reviewing the current trends, Ben J. Wattenberg commented:

> The long-standing differential between rates of men and women going to college has been sharply narrowed—probably permanently. They've come a long way and they're not going back to teen age marriage and three fast kids.[46]

Increased education is associated with an alteration in female identity because of the breadth of experience and altered self-conceptions afforded through such change. However, the aggravations of changed sex role identity are not found in the fact of the equalization of educational attainment between men and women. Rather, it is to be found in the extent to which there remains an inconsistency between the prevailing cultural ideology and the experiences encountered by women as they move into the work world afforded them by their education.

In 1970, for example, the following statistics portrayed the work situation for females: four of every ten workers in the United States were female; half of all women workers were employed in a handful of job categories such as office worker, salesclerk, teacher, librarian, or beautician. In the overall job category, the median annual income for men (in 1969 dollars) was $7,610; women earned $3,649. Even for those women gainfully employed in the professions in the 1970s, women still tended to lag behind men. The median salary of female social scientists was $7,678, while males earned $13,356. The comparison of average salaries of men and women employed in high schools and elementary schools also bear out these types of differences. Where men earned an average salary of $9,002 in secondary schools and $8,013 in elementary schools, women earned $6,439 and $6,346 in comparable positions.[47]

Many factors accounted for this discrepancy: the lack of paid maternal leaves for women; a desire by men not to be dominated by women; the early socialization process that instructed women not to compete with men; and the legal structure which, in many states, required a woman to move to a new job with her husband at the risk of divorce, whereas men were not. Nonetheless, the obvious discrimination in job opportunities, pay, and promotion of women is inconsistent with the American ideology of the privilege of individuals to chart their own lives.[48]

Historically, of course, women have always involved themselves with the economy of the nation. In fact, as Alice Rossi has noted, this is probably the first time in history that adult women were expected to be fulltime mothers. She writes:

> In the past, whether a woman lived on a farm, a Dutch city in the seventeenth century, or a colonial town in the eighteenth century, women in all strata except the very top were never able to be full-time mothers as the twentieth century middle class American woman has become. These women were productive members of farm and craft teams along with their farmer, baker or printer husbands and other adult kin. Children either shared in the work of the household or were left to amuse themselves; their mothers did not have the time to organize their play, worry about their development, discuss their problems.[49]

Work today in industrial urban society, however, is removed from the home for both females and males. Conveniently, the total number of women employed in the labor force increased with the simultaneous introduction of time- and labor-saving devices and the availability of positions that could be most efficiently filled by women. Wrought by the introduction of advanced technology and increased education, however, these changes are matched with other social conditions that frustrate the move of many women from housewife-mother to that of housewife-mother-worker status.

For example, when many of today's wife-mothers seek employment outside the confines of home, they cannot leave their children on their own resources as during the earlier periods of our history. The psychology of Dr. Spock and other twentieth century child development specialists left too deep an imprint on the requirements of "healthy" childrearing to allow mothers to "desert" their children to city streets unless totally necessary. Yet, quality child care centers have not yet been made available; relatively depressed female salaries do not allow employment of desirable mother substitutes; since the American family is nuclear and neolocal, help from grandmothers and aunts is not always readily available.

Other inconsistencies

Women who want to return to more specialized work after a period of housewivery frequently find that their years of advanced education have become obsolete in a year or two without refresher courses. Such courses are not usually readily available to the suburban woman who must, therefore, not only seek educational opportunities, but also work in locations far removed from her residence.

Two other aspects of American life have drastically changed the woman's role in America. First, due to a desire to escape tax laws and their lesser longevity, men have gradually transferred the wealth of America into the hands of women. More women than men, for example, owned stocks in American corporations in 1970.[50] While they seldom exercised their power in the name of women's liberation, women have become the largest absentee owners of America's productive facilities. Men retained control over the administration of America's capitalist system as women emerged as the de jure owners.

Second, the increasing demand for liberalized divorce laws also gave women exceptional economic power. In 1910, there was approximately one divorce out of seventeen marriages. Today, as we have already discussed, the rate is more than two out of five marriages. Liberalized divorce laws beginning in the 1890s allowed women the control of their children while remaining dependent on their ex-spouses in the form of alimony.[51] This was due to the peculiarly American view that only women were fit to raise young children and that they should be supported financially while doing so. Contrast is provided in the traditional terms of divorce and child custody in Moslem nations. Men were able to divorce their wives by repeating the words "I divorce you" three times; further, they were not obligated to pay their ex-wives alimony, and all male children automatically fell into the custody of the father. Female children, at the choice of the father, could be placed under his custody after the age of seven.[52]

By liberalizing the law, granting alimony, and providing geographical mobility for women, divorce "American style" granted women extraordinary advantages including control over children and a man's income.

Transformation of sex role over a lifetime

Based on the work of French scholar Arnold van Gennup, a conceptualization of the series of self-definitions over an individual's lifetime and related social events that define points of identity transformation has been introduced and explicated by Everett Hughes.[53] We know that the same kinds of incidents that lead to the revision of identity of one woman is likely to have consequences to other persons of the same generation, occupation, and social class.

What this suggests is that beyond the problems of sex role, which emerge as a result of education, work, and other opportunities, perhaps another factor can be added in the explanation of the emergence of the current women's liberation movement.

A number of otherwise innocent appearing statistics bear on the type of analysis suggested here. A woman's life expectancy, for example, is a little more than 74 years. Children are spaced approximately two years apart, and their average marriage age is approximately 20 years of age.[54] This means that even if a woman chooses to follow the traditional housewife role, she can expect to alter her activities when she is approximately 43 years old, thus leaving most women thirty years to assume a more varied life. However, many alternatives open to younger women are closed at that point. Few concessions are proffered by society to help middle-aged women confront the dilemma of finding rewarding activities to fulfill their lives.

In view of these conditions and the modifications necessary to accommodate women who must work outside the home, it is not surprising that discontent should be voiced by the more articulate middle-class woman.

PRECIPITANT

Betty Friedan's *The Feminine Mystique* (1963) provides an early and concrete voice in the current wave of the women's liberation movement. As the historical background and the situation regarding work, educational, and other inconsistencies suggest, however, the most recent attempts by women to obtain equity are a result of many previous complex changes.

The actual mobilization of women was enabled by at least two precipitant factors:[55] first, many college women were involved in the progressive and radical movements of the 1960s which allowed them to develop political skills. Robin Morgan, in *Sisterhood Is Powerful*, confirms the relationship of participation in other movements and the emergence of women's lib. She wrote:

> The current woman's movement was begun largely though not completely, by women who had been active in the civil rights movement, in the anti-war movement, in student movements, and in the left generally.[56]

Second, women found contradictions in the ideologies of some of these movements which, in turn, led them to formulate ideas bearing more directly on their own role, status, and rights. As John Howard has noted:

> All of the radical movements of the 1960's called for a redefinition of social roles: blacks could no longer shuffle; students would no longer grovel; the male would no longer have to define his manhood as a readiness to kill for his country.[57]

Women, aware of the inconsistencies, almost *had* to take a stand.

REFORM: WOMEN ON THE MOVE

The leadership of the women's liberation movement comes from urbanized upper-middle-class women. They are the most educated and frustrated in their efforts to compete in a male dominated social structure. They also have more time to articulate their complaints. Historically, the leadership of the feminist movement also was drawn from the most outspoken advocates of other social causes: Quaker women, for example, who were not only prevented from voicing their opinions, but were not even allowed to sit on the floor where debate about the abolitionist movement was being conducted, took the lead in early feminist movements. The major difference between the early and the more recent women's liberation movement is the lack of a single issue on which to focus attention and provide a point of defining success. In the earlier movement women focused on the desire to vote. Today they demand equity on all fronts: economic, political, and social. The lack of a specific unifying issue in the 1960s and 1970s, perhaps, accounts for the dissension found in the organization of women today.[58]

Stages in the movement

As multilayered, multifaceted, and fragmented as the reform movement may appear, it has progressed over the last decade through at least three distinct phases.[59]

Consciousness raising sessions, the first phase of the current movement, although still being conducted in many homes around the country, are now a thing of the past for those women leading the way. These sessions ranged from discussion groups to a form of group therapy. Such topics as the historical role of women, discrimination against women, lesbianism, and the specific problems faced by each member were discussed. By communicating their complaints and ailments, many women realized that their problems were not unique. Eventually, some women's groups even sponsored consciousness raising sessions for men: mainly husbands and male friends.

As consciousness was aroused in groups of women around the country, the focus of the movement shifted to agitating for specific reforms such as equal pay for equal work, day care centers, and liberalized abortion laws. As ground was broken on these fronts, the next logical step was a move into national politics.

In 1972, formally organized seminars were conducted around the country by the National Women's Political Caucus. The purpose of these seminars was to "awaken, organize and assert the vast political power represented by women." The first effect of these efforts to concentrate on politics (the third phase of the women's reform movement) was evidenced in the 1972 national political conventions. Whereas in 1968 only 13 percent of the Democratic National Convention delegates were women, in 1972 fully 40 percent of the delegates were women. Women composed 35 percent of the Republican National Convention in 1972; and in both Democratic and Republican parties, numerous women participated on subcommittees as chairwomen and candidates.[60]

In 1974, flamboyant congresswoman Bella Abzug trumpeted, "this is the year of the woman." Her prediction was not far from wrong; more women ran for elective office that year than ever before and more of them won office. In Connecticut, Ella Grasso took over the Governor's office as the first woman ever elected to such an office on the basis of her own merits; New York chose a female lieutenant governor; and in Nevada the madam of a local brothel almost succeeded in winning a state assembly seat.

Nonetheless, the Equal Rights Amendment (ERA), which simply guarantees women the same rights as men, was defeated in one of the most liberal states in the nation (New York) in 1975. The same amendment already had been approved by the New York State legislature as well as in a majority of other states in the union. This defeat bodes ill for equality of the legal status of women. The immediate hope for the women's movement, politically, would appear to be in doubt.

The spread of consciousness

Spearheading and effecting a successful social reform would be virtually impossible if the problems and obstacles are seen as the plight of only a select group of persons. A larger base of support must be obtained. Thus, leadership provided by associations of women promoted social changes with consequences for the majority of women who were not aware of or fully committed to changing their relationship to males at work and in the home. In the era of mass communication and the ubiquitous television the story of women's problems, alternative solutions, and suggested remedies traveled rapidly to women located in different places in the social structure. This is confirmed by a story of four women, reported in the *New York Times*. Previously employed as garment workers, these women sought jobs as miners. Mrs. Anderson, one of the four women, said: "We were sitting around in the cafeteria talking about equal rights. I had been watching a show on television the night before. There was one of those women's lib people on from New York. I don't remember her name . . . but when I thought of men making all that money in the mines, I figured we could too."[61]

Just as support for the women's liberation movement from different occupational groups is obtained, as the movement itself has proceeded from consciousness raising sessions onto specific issues such as child-care centers, equal pay, and abortion laws, support has been obtained from women in less privileged societal positions as well. Thus, women from the black, Mexican-American, and Indian communities are being drawn into the multitude of voices calling for fair, equal positions in society.[62] From this broadened base of support, as well as the changed urban conditions we have discussed, we speculate that the social movement known as the women's liberation movement of the mid-twentieth century will continue. However, the full extent to which this social movement can be expected to succeed in its goal of complete equalization of males and females depends in part upon the nature of the support it is able to obtain from all people. Moreover, the success of the movement is expected to depend on the ability of women to prove themselves indispensable to the economy and unified in terms of political power. At this writing each of these points remains an open question.

DISCUSSION: AN ONGOING REFORM MOVEMENT

The women's liberation movement of the 1960s derived from many sources. Inequities, as well as incongruities of position and activities within a society espousing freedom and equality of opportunity for all, should be considered as the prime ideological precursor to the reform attempt. Conflict of interests maintained at an ideological level, however, cannot account for the emergence of the movement in the 1960s.

By 1960, because of industrialization and urbanization, a large number of women already were employed outside of their homes and were educated. Increased education and work opportunities provided two important stimuli for many females. Legal changes pertaining to financial holdings and divorce, as well as a longer life, also proved important conditioners to the emergence of the reform movement. All of these functioned to increase personal resources, thus altering the formerly dependent status of women. Women, regardless of various labors in the past, have been defined as dependent on males, both politically and economically. Males, in spite of social changes, retained the power to define the conditions of the female in society. The already changed position of urban women in America and the impetus of the demands of other oppressed groups, in our opinion, accounted for the 1960s movement.

The history of the feminist movement over the past century provides many parallels supporting our discussion. For example, the disparity between the urban work conditions and ideology derived from the Enlightenment also served as an impetus for the feminist movement of the 1800s. A vivid account of the work conditions was presented by Andrew Sinclair:

> . . . factory conditions at the turn of the century stank in the nostrils. Laundresses worked, stripped to the waist, for twelve hours a day in temperatures above one hundred degrees Fahrenheit. Machines were unguarded and could amputate fingers or hands. Poisons fouled the air in many industries; women breathed brass and glass dust, naptha and paint fumes and the exhalations of lead and phosphorus. There were hardly any washrooms in the factory. Pools of oil and grease lay on the floor, inviting tragedies such as the Triangle Shirtwaist Fire and its murder of one hundred and forty-five girls.[63]

Led by a segment of the feminist movement of the time, strikes of female employees were planned, political lobby groups were organized, and even a few abortive attempts to create a female labor union were made. These actions signaled the demand for equal and humane treatment of the female worker. Great headway has been made since that time, yet injustices remain.

Observations that can be made today provided the same basis for the incipient feminist movement in the mid-1800s. Female participants in the abolitionist movement encountered many contradictions between the ideology of freeing other individuals while themselves remaining constrained. Female participants in meetings promoting these causes were relegated to the balcony, albeit after heated debate. These women, as today's women, were moved to act on their own behalf on the basis of these types of inequities. Further, it was not a historical accident that many of the early leaders of the 1800 feminist movement were of Quaker tradition.[64] At a time in American history when women, like children, were not encouraged to be highly verbal, Quaker women, as well as men, were allowed to bear witness through public speaking. The skills in public speaking thus acquired served these early feminist activists well. They, like the better educated, more articulate women of the middle class today, were better able than the average women to increase others' awareness of their mutually shared plight and propose appropriate measures to remedy the existing situation.

Regardless of the many parallels between the early feminist movement of the first part of the twentieth century and that of the present decade, one difference can be cited. Today change is advocated on many fronts. There will be few, if any, women who will be completely satisfied with any specific changes. Technology, however, and urbanization have provided many opportunities that did not exist a century ago. The changed social conditions and the ease of relaying the commonality in plight through the mass media lend some credence to an optimistic position regarding the final outcome of the reform movement this time around.

Case 3
Urban educational reform

For most Americans, happiness is an education. Educational attainment in American society is the mark of personal achievement, increased income, and a prestigious occupation.[65] The image of what an education can do for an individual's upward social mobility, coupled with the prominent American cultural themes of individualism and equality of opportunity, account in part for the massive outcry for reform of the education system.

An overwhelming concern with public education first coincided with the flood of new migrants into American cities. The urban upper classes wished to create docile urban workers and citizens; many urban migrants accepted the belief that education would open the city's economic doors. Thus, in a society of phenomenal technological change and population shifts (described in chapter 3) some Americans felt that the educational institution, as well as business and the government, had failed them. Concentrated in segregated areas of the urban core, the disadvantaged vocally demanded more, improved education.

THE SETTING: INEQUITY AND THE PUBLIC SCHOOLS

Indeed, statistics support the accusation of inequities in the distribution of education in America. William Sewell and Vimal Shah, for example, examined the careers of 9,000 high school seniors in the state of Wisconsin between 1957 and 1965.[66] The purpose of the study was to determine the impact of social origins on educational attainment. Their results indicated that those in the highest socioeconomic quartile had a chance 2.5 times greater than those in the lowest quartile of continuing in some kind of education after high school. Moreover, individuals in the highest quartile were four times more likely to attend an institution of higher education, six times more likely to graduate, and nine times more likely to attend graduate or professional school than those in the lowest quartile. These investigators also found that a high intelligence did not guarantee a college education, since the great majority of intelligent lower-class males failed to graduate from college. Even if they did enter college, lower-class males of high intelligence were three times less likely to graduate than were comparable people from the upper classes. Other studies also have confirmed that a strong inequity exists.[67]

Research supports the contention that the problem of inequity begins early in the educational careers of many groups of children. Of course, variation in individual characteristics and life experiences had long been associated with more (or less) difficulty in accomplishing the tasks assigned by the schools. Generally speaking, differences between the school performance of middle-class children (largely suburban) and lower-class children (largely urban) have been made glaringly evident. Children from middle-class homes have been reported to experience less difficulty in classroom achievement; whereas children from lower socioeconomic homes were found not to perform at the same level as most middle-class children.[68] In fact, as ghetto children (who are disproportionately black) pass through the grades, they have been found not only to become increasingly alienated but also to perform less adequately than their white middle-class counterparts. That is, the gap between the urban ghetto child and the middle-class suburban child widened with each successive year in school.[69] Surely, in spite of evidence presented by scholars such as Arthur Jensen and others,[70] the school must be held responsible for assessing its role in this situation. This is true in spite of the fact that some of the criticism directed at the school may itself be questioned.[71] Regardless of eventual conclusions concerning the interrelationship of the home, individual genetic difference, subculture, and school in terms of effect on education, the school cannot be absolved from the responsibility of seeking modes of responding to the problem.

Indeed, in response to the demand for reform of the educational system, the public schools have introduced hundreds of new programs.[72] That the public schools have been shaken and subjected to public scrutiny and change is suggested by concepts such as "accountability," which has been readily accepted and incorporated.[73]

Although the specific practices varied from school to school, all of the changes introduced into the public schools appeared to have two common goals: remediation—that is, an attempt to fill social, cultural, and academic gaps in children's experiences; and prevention—the forestalling of continued failure in schools. The decades of the 1960s and 1970s can clearly be recorded as a period of attempted educational reform.

Higher education: student activism

The pattern of university reforms differed in accord with the needs, interests, and demands of the student bodies. The period of the 1960s was punctuated with the voices of various student groups and commonly identified as an era of student activism. A review of the history of student activism by Richard Flacks[74] suggests the following developmental stages in the youth movement:

During phase one (1960–64) thousands of student activists became involved in the civil rights movement in the south, Appalachia, and northern urban ghettos. "Nonviolent, direct action and passive resistance were seen as radical weapons in a struggle for social reform."[75]

The Berkeley campus and the free speech movement heralded, according to Flacks, the second phase of student activism. The free speech movement advocates used the tactics and spirit of the civil rights movement in relation to university issues. The Berkeley student uprising dramatized the changes the universities had undergone during the previous decade. The university, it was argued, had become "an important element in the defense establishment; its educational function was decisive in providing the manpower to operate the corporate and governmental organizational structure; its policies regarding admissions, personnel, curriculum, and research had substantial effects on change related to blacks and other ethnic minorities; and its internal life and administrative structure symbolized the general social consequences of bureaucratization just as the gap between its rhetorically proclaimed ideals and its actual practice typified the chasm between the ideal and the real that prevailed in the society as a whole."[76]

University reform activities, after Berkeley, swept American campuses. Such activity did not generally take the form of overt protest, but surfaced as rallies, petitions, or experimental schools. In response to the pressures exerted by students, many colleges and universities altered their operation. Yielding to the demand of students that they be permitted some voice in their academic experience and that there be an end to restrictive social and political life, various universities and departmental committees opened their meetings to representatives from the student body. Students formally evaluated their professors, a virtually unheard of activity in previous years. The requirements for graduation were altered in many schools as students expressed their dissatisfaction with the type of education they were being forced to accept. Many students complained of the irrelevance of some types of educational experiences for the "real world"; along a similar but more specific vein, some students expressed a desire for an increased spectrum of opportunities in vocational choice.[77]

Student activism underwent further transformations between the 1969 and 1970 school year. According to Flacks, during this period the scope and intensity of student protest reached its peak. He wrote:

> Student protest tended to shift from the campus to the surrounding youth "ghettoes," and street fighting, "trashing" and burning became visibly more prevalent than nonviolent civil disobedience was.[78]

Although educators and the public were concerned that student activism would continue into the 1970s,[79] such was not the case. Perhaps, as Flacks suggests, campus confrontation and student revolution had reached an end "not because it failed, but because it reached the limits of its possibilities."[80]

Whatever the case may be, the youth movement of the 1960s clearly has succeeded in effecting a transformation of the consciousness of an entire generation[81] in regard to sexual freedom, materialism, patriotism, religion, marijuana, and saving money.[82] Further, the change extended beyond the boundaries of the college campus; there has been a decided increase in the proportion of noncollege students who have accepted many of the new values of college students.[83]

College student activism also left a deep and lasting imprint on the structure of the university. Edgar Z. Friedenberg has written:

> [Universities over the country have taken measures as] ways of providing more status for students and more respect for them; indeed there are few campuses beyond the most parochial in which student sentiment and values are ignored today.[84]

Education and conflict

All changes in the educational institution, both at the lower and higher levels, should be viewed in a broader context. At the risk of oversimplification, three factors—the American value of egalitarianism, the rapidity of growth in number of students, and the multifaceted interests served by the university—may be underlined as important to an understanding of the changes that have taken place.

In spite of the inequities noted in the distribution of higher education, American higher education has never been the monopoly of those in the highest strata. Higher education has long been a mode of allowing many young men of rather modest means to make contacts and prepare for new occupations and social orbits. The faculty was charged with supervising discipline and "character building."[85] Egalitarianism was most associated with the establishment and evolution of land grant colleges.[86] These institutions, however, tended to follow as their model the smaller private institutions.[87]

In more recent times the response to the question, "who shall be educated?" has been, "almost everyone." In 1970 over 60 percent of the high school graduates were enrolled in institutions of higher education.[88] Between 1950 and 1970 a threefold increase occurred in students enrolled in four-year colleges; two-year college student populations increased by eightfold.[89] In spite of the phenomenal growth in the number of two-year colleges, the difficulty of implementing other alternatives to the existing system of colleges is noted by Riesman and his associates:

> . . . egalitarianism has the ironic consequence of making it difficult to give status to post secondary alternatives such as vocational and technical education, home study, and in-service training. High school graduates in general want to attend a "real college," just as on graduation from college they want to find white collar jobs which retroactively justify their having gone to college.[90]

The growth in the number of students is not the most important problem colleges and universities face. In line with our focus on conflict, it is germane to consider the multifaceted nature of the interests served by the university and the problem of redirecting goals and the appropriating of resources. The American university, according to Clark Kerr,[91] has three different goals: (1) scholarship and undergraduate education; (2) scientific research and graduate education; and (3) servicing the local and national economy by providing trained personnel.

The conflict between the goals set by each of the functions noted by Kerr derives from the priorities set by the participants and decision makers in the university. A survey by Gross and Grambsch of the goals of more than seventy institutions of higher education, for example, indicated that self-interest was the top priority of faculty members.[92] The protection of academic freedom, prestige of the college, and their own research ranked among the first seven goals thought to be most appropriate for a university. Faculty, administrators, and students, then, would appear to hold interests of a potentially conflictful nature, since it can be assumed that students prefer professors to teach rather than write or do scholarly research.[93] Even if a university should focus on undergraduate education, however, the question remains as to whether this should mean a liberal arts, vocational, or a scientific emphasis.[94]

The traditionally conservative undergraduate education provided by the faculties of most colleges and universities was congruent with the expectations of the more carefully selected students admitted than it is today. Certification for jobs and a liberal education of a relatively select group of students was not impossible. As the City University of New York faculty task force on higher education reported:

> Just as a broad spectrum of students was gaining access to higher education, the measures of selection and evaluation were increasingly focused on narrow concepts of academic ability.[95]

As the internal operation of universities and colleges around the country changed, so did the policies governing admission to many large universities. A larger proportion of working- and lower-class people obtained access to higher education than ever before because of veteran's benefits, special financial aid, and the altered criteria for admissions.[96] The ethnic composition of many of these colleges reflects the new population in urban areas. All of these changes affected the educational processes in many universities and colleges.[97]

In spite of the student activism of the 1960s, some people might call the educational reform a quiet reform. The case study to follow is an example of educational reform at the City University of New York (CUNY). Unique among urban institutions of higher education, CUNY was completely tuition free and admitted any high school graduate of New York City until 1976. The effect of innovation, in this instance, on the internal processes of the school has not always been quiet.

PRECIPITANT: DECISION TO CHANGE CUNY

An overview of elementary statistics of CUNY indicates that during the decade of the 1960s CUNY grew to be the third largest system of higher education in the United States. Expansion since 1963 included the addition of six senior colleges to the four in existence in 1963, four community colleges to the existing four, a graduate school, and an affiliated medical school. Enrollment mushroomed from under 110,000 students in 1963 to 260,000 students in 1973.[98] As the report of the University Faculty Senate Task Force indicates, the growth did not occur because of increases in the number of qualified high school graduates in 1973 compared to 1963; rather the expansion occurred because of a "broadened conception of the University's role, which included a commitment to extend to a wider spectrum of the population the opportunities and advantages of higher education that had been of such great personal and social benefit in the past."[99]

A discussion of the possibilities of extending educational opportunities to the residents of New York City was recorded as early as the 1940s in the report of the chairman of the board. It was noted at that time:

> An enforced policy of rigid selectivity gives us a student body of distinctly superior intelligence, but it also means that approximately seventy five percent of the graduates of our city high schools have no present prospect of a free college education. The citizens of our city can no longer remain complacent about so restrictive a policy.[100]

The eventual decision, almost two decades later, to open the school to all high school graduates was probably triggered by the series of students who through their revolt demanded the new policy, as well as the initiation of a black studies program, community control over CUNY, and faculty status for teachers involved in programs aimed at underprivileged minority groups.

In fact, the intention to open CUNY to any New York City high school graduate had been publicly announced five years before, but with a gradual program to implement it. Both alumni and many faculty members (primarily white and Jewish) had opposed even a gradual change. They offered a series of alternatives, including honors programs, which would have in fact, if not in name, excluded many of the new populations emerging in New York City.[101] The alternative solution was rejected by the larger CUNY faculty. The main reason behind the initiation of the open admissions policy proposal was the visibly and rapidly changing demographic nature of New York as blacks, Puerto Ricans, and other minority groups gained predominance in the lower public school system and increased their political power.[102] As the socioeconomic composition of high schools changed, the university system also altered to accept the products of the system.

In 1970, strongly influenced by changes in the city's demography (and by subsequent alterations in the ethnic, economic, and political composition of New York), the city's Board of Higher Education published the following goals for the open admissions program:

1. It shall offer admission to some university program to all high school graduates of the city.
2. It shall provide remedial and other supportive services requiring them.
3. It shall maintain and enhance the standards of academic excellence of the colleges of the university.
4. It shall result in ethnic integration of the colleges.
5. It shall provide mobility for students between various programs and units of the university.
6. It shall assure that all students who would have been admitted to specific community or senior colleges under the admissions criteria which have been used in the past shall still be so admitted. In increasing educational opportunity for all, attention shall also be paid to retaining the opportunities for students now eligible under present Board policies and practices.[103]

REFORM: OPEN ENROLLMENT

In 1963, entrance into one of the four senior colleges in existence at the time was limited to the top quarter of the city's high school graduates. This meant that students must have had a high school grade average of 82 percent or higher, or the equivalent as demonstrated by achievement tests. By contrast, only about 47 percent of the freshmen admitted to the senior colleges in the fall of the 1973 school year had grade averages of 80 percent or higher.[104] In fact, approximately 14 percent of the students admitted to CUNY had averages below 70 percent. Particular colleges within the system have faced even more drastic change since 1970 that can be relayed in the statistics for the overall system.

Focus: City College of New York (CCNY)

The City College of New York (CCNY), a branch of CUNY regarded as the Harvard of public education, having produced such diverse and prominent figures as politician Abraham Beame (mayor of New York), scientist Jonas Salk, and statesman Bernard Baruch, experienced a special trauma. In the five years preceding open enrollment the average high school score for entering freshmen was 83.4 (or a comparable score on the SAT). The number of freshmen with high school averages over 90 decreased from 773 students in 1970 to 453 students in 1972 to 290 students in 1974.[105] Students who performed conspicuously well in high school and chose to attend CUNY apparently decided against CCNY, requesting admission to other colleges such as Queens, Hunter, and Brooklyn College. Within four years

CCNY dropped from first to fourth place in the CUNY system as the first choice of students.

Change in the student composition presented many challenges to the university as a whole. For example, the wide range of college students added as a result of open admissions posed significant questions about the quality of education the students received, the educational priorities to be set by the various units, and the proper ways to educate *all* students, both good and poor in academic achievement.

As a result of the altered admissions policy, another change in the composition of the students can be noted: in 1969, blacks, Puerto Ricans, and Spanish surname students represented less than 20 percent of CUNY's first-time freshmen. By 1973, three years after the inauguration of open enrollment, these students constituted 41 percent of the entering freshmen. This increase occurred in spite of the drop in the proportion of these minority group members graduating from local high schools.[106]

For specific units of CUNY the change in student body composition was more drastic than the average figures cited. City College, for example, changed from a predominantly Jewish student body in the 1960s to a student body more closely reflecting the ethnic composition of New York City by 1976. The black student population in 1969 was 8.5 percent of CCNY's student population. By 1974 the figure was 33 percent. Puerto Rican students increased from 4.9 percent to over 15 percent during the same period. Those who regarded themselves as Jewish dropped from 63 percent in 1966 to 26 percent in 1971 to 20 percent in 1974.[107] Further, while CCNY students have always been relatively poor, open admissions increased the number of poverty level students. Entering freshmen reporting a family income of less than $6,000 a year rose from 17 percent to 24 percent between 1969 and 1971; middle-class students (with family incomes up to $10,000) fell from 44 percent to 31 percent.[108]

In effect, some of the goals set by CUNY in implementing the policy of open admissions to all high school graduates of New York City were achieved. Certainly, educational opportunity was opened to larger numbers of students than in prior years. Further, low achievement of students during their high school years was not held against them.

Changes within the classroom

The changes wrought by the heightened access to a college education in New York City were varied. An immediate need to institutionalize supportive teaching was felt. The response of the colleges, most commonly, was through the development of increased advisory staff, tutorial instruction, and the initiation of remedial classes. The report of the CUNY Faculty Senate Task Force indicated that approximately 15 percent of the regular admissions students to senior colleges and 40 percent in the community colleges required remediation of some sort.[109]

English and mathematics departments were the most pressured areas on most campuses. Basic skills in these disciplines, not acquired in high school, had to be mastered before other academic areas could be developed. At CCNY it was found that by 1971 fully 68 percent of all entering freshmen were required to enroll in basic writing courses.[110] The mathematics faculty also instituted remedial courses and watched the enrollment grow from 520 students in 1970 to 1,650 students in 1972.

The initiation of these remediation programs had different effects on faculty compositions. The English department hired many new, temporary personnel whose qualifications did not meet traditional college standards. In 1973, for example, only eight of the forty-two instructors who devoted most of their time to teaching basic skills had achieved a Ph.D.[111] Unlike the English department, however, the mathematicians voted to share remediation work among all ranks.

The immediate or long-term results of the many remediation programs are difficult to evaluate. As was observed by the coordinator of the Open Admissions Office in 1972:

> It is unclear how much improvement in the quality of student performance—however we judge this performance—can be expected from a successful course. It is clear that students' academic characteristics will not change radically in one semester or in one year.[112]

Four research teams were assigned to assess the remediation attempts at CCNY. The results have been mixed.

The first study examined the impact of remedial mathematics on student performance in that field. Essentially, the report of the committee concluded that one semester of remedial work would have allowed the student to have been placed one course higher in mathematics than when he originally entered college.[113]

The second piece of research concerned the reading level of students who enrolled in college skills courses. The researchers found a significant improvement in reading ability; yet, most of the students who completed these courses still could not read at the level of high school graduates. In the most elementary course the mean reading grade level increased from 9.9 to 10.4; in a more advanced course, reading ability rose from 11.4 to 12.1 in one semester. (These figures, of course, do not include the 29 percent of students who chose to leave college.)[114]

A third investigation conducted in 1974 analyzed sociology students who had been instructed to attend special tutorial classes. At the beginning of the term, all of these students had been flunking their course work. At the end of the term the following grade distribution was recorded:

Final grade	*Percent of students failing at midterm*
A	0
B	7
C	35
D	20
F	38

The major instructors of the course did not know who was receiving tutorial attention; therefore, they could not bias their grading. Nonetheless, it must be noted that only approximately one-half of the number of students told to attend tutorial sessions actually attended. Of the group who did not attend the tutorial sessions, the study showed that fully 85 percent failed the course.[115]

In the most comprehensive study a group of students who required remedial reading and arithmetic course work but who did not receive it were matched to students of the same entering level but who had engaged in remedial work. Discouragingly, the difference between the two groups was small. A multiple regression analysis indicated that the amount of variance accounted for by remedial courses was, in fact, miniscule.[116]

The four research studies indicate that remedial programs improve the basic skills of students with limited academic aptitude. However, the studies also indicate that early failure to attain college achievement levels cannot be easily remedied.

In an effort to maintain the standards of a college education, many departments worked on improving teaching techniques within the classroom and providing additional introductory coursework (sometimes differentiating those students who were majors in a particular field from those who were nonmajors but were obliged to take the course to fulfill basic requirements for graduation).

As a specific example, the history department at CCNY introduced courses designed to make the study of history relevant to new students; and political science combined with remedial teachers in English and arithmetic to offer an integrated sequence of courses at the freshman level. The biology department introduced a sequence of courses at the freshman level using new technology in the laboratory designed to facilitate individualized instruction.

While the long-term results of the many attempts cannot be easily measured, the tentative existing evidence suggests some difficulty in expecting all students to achieve academically responsible standards of college work.

The results of the biology experiment were discouraging. This program was implemented by Professor Gerald Posner in 1972 to allow students more time to concentrate on their personal academic weaknesses. To repeat regular classroom work, students were given the opportunity to use modified audio-tutorial equipment.[117] As an evaluation of the program, Posner compared four groups of students: SEEK enrollees who took the experimental course (SEEK is a program designed to help students from economically poor backgrounds; students for this experiment were drawn by lot from high-density poverty-stricken areas), open admissions students, regular students enrolled in the experiments, and students who took the traditional introductory biology course given at CCNY. Evaluation of the experiment was done by a comparison of grades.

Although it cannot be known what grade distribution would have occurred if many of the students had not taken the multimedia approach to the study of biology, even a cursory glance at the grade distribution in Table 4, however, indicates that the particular educational technology introduced in these classes offered little academic support for many biology students.

A report of the grade distribution of eighteen undergraduate colleges within the CUNY system provides more information about the academic environment within the various colleges. Seldom a source of concern to faculty, but frequently discussed by students, the report indicates that with few exceptions the open enrollment program "did not cause any consistent shift in grading practices throughout the university."[118] A comparison of grading at CUNY before and after open admissions shows no consistent trend. Since we have used City College as our specific case, it should be noted that CCNY records indicate "a decided decline in grades at City College from 1967 to 1972 which could indicate that fewer students were able to meet traditional standards."[119] A summary conclusion, based on this admittedly inadequate evidence of academic standards, would indicate that those criteria of evaluating students in the 1960s (and perhaps before) were main-

Table 4. Biology grades of multimedia project students*

	SEEK students (N† = 61)	Open admissions students (N = 34)	Regular students (N = 71)	Traditional coursework students (N = 436)
A and B	5%	12%	32%	23%
C and D	5	9	1	36
F and Incomplete	87	79	66	41
Other	3	0	3	0

*Adapted from Gerald Posner, "Interim Report to the General Electric Foundation," City College of New York, 30 May 1972.

†Number of students in study group.

tained after the open-door policy was introduced.

Supportive of the conclusion stated above, a study of the overall retention rate of students enrolled in CUNY indicates that 52.4 percent of the students (compared to 70 percent prior to open admissions) remained in college to graduate as of 1974. For the senior colleges the survival rate was 50.4 percent, which, according to *New York Times* reporter Gene I. Maeroff, "compares with the 58.5 percent that the American Council on Education study found for four-year colleges throughout the country."[120]

It can be questioned whether colleges and universities can take pride in a high failure rate even though this is taken as positive evidence that traditional college standards are being met. The frustration and heartbreak concomitant with failure to obtain a college education could lead to individual and social problems not yet measured or evidenced.

Of course, much will depend on outside forces such as the state of the economy and the availability of jobs for dropouts and graduates alike. On the surface the interests and values of the open admissions student reflect the classic immigrant story of another era. Professor Alice Chandler reported her impressions of student themes written by open admissions students.

> The [narratives] represent a composite of poverty, hard work, and aspiration, in which the pressure of economic necessity takes precedence over such values as personal freedom or self development. Many of the students recognize the value of their elders. They however, see themselves as free from such value systems, spared both the economic and spiritual deprivation their parents have suffered because of the opportunities and education available to them.[121]

Perhaps to have been enabled to try will be enough; a few will have succeeded. That would appear to be the most optimistic position that can be taken.

Changes in campus life

The not so quiet part of educational reform occurred on different college campuses with varied manifestations. Tensions mounted for students who remained in the colleges: students moved against both faculty (and vice versa) and other students.

Accustomed to eager, argumentative students, many faculty members on college campuses such as CCNY simply withdrew, confining student contact to brief classroom encounters. Traditionalist academicians lamented over the many new programs of studies introduced to accommodate the diversified student body such as Afro-American studies, Puerto Rican studies, and Jewish studies. By 1974 faculty members openly deplored what they regarded as a lack of intellectual rigor in many of these new programs.

Asian studies students charged the president of CCNY with not having investigated the reappointment of three instructors in their department and demanded a "direct response." The dispute between faculty-administration and students centers on the direction each group feels the department should take and the appropriate staff members to handle that program. The students favor a more community-oriented program with the academic emphasis on Asian-American studies. They feel that the faculty is more interested in the traditional academic qualifications of their peers than in providing a community experience. The faculty opinion, expressed in the words of Chairman Winberg Chai, is that "professionalism is absolutely necessary. It's necessary to Asian Americans for their social mobility."[122]

In *The Source*, a newspaper published by Jewish students, student ombudsman, David Romanoff, charged the officers of the Student Senate (controlled by black students) with "conducting a clear case of racism" for denying him admittance to a student executive meeting while permitting Vice Provost of Student Affairs, Dean Herbert Deberry (a black), to attend.[123]

The 1975 academic year ended with a melee between a small group of students, minority construction workers, the police, and construction workers on the CCNY building site. Students had been agitating about the proposed reduction in fellowship funds and the alleged failure of the university to hire adequate numbers of minority construction workers. The incident proceeded as follows:

> About 8:00 on Wednesday, May 14, 1975, several of the minority workers and students broke into the construction site and set fires. Students gathered to listen to speeches. As the tension gathered, there were a few fights, one with one of the policemen standing around. Reinforcements of police were called in. Students started throwing rocks, hitting policemen and other students.
>
> The scene remained a shouting terror for hours. Every time one of the rebelling students was shoved by a policeman, the construction workers cheered. Any time somebody hit a policeman, the protesting students and minority construction workers cheered. Every time it seemed quiet, the administration cheered.[124]

CCNY secretaries (who service an average of thirty professors and 200 students) refused to set foot on the campus at night or during unguarded holidays; students marched together in groups for mutual protection.

Previously, in 1974, concerned faculty members met and endorsed several new policies for CCNY, which if effectively implemented could improve the education of all students. In effect, the following policy changes were suggested.[125]

1. A reassessment of educational priorities as reflected in budgetary matters.
2. Improvement in the programs available to honors students.
3. Greater assurance that all students are properly prepared before being pushed on to more rigorous academic programs.
4. The utilization of New York City as a laboratory of urban experiences.
5. The development of a vigorous international academic program.

This set of recommendations suggests that these faculty members are more concerned about the quality of education of their students than the faculties and administrators surveyed by Gross and Grambsch.[126] Taken together, these recommendations could go far in fulfilling CUNY's promise to the children and residents of New York City.

The suggested reassessment of the budget in terms of educational priorities, if conducted thoughtfully, could influence the type of education that could be pursued by the students. This reassessment means more than considering the amount of paper to be purchased or the number of students occupying seats in a classroom. Improvement of both the honors curriculum and the tutoring assistance given to those with less than an adequate background for college level work can result only in an improved education for all students.

Ethnic parochialism breeds racism; hence the local and international flavor of the suggested policy revisions were included.

Such proposals and innovations attempted at CUNY and elsewhere indicate the energy and vigor that still abound in this institution—in spite of its problems.

WHERE TO FROM HERE?

Unlike other commodities, education need not be scarcely distributed. The problem is the type and quality of education that can be offered when education is massified. All individuals theoretically have the opportunity to maximize their desires and potential in regard to education. Attached to certification and the hierarchy of occupations and professions, however, those who "have" jealously guard against the intrusion of those who aspire.[127] Ironically, in a society espousing the freedom of opportunity to compete, those who "have not" are disproportionately minority group members.

Moving with the tide of social movements in the 1960s, one of the many educational reforms in New York City was the elimination of inequitable access to higher education. As of 1970 anyone with a New York City high school certificate could enter one of the many branches of CUNY. The university even sought out students from disadvantaged areas of the city and arranged for stipends in programs such as SEEK.

The educational reform of providing open access to higher education, however, brought with it many other consequences not easily resolved. Tutoring, new modes of introducing information, and innovative programs were instituted to meet the needs of the students. Although contributing diversity to college and university life that could potentially enrich the lives of all students, most of the programs found the job of trying to remediate learning problems a difficult one. Afraid of lowering standards and becoming an appendage to the public school system, many of CUNY's faculty did not reformulate priorities or alter traditional concepts of a liberal education.

The myth of receiving a college degree and accompanying benefits became an unfulfilled promise for those who went through CUNY like a revolving door. For those who remained, tensions between students and between students and faculty hindered the maximum benefits that might be obtained from a college experience.

The program of enhanced access to higher education occurred on the eve of American economic problems. Economic inflation and recession came to the forefront of American problems in the mid-1970s. Consequently, in a conference called by the National Scholarship Service in Chicago, participants charged that the doors of higher education were again closed to minority group members. This time the basis of inequitable recruitment has been laid at "the rising cost of education, growing competition for educational resources, racism and complaints by middle class white Americans that too much attention and money were being devoted to minorities, especially blacks."[128] The conference resolution called for "plans and strategies that would ensure survival of minorities through continued and expanded participation in the educational process at the congressional, state, and local level."[129]

Whether because of the reasons cited by the Chicago conference or sheer economic need on the part of individual minority group college students, it would seem that for a while, at least, the expansion of educational opportunities for minorities has dropped from its previous high. A survey by the American Council of Education showed that 7.8 percent of the 1.6 million freshmen who entered American colleges and universities in 1973 were black. In 1972, 8.7 percent were black. In addition, the total proportion of all minority group members (Spanish surname, Oriental, Indian, and black) dropped from 14.8 percent of the freshman class of 1972 to 13.0 percent in the 1973 freshman class.[130] As college education has become more expensive and inflation has chipped away at the family budget of all American families, William Boyd, executive director of the Educational Policy Center (a nonprofit organization), reported that "students from poor families lose out as financial aid officers are reallocating funds to benefit the middle class."[131]

Has the promise for a college education such a short life? Might not national and local priorities be reassessed so that the most appropriate education can be provided to all people who want it? Cannot educators reconceptualize the requirements of education to accommodate the needs and the backgrounds of both the "haves" and the "have nots"? These are some of the questions in urban higher education. Will Americans let educators off the hook?

By 1976 it appeared most unlikely that New York City would have the resources necessary to maintain its educational programs at the former level. Because of a majestic chasm in its budget and the unwillingness of the city or the state to completely support it, CUNY imposed tuition for the first time since its inception. This fact greeted students in the 1977 fall semester. The late 1970s will probably also see the demise of many City University units. This will, in effect, force a higher standard for admission and increased competition for available positions in the remaining schools. Such actions especially hinder the growing populations of black and Hispanic-Americans in New York City. The commitments of the 1960s, like so many others in the past, are evidently subject to conditional specification by those who have power.

SUMMARY: THE RISE AND EVOLUTION OF REFORM MOVEMENTS

"I recognize when power moves," Richard Daley, the mayor of Chicago, commented at the Democratic convention in 1974, "and I . . . compromise."[132] Daley, one of the last of a breed of "bosses" who controlled American cities for a decade,[133] shrewdly assessed the nature of reform movements. In an urbanized, relatively democratic society the "power brokers" will accede to the demands of groups who have mustered enough economic or political power to potentially threaten them. In this particular case, Daley recognized that the growing influence of urban minorities and women required certain changes in the Democratic party structure. Therefore, despite the opposition of organized labor, his major political ally, the mayor chose the path of compromise that, at least on paper, granted some concessions to outspoken groups without eroding his own political power base.

As illustrated in the cases just presented, reform movements are attempts to change the status quo by *nonviolent* means. Sporadic violence may occur during the process of reform; the Meiji were threatened by revolts,[134] feminists fought with the police, and student revolutionaries occupied buildings during periods of educational reform. Violence, however, has been relatively mild and constrained during periods of attempted reform. Partially, this is because the reformers and their opponents agree on basic values. Thus, cleavages do not run as deeply as during periods of revolution. Generally, the existing elite is—by choice or necessity—relatively flexible and open to limited change, particularly if they believe that their own power is not seriously threatened or they require the reformists as allies.

The ruling group, however, may miscalculate their position; once the Tokugawans allowed the "winds of change" to alter their society there could be no return to the old order. Conversely, reformers may believe they have achieved a great success, when in fact their position in society has not been greatly altered; for example, the city of New York initiated an open admissions policy, but this has not revolutionized the position of large numbers of lower-class blacks.

The rise of reform movements

Reform movements, whether they succeed or fail in realizing their goals, are peculiarly urban in nature. Of course, there have been coups d'etat, court intrigues, assassinations, and struggles for power outside the city. Yet, only the birth of an Athens, Rome, London, Paris, or Tokyo provided the conditions for mass movements aimed at transforming society or some institution within society. The tolerance of cities for novelty, the exposure to new ways of living, and changed attitudes and values, as well as the emergence of new social groupings, laid the basis for reform.

Of course, we realize that just as the urban setting provides conditions for reform, it also provides a basis for tyrannies far more draconian than those found in preurban societies. The mass media, for example, which is so pervasive in industrial urban societies, can be used by reformers as a weapon for enlightenment. For dictators, such advanced inventions as the radio and mass education can be powerful instruments for suppressing dissent and spreading propaganda.

There have been many reform attempts

that have died along the way. We also should examine some of the unsuccessful attempts since they serve as an additional test of the validity of our generalizations about social movements, which can, in fact, transform a society.

The list of unsuccessful reform movements is long, sad, and varied. One might recall the radical reconstruction attempts after the American Civil War, the prohibitionists of the early twentieth century, the Republicans who eventually fell in Spain's Civil War (1930s), and the French attempt at decentralization (1950s).

The radical reconstructionists who attempted to change the southern United States after the Civil War proposed a program that would ensure freedom and justice for blacks in the South.[135] They gained control of Congress in 1866 and passed a number of bills prohibiting any state from infringing on the rights of its citizens, providing that all citizens, including blacks, should be allowed in the electoral process, and prohibiting the participation of rebellious southern leaders in the political process.[136] The southern states, although defeated in war, refused to accept these provisions. In response, the Ku Klux Klan was organized in 1866 and persecuted white or black citizens who cooperated with the new laws.

By 1872 the unreconstructed white southerner was admitted to Congress, and the hope of radically changing the American South died. The reasons for the failure of the reconstruction are clear: radical reformers attacked the power base of the South; they had no support from an indigenous secondary elite. Further, they failed to provide an economic base from which freed slaves could assert their potential influence.[137]

During another period of American history, prohibitionists such as Susan B. Anthony, Horace Mann, and Wendell Phillips attempted to alter the drinking habits of Americans. By mobilizing women, the prohibitionists were able to swing several political campaigns in the late nineteenth century for candidates who viewed drinking as immoral.[138] In 1919 these candidates managed to pass the Eighteenth Amendment to the Constitution, which prohibited trade in liquor. On the whole, the American public ignored the liquor prohibition. The Roaring Twenties were filled with a liberal supply of illegal liquor.

By 1933 the Twenty-first Amendment ended prohibition, and the Prohibition Party passed into obscurity. It had run counter to a value system condoning the free use of liquor, an elite that essentially ignored the rules, and a mass of people who regarded the party as a group of naive fools. Without the force of outside help to enforce their own beliefs, the prohibitionists were doomed to failure.

In a totally different cultural context, the Republicans of Spain attempted to establish, by nonviolent means, an alternative to replace Spain's dictatorial monarchy. Temporarily, a rough coalition of liberals, anarchists, socialists, and Communists succeeded. A small group of middle-class liberals deposed Alfonso XIII without violence in 1931.

The new government counted on the support of more revolutionary groups. Once in power, however, the liberals who headed the government could not control the strikes headed by the Communists, the urban terrorists, or the revolutionary passions of Fascists. In fact, the liberals lacked the support of most power groups in Spain: the army, the church, and the landholders.

The army under General Franco revolted and eventually destroyed the moderate Republicans. Franco received the support of the Spanish elite in addition to Germany and Italy.[139] This attempt proved more successful.

In France in the 1950s Pierre Mendès-France tried with some degree of frustration to reform his nation. The Mendesistes elected their hero to be head of the republic and allowed him to liquidate the former French empire in Indochina and North Africa. Mendès-France's goal, however, included the fiscal reform of the nation, the modernization of agriculture, and the decentralization of political power from Paris to the provinces.[140] His program was defeated in the election of 1956, thus paving the way for a resurgence of anger in the ranks of the army and the ascension of General Charles de Gaulle to power.[141] Mendès-France had managed to alienate his most powerful source of support: capitalistic middle-class people, the army, the farmers, and the Parisians.

Each of the reform movements that failed, although urban in nature and leadership, attempted to fulfill goals that were ahead of the time. Each lost, or never obtained, the support of secondary elite and could count on no outsider for support of its cause. In addition, each movement tended to alienate the urban masses.

Long-lived reform movements usually have arisen after many changes have already occurred. In one sense, they may be viewed as a way of conferring congruent status on groups that have already moved along the path of change. Hence, reform may be largely symbolic in nature.

In Japan, the samurai had achieved significant economic and technological competence long before the Tokugawan regime realized its need for them. In America, through the process of education and the spread of work and income from outside the family unit (all concomitant with urbanization and industrialization), women achieved social change unmatched by their political and social status. Demands were made to equalize their position in these regards. Similarly, preceding urban educational reform, American cities had already undergone demographic and, consequently, political change.[142] Yet, economic inequities remained. Educational reform, then, was demanded to provide equal access to the marketplace.

It is the secondary elite in cities that take the lead in reform movements. These groups are socially and economically similar to the ruling elite in the area; however, the leaders and most of the early followers are not the oppressed masses, but rather those who have already garnered some form of power, but not the full position they wish to achieve. Thus, in Japan the samurai stood near the top of the social pyramid; in America, middle-class, well-educated women took the lead in the feminist movement; in urban colleges, the articulate leadership for educational reform emerged from relatively well-to-do, intellectually advanced students and faculty rather than from community groups (such as the poor in Harlem) who were, in fact, those who suffered most from exclusion from higher education.

Often, a significant outside force—military, ideological, or economic in nature—aids the growth of reformist movements. In Japan, it took the arrival of Admiral Perry's fleet to precipitate a reform movement that had been germinating for many years. In America, one may speculate, both the women's liberation movement and the student revolt received inspiration and some impetus from the civil rights movement and the inequities of the war in Vietnam in the 1960s.

We have concentrated for the most part on three case histories. Yet, in viewing the sweeping maze of history, the same generalizations appear applicable to other successful reform movements. The demand for the vote in nineteenth century England, as one more example, emerged in (1) an urban setting; (2) after a growth of economic power of merchant and industrial classes; (3) under the leadership of a secondary elite of merchants; and (4) after the shocks imposed on England by the success of the French Revolution.[143]

The success of urban reform movements

America has been swept with many faddish reform movements such as Prohibitionism of the 1920s and the Progressive Party of the 1940s, which flourished briefly, changed a law or two, brought eminence to their leaders, and then died without effecting lasting changes in society.

Why have some reform movements succeeded in transforming an entire society (as did the Meiji) while others died? The reasons lie, we believe, in the following conditions:

1. A reform movement must have a solid urban base, access to the mass media, and must be congruent with changes that have already taken place. William Jennings Bryan and his Populist movement, for example, expired precisely because they set themselves firmly against the urbanizing trend of American society. Educational changes in New York, however, partially succeeded because they accurately reflected the altered demographic composition of the city.

2. A reform movement must represent the interests of powerful urban groups that already possess the skills, knowledge, and economic expertise necessary to make them indispensable to the functioning of an urban society. Labor unions, for example, advanced their cause exactly in step with the economic indispensability of their members in an urban society. The civil rights movement as of the 1970s, on the other hand, lost some of its momentum because a gap emerged between the urbane, black, rich middle-class group and the unskilled urban mass that possessed decreasing economic power in a highly technological society.

3. A reform movement succeeds if its leadership is crucially needed by the existing rulers. When the Tokugawa regime, for example, was forced to seek the support of previously ignored samurai, or the Democratic party in America acknowledged the voting power of women in its ranks, the seeds for successful reform were laid.

4. A reform movement succeeds most easily when its leaders do not attempt to strip away all of the existing symbols of the ruling elite.

5. Naturally, a reform movement may gain critical support from an outside force. Educational reformers in New York, for example, could always evoke the threat (not yet fully realized) of guerrilla warfare in the slums to enforce their demands. Similarly, Japanese reformers counted on the aid of a variety of European nations in their attempts to modernize the nation.

6. Reformers may anticipate greater success if they attempt to change a noncrucial institution within the society than if they mount an attack upon the most substantial bases of power of the existing elite. New Yorkers allowed a transformation in the nature of CUNY partially because it is regarded as a peripheral institution: privileged, white Anglo-Saxons who control the citadels of power in New York were not directly threatened. Educational reform for them was relatively harmless since their own children would continue to attend private schools and Ivy League colleges. Similarly, American males can afford to liberalize hiring policies for women, use the title of "Ms.," and encourage their wives to attend consciousness raising sessions, since the men have little fear that they will completely lose control of the business and political institutions of America.

Few urban reform movements can fulfill all of these prerequisites to success. Yet, a movement forces those who control our cities to some degree of compromise.

In contrast to reform movements, urban riots erupt spontaneously, lack a coherent program, take on a violent, sometimes anarchic nature, and usually draw their support from the lowest echelons of the city. By their nature, therefore, riots are merely passing armies fighting in the night. Yet, in their effects, as opposed to any consciously promulgated policy, and in the symptoms of social malaise that they expose, riots also may be a stimulus to significant societal changes.

Issues for further discussion

1. What are the significant differences between the Meiji reforms in Japan and the American women's liberation movement? What similarities may be cited?

2. Can equality of opportunity in higher education be achieved in contemporary America?

3. Under what conditions does a reform movement succeed in fulfilling its aims?

4. What elements in the urbanization process have contributed to the growth of reform movements?

5. Aside from the case histories cited in this book, examine other attempts at reform and explain their success or failure (e.g., the French-Canadian movement to ensure equality of language and opportunity).

FOOTNOTES

1. See John H. Hall and Marins B. Jansen, *Studies in the Institutional History of Early Japan* (Princeton, N.J.: Princeton University Press, 1968), and G. B. Sansom, *A History of Japan: 1615–1867* (Stanford, Calif.: Stanford University Press, 1963).
2. R. P. Dore, *Education in Tokugawa Japan* (Berkeley and Los Angeles: University of California Press, 1965), chap. 1.
3. Ibid.
4. Ibid., p. 12.
5. Ibid., pp. 14–32.
6. Ibid., pp. 317–322.
7. Ibid., p. 304. For a more detailed breakdown of different types of samurai and their role in the reformation see Albert Craig, "The Restoration Movement in Chosen," *Journal of Asian Studies* (Feb. 1959).
8. Ibid., pp. 160–61. Also see G. B. Sansom, *The Western World and Japan* (New York: Alfred A. Knopf, 1970).
9. Edwin O. Reischauer, *Japan* (New York: Alfred A. Knopf, 1970), p. 23.
10. See Sansom, *Western World and Japan.*
11. Henry Rosovsky, *Capital Formation in Japan* (New York: The Free Press of Glencoe, 1961).
12. Thomas Smith, *The Agrarian Origins of Modern Japan* (Stanford, Calif.: Stanford University Press, 1959).
13. Reischauer, *Japan.*
14. Ibid.
15. John Johnson, *The Role of the Military in Underdeveloped Nations* (Princeton: Princeton University Press, 1962).
16. Ibid.
17. Reischauer, *Japan,* p. 134.
18. Rosovsky, *Capital Formation in Japan.*
19. Reischauer, *Japan,* p. 133.
20. Paul A. Baran, *The Political Economy of Growth* (New York: Monthly Review Press, 1960).
21. Ibid.
22. Ibid.
23. Ibid.
24. Rosovsky, *Capital Formation in Japan.*
25. James Abegglen, *The Japanese Factory* (New York: The Free Press, 1958).
26. Ibid.
27. Dore, *Education in Tokugawa Japan.* The remnants of this type of education can still be found in Japanese education. See, for example, Chie Nakane, *Japanese Society* (Berkeley and Los Angeles: University of California Press, 1970).
28. Reischauer, *Japan,* p. 137.
29. Ibid.
30. Ibid., p. 142. See also, Sansom, *Western World and Japan,* pp. 339–374 for a detailed account of Western influence on Japan's political development.
31. Ibid., p. 143.
32. Ibid., p. 112.
33. See Sansom, *Western World and Japan,* especially pp. 223–308.
34. Ibid., pp. 378–394.
35. Reischauer, *Japan.*
36. Ibid., p. 118.
37. Robert Bellah, *Tokugawa Religion* (New York: The Free Press, 1957).
38. Frank Corrigan, "For Women: A Long Way to Go," *New York Times,* 24 November 1970, p. 56.
39. Judith Hole and Ellen Levine, *Rebirth of Feminism* (New York: Quadrangle Books, 1971), especially chaps. 1 and 2.
40. Corrigan, "Long Way to Go."
41. See William Goode, *World Revolution and Family Patterns* (New York: The Free Press of Glencoe, 1963).
42. U.S. Department of Commerce, Bureau of the Census, *Statistical Abstracts,* 1975.
43. Talcott Parsons and Robert F. Bales, eds., *Family Socialization and Interaction Process* (Glencoe, Ill.: The Free Press, 1955).
44. See, for example, Robert Blood and Donald M. Wolfe, *Husbands and Wives* (New York: The Free Press of Glencoe, 1960), and Mirra Komarovsky, "Class Differences in Family Decision Making on Expenditures," in

Sourcebook in Marriage and the Family, ed. Marvin Sussman (Boston: Houghton Mifflin, 1963), pp. 261–266.
45. Thomas Woody, cited in Gladys E. Harbison, *Choice and Challenge for the American Woman* (Cambridge, Mass.: Shenkman Publishers, 1967).
46. Ben J. Wattenberg, *The Real America* (New York: Doubleday & Co., 1974).
47. U.S. Department of Commerce, *Statistical Abstracts,* p. 362.
48. Corrigan, "Long Way to Go."
49. Alice Rossi, "Equality Between the Sexes: An Immodest Proposal," *Daedalus* 93 (Spring 1964): 2.
50. Jessie Bernard, *Women and the Public Interest* (Chicago: Aldine-Atherton, 1971).
51. Jessie Bernard, *The Failure of Marriage* (New York: World Publishing, 1972).
52. See Abdullah Lutfiyya, *Baytin* (The Hague: Mouton Publishers, 1967). Apparently, according to this report, men now pay a small advance "dower," and in later years are expected to pay a larger second dower which cements the marriage. Divorce, therefore, is not a simple matter since the second dower must be paid in any case.
53. Everett Hughes, "Dilemmas and Contradictions of Status," *American Journal of Sociology* (1945), pp. 353–359.
54. This figure is for white women in the 1960s. For nonwhite, life expectancy has been a little more than 67 years of age. See Gladys E. Harbison, *Choice and Challenge,* p. 12.
55. John R. Howard, *The Cutting Edge* (Philadelphia: J. B. Lippincott Co., 1974).
56. Robin Morgan, ed., *Sisterhood Is Powerful* (New York: Random House, 1970), p. xx.
57. John Howard, *The Cutting Edge,* p. 145.
58. Ibid.
59. Dierdre Carmody, "Feminist Shifting Emphasis from Persons to Politics," *New York Times,* 22 August 1972, p. 45.
60. Ibid.
61. Georg Vecsey, "Four Women Seek Jobs as Miners and Man's World is in Conflict," *New York Times,* 9 September 1972.
62. Carmody, "Persons to Politics." Also see "Feminism: The Black Nuance," *Newsweek,* 17 December 1973, p. 89.
63. Andrew Sinclair, *The Emancipation of the American Woman* (New York: Harpers, 1965), p. 307.
64. Eleanor Flexner, *Century of Struggle* (Cambridge, Mass.: Harvard University Press, 1959).
65. Christopher Jencks and associates, *Inequality: A Reassessment of the Effect of Family and Schooling in America* (New York: Basic Books, Inc., Publishers, 1972) has challenged this assumption. The thesis argued by Jencks has been subject to much debate. See, for example, "Inequality in America: A Problem Too Vast for Schools to Overcome?" Carnegie Corporation of New York (Fall 1972). We recommend that interested persons pursue more detailed reading on this subject on their own. Our concern, in this section is not with the truth or falsity of the assertion, but with the general acceptance of it by the larger population.
66. William Sewell and Vimal Shah, "Socioeconomic Status, Intelligence and the Attainment of Higher Education," *The Sociology of Education,* vol. 40 (Winter 1967).
67. See, for example, Willard Wurtz, "Income and College Attendance," in *Poverty in Affluence,* ed. Robert E. Will and Harold Votter (New York: Harcourt, Brace and World, 1965).
68. See D. S. Leventhal and D. J. A. Stedman, "Factor Analytic Study of the Performance of 340 Disadvantaged Children on the Illinois Test of Psycholinguistic Abilities" (paper presented to the Society for Research in Child Development, New York, March 1967), and Frank Hooper, "The Appalachian Child's Intellectual Capabilities—Deprivation or Diversity?" in *Educating the Disadvantaged,* ed. Allan C. Ornstein, Russell C. Doll, Nancy L. Arnes, and Maxine Hawkins (New York: AMS Press, 1971), p. 15.
69. R. T. Osborn, "Racial Differences in Mental Growth and School Achievement: A Longitudinal Study," *Psychological Reports* (1960), p. 7.
70. Arthur R. Jensen, "How Much Can We Boost I.Q. and Scholastic Achievement?" *Harvard Educational Review* 39 (Winter 1969): 1–123 and R. Herrnstein, "IQ," *Atlantic Monthly* 228 (Sept. 1971): 43–64.
71. See, for example, Jonathan Kozal, *Death at an Early Age* (Boston: Houghton Mifflin, 1967); Charles Silberman, *Crisis in the Classroom* (New York: Random House, 1970); Paul Goodman, *Compulsory Miseducation* (New York: Vintage Books, 1968); and Jerry Farber, *The Student as Nigger* (New York: Pocket Books, 1970).
72. See, for example, David Street, ed., *Innovation in Mass Education* (New York: John Wiley & Sons, 1969).

73. See, for example, John E. Morris, "Accountability: Watchword for the 70's," in *Innovation in Education for the Seventies,* ed. Julia E. DeCarlo and Constant A. Madon (New York: Behavioral Publications, 1973), pp. 3–11.
74. Richard Flacks, *Youth and Social Change* (Chicago: Markham Publishing Co., 1971).
75. Ibid., p. 77.
76. Ibid., p. 83.
77. Also see, Daniel Bell and Irving Kristol, eds., *Confrontation* (New York: Basic Books, Inc., Publishers, 1969).
78. Flacks, *Youth and Social Change,* p. 200.
79. Margot Hentoff, "The Ungreening of Our Children," *Newsweek,* 12 May 1975.
80. Flacks, *Youth and Social Change,* p. 101.
81. Daniel Yankelovich, *The New Morality: A Profile of American Youth in the 70's* (New York: McGraw-Hill Paperbacks, 1974).
82. Ibid.
83. Ibid., especially pp. 55–115.
84. Edgar Z. Friedenberg, "The University Community in an Open Society," in Ornstein, Doll, Arnez, and Hawkins, *Educating the Disadvantaged,* p. 139.
85. David Riesman, Joseph Gusfield, and Zelda Gamson, *Academic Values and Mass Education* (New York: McGraw-Hill Book Co., 1970), p. 3.
86. See Lawrence Veysey, *The Emergence of the American University* (Chicago: University of Chicago Press, 1965).
87. Riesman, Gusfield, and Gamson, *Academic Values and Mass Education,* p. 4.
88. *Standard Education Almanac* (Los Angeles: Academic Media, 1970).
89. Ronald G. Corwin, *Education in Crisis* (New York: John Wiley & Sons, 1974), pp. 58–59.
90. Riesman, Gusfield, and Gamson, *Academic Values and Mass Education,* p. 11.
91. Clark Kerr, *The Uses of the University* (Cambridge, Mass.: Harvard University Press, 1963), pp. v–vi.
92. Edward Gross and Paul Grambsch, *University Goals and Academic Power* (Washington, D.C.: American Council on Education, 1968).
93. Riesman, Gusfield, and Gamson, *Academic Values and Mass Education,* p. 11.
94. See, for example, Robert M. Hutchins, *The Learning Society* (New York: Praeger Publishers, 1968).
95. Cited in George Fischer, *Urban Higher Education in the United States* (New York: The City University of New York, 1974), p. iii.
96. Burton Clark, *The Open Door College* (New York: McGraw-Hill Book Co., 1960), and Corwin, *Education in Crisis,* p. 95.
97. For two case histories, see Riesman, Gusfield, and Gamson, *Academic Values and Mass Education.*
98. *Report of the University Faculty Senate Task Force on the Educational Mission of the City University of New York,* pamphlet (Oct. 1974).
99. Ibid., p. 1.
100. Ibid., cited on p. 17.
101. The debate and offering of a special series of honors classes has been, in fact, widespread. See, Riesman, Gusfield, and Gamson, *Academic Values and Mass Education,* p. 13.
102. Michael T. Kaufman, "Bitter Local School Dispute Reflects Citywide Concern," *New York Times,* 1 April 1974, pp. 33, 55.
103. *Report of the University Faculty Senate,* p. 32.
104. Ibid., p. 30.
105. Eleanor Hall, Elain El-HKawnees, Helen Austin, "Descriptive Profile of the 1970 Freshman at the City University of New York" (New York: University Research Corporation, Sept. 1971).
106. *Report of the University Faculty Senate,* p. 8.
107. Hall, El-HKawnees, and Austin, "Descriptive Profile."
108. Ibid.
109. *Report of the University Faculty Senate.*
110. Alice Chandler, "The Proficiency Examination in English: A Report," mimeographed (New York: City College of New York, 1972).
111. Joel Perlman, "Open Admissions at City College: A Report After Two Years," mimeographed, 8 February 1973.
112. Ibid.
113. Dan Berger, "The First Year of Remedial Mathematics Under Open Admissions," Research Report 39 (City College of New York, 1972).
114. Michael Ribaudo and Geoffry Greenhaus, "College Study SEEK: An Initial Report," Research Report No. 10, mimeographed (City College of New York, March 1971).
115. Jane Zeff, "Performance of Tutored and Non-tutored Students," mimeographed (Department of Sociology, City College of New York, 1972).
116. Perlman, "Open Admissions," p. 49.
117. Gerald Posner, "Interim Report to the General Electric Foundation," mimeographed (City College of New York, 30 May 1972).

118. Gene I. Maeroff, "City University Grading Process Found to Vary," *New York Times,* 2 September 1974.
119. Ibid.
120. Gene I. Maeroff, "City U. Puts Dropout Rate Near 50%," *New York Times,* 1 September 1974, p. 1.
121. Alice Chandler, "Proficiency Examination."
122. Liz Carver, "Asians Demand Rehiring of Teachers," *The Campus* 136 (City College of New York) :4, 7 March 1975.
123. Mark Czarnolewski, "Romanoff Charges Racism and Foulplay," *The Source* 4 (The Jewish Voice of City College) :2, 13 March 1975.
124. "Violence Breaks Out on Campus," *The Source* 4 (The Jewish Voice of City College) :5, 19 May 1975.
125. Proposal that emerged out of a meeting of professors from the Social Division, City College of New York, mimeographed (Winter 1973).
126. Gross and Grambsch, *University Goals and Academic Power.*
127. See, for example, Martin Carnoy, *Education as Cultural Imperialism* (New York: David McKay Co., 1974).
128. Paul Delaney, *New York Times,* 20 October 1974.
129. Ibid.
130. Gene I. Maeroff, "Minorities Drop in U. S. Colleges," *New York Times,* 3 February 1974.
131. Ibid.
132. Quoted from the *New York Times,* 8 December 1974, p. 1.
133. For a biographical account, see Mike Royko, *Boss: Richard J. Daley of Chicago* (New York: E. P. Dutton & Co., 1971).
134. Irwin Schiener, *Christian Converts and Social Protest in Meiji Japan* (Berkeley and Los Angeles: University of California Press, 1970).
135. Max Savelle, *American Civilization* (New York: The Dryden Press, 1957), pp. 384–389.
136. Ibid., p. 387.
137. Ibid.
138. Louis Fetter, *American Social Reform* (New York: Philosophical Library, 1963), pp. 624–625.
139. Hugh Thomas, *The Spanish Civil War* (London: Eyre and Spottiswoode, 1961).
140. Edward R. Tannenbaum, *The New France* (Chicago: University of Chicago Press, 1961).
141. Ibid.
142. Allen P. Grimes, *Equality in America* (New York: Oxford University Press, 1964).
143. See G. M. Trevelyan, *History of England,* vol. 3 (New York: Doubleday & Co., 1953).

SUGGESTED READINGS

For a readable, comprehensive history of the transition between Tokugawa and Meiji Japan, see G. B. Sansom, *The Western World and Japan* (New York: Alfred A. Knopf, 1970).

Simone de Beauvoir, *The Second Sex* (New York: Alfred A. Knopf, 1953) was the first and still classic statement of women's condition in the twentieth century. For a more recent statement, see Judith Hole and Ellen Levine, *Rebirth of Feminism* (New York: Quadrangle Books, 1971), and Cynthia Fuchs Epstein, *Woman's Place* (Berkeley and Los Angeles: University of California Press, 1971).

For a look at educational systems and innovations of the 1970s see Seymour B. Sarason, *The Culture of the Schools and the Problem of Change* (Boston: Allyn & Bacon, 1971), and Julia E. DeCarlo and Constant A. Maddon, *Innovations in Education for the Seventies* (New York: Behavioral Publications, 1973).

A specific case of political reform during the progressive era is provided by Melvin G. Holli, *Reform in Detroit* (New York: Oxford University Press, 1969). A description of a reform movement that attempted to infuse urban values into a rural setting is provided in *Mississippi: The Long Hot Summer,* by William M. McCord (New York: W. W. Norton & Co., 1965).

G. M. Trevelyan, in his *History of England* (New York: Doubleday & Co., 1953) provides an eloquent portrayal of that nation's gradual evolution from tyranny to constitutional monarchy. In *The Case for Modern Man* (New York: Harpers, 1956) Charles Frankel defends the ideological basis of liberal hope that societies can be reformed.

chapter 6

Strife: urban riots

The violence of the oppressor has generally been more effective than the violence of the weak and the oppressed.

Barrington Moore, Jr.

If the social kindling is ready, almost any event—real or imaginary, trivial or crucial—can ignite a riot. Pogroms in Russia often were precipitated by the myth that Jews annually sacrificed Christian children as part of their religious celebrations. Riots in Ceylon in 1958 began with the story that a Sinhalese baby had been boiled in a barrel of tar. The "Great Mutiny" in India (when entire regiments of troops massacred officers and ran through the streets) was started by a belief that the soldiers' bullets had been greased with forbidden pork fat. And the riots in Kashmir, West Bengal, and East Pakistan in 1964 were prompted by the supposed theft of a hair of the prophet Muhammad from a mosque in Kashmir.

Events symbolic of the social conditions or contradictory to the basic ideology of the group may start a conflagration. Our task in this chapter is to untangle some of the underlying social factors that turn a rumor, or an otherwise commonplace event, into a violent urban conflict.

We have chosen to investigate three riots—unplanned, spontaneous, and in many ways self-destructive—that plagued America in the twentieth century. The white attack upon blacks in East Saint Louis in 1917, the eruption of Watts in 1965, and the Houston police riot of 1967, all occurred within the context of urban ethnic conflict. While the three situations were precipitated by different events and occurred within varied social conditions, we believe that a common pattern for the phenomenon can be induced from the evidence.

Case 4
East Saint Louis, Illinois, 1917

Located across the Mississippi from Saint Louis, Missouri, East Saint Louis was an industrial, scabrous city of approximately 500,000 people, with a reputation as a violent, lawless town by the beginning of the twentieth century. Deserted by its middle class and ruled by a corrupt political machine, the city flourished on vice and untrammeled attacks by employers on labor. At the turn of the century a great influx of Southern blacks migrated to the city with the hope of a better future.[1]

As the city grew, competition for housing, jobs, and job security increased to the point where a variety of observers correctly predicted that a race war would soon break out. "Race feeling is at a fever beat," R. H. Leavell reported, "the hatred is increasing daily."[2] A union organizer said, "It was a terrible feeling in the air. Everyone felt that something terrible was going to happen."[3] They were all too correct: between May and July of 1917, thirty-nine blacks and nine whites were killed, the black section of East Saint Louis was devastated by arson, an untold number of blacks died in the fires, and thousands of blacks fled from the city in fear of white hatred.

THE SETTING

It is not uncommon that outside observers can correctly predict situations where a riot is imminent. Few persons have been able to state exactly when or where a riot will occur; many, however, have detected the atmosphere of antagonism and hostility that precedes one. A number of conditions helped to create the volatile situation that led to the East Saint Louis explosion.

Black migration and threat

First, the city experienced a large migration of blacks from the South who not only competed directly for jobs, housing, and job security with whites, but also openly demanded equal rights. The black population of the city tripled between 1900 and 1915. The riot erupted just after white union workers lost a strike at the Aluminum Ore Company. They blamed the black migrants for their defeat.[4] Rumors circulated that blacks had been directly recruited in the South for exactly the purpose of breaking union strikes; indeed, meat-packing company officials confessed that they had "imported" blacks. Thus, the economic stage was set for a direct confrontation.

Second, the great upsurge in the black population was viewed by whites as a political conspiracy. Much of the public believed that blacks always voted Republican; thus the great battle cry of the Democrats in 1916 was a warning against political colonization.[5] Even President Wilson's attorney general openly stated his feeling that black migration was caused by political forces and that election frauds would be prosecuted vigorously.[6] In fact, when the Justice Department interviewed black migrants in many cities—including East Saint Louis—they found that the sole encouragement for blacks to leave the South was the hope of economic advancement. Nonetheless, after the election (in which Republicans swept East Saint Louis), the Justice Department continued to hint at a political conspiracy between blacks and Republicans.[7] Although the Democratic-controlled department never launched a lawsuit on the matter, it was widely believed that blacks had been used to tarnish the facade of democracy. In East Saint Louis, labor union leaders who had supported Wilson linked political and economic charges together and joined in the accusation that the black migration was a double-headed capitalist conspiracy.

Third, job security for whites in East Saint Louis was virtually nonexistent. Laborers were forced to move from plant to plant, and there was no guarantee that their jobs would continue beyond a period of a few weeks or months. The coming of World War I gave union organizers a rare chance to fight for job security. Employers, however, protected their position by supplying a surplus of black labor. In fact, as Elliot Rudwick has shown, the arrival of black labor did not cause unemployment among whites.[8] The number of employed whites actually increased during wartime. Yet, blacks remained a direct threat to labor in its attempts to organize all workers in a united front against management.[9]

Fourth, labor unions on the local level systematically excluded blacks from their ranks, further alienating them from the white economy. Eugene Debs later condemned the entire labor movement for its prejudice. He viewed the riot as "a foul blot upon the American labor movement. . . . Had the labor unions freely opened their door to the Negro instead of barring him . . . and, in alliance with the capitalist class, conspiring to make a pariah of him, and forcing him in spite of himself to become a scab . . . the atrocious crime at East Saint Louis would never have blackened the pages of American history."[10]

Debs' attack would appear to have been justified, and yet it ignored a basic fact:

the majority of both white and black workers were unskilled and nonunionized. Employers had stringently opposed any efforts to organize unskilled laborers. Thus, as Elliot Rudwick has observed, "the race riot grew out of competition, not between organized white labor and unorganized Negro labor, but between unorganized and unskilled whites and Negroes."[11] It was truly a people's war.

Fifth, the black migrants had objectively gained in economic, political, and even social status; suddenly in their newfound havens of Northern cities, they were threatened by white resentment and white attempts to keep the black man "in his place." While the blame for the riot falls mainly on the white population, it is also evident that blacks were ready, although hardly eager, to fight.

Sixth, the usual forces of resentment—city hall, the police, and the National Guard—were either unwilling or unable to apply the coercion necessary to keep whites under control. Despite a series of incidents in May of 1917 and repeated warnings that a riot would erupt, external restraints were not applied. Partially, this laxity was due to the political climate of the city, which demanded that the mayor should appeal to all segments of the working classes, black or white, and thereby paralyzed him from taking any decisive action. It must be recognized, too, that many (if not most) of the police and National Guardsmen were sympathetic with the white rioters, deliberately turning their backs upon arson, murder, and assault.

PRECIPITANTS AND ACTION: RIOT

Fact and rumor—a combustible mixture

The first outbreak of violent action occurred on 28 May 1917. On the eve of 28 May representatives of the local trade union, protesting the presumed use of black laborers imported from the south, gathered outside of the city council building. They were preceded by female members of the union demonstrating against the "threat of Negro lust" to white womanhood.[12]

The protesters believed that the Aluminum Ore Company, one of the city's largest employers, had brought in blacks as strikebreakers. As one advertisement before the meeting suggested, "Negro and cheap foreign labor . . . tear down the standard of living of our citizens."[13] During the meeting even the mayor of East Saint Louis condemned the waves of black migration to the city; further, the city clerk, a lawyer, publicly exclaimed, "there is no law against mob violence."[14] Violent action was yet to erupt.

When the white laborers emerged from their meeting, rumors were circulated about a white woman who had been insulted by a black person, two white girls who supposedly were shot, and a black man who was accused of having killed a white man during a robbery. Factually, as far as can be determined, a black holdup man had accidentally wounded a white person.[15]

Incensed by the stories, the white laborers roamed the main streets of the black section of the city beating, kicking, and shooting any black person unfortunate enough to be there. Most of the police force refused to take any action. Two detectives, however, Samuel Coppedge and Frank Wadley, succeeded in preventing the burning of the black ghetto.[16] Ironically, these same men were shot during subsequent confrontations in July of the same year, and their deaths served to ignite more riotous behavior.

The escalation of the violence

After the early riot in May, the police systematically stopped all cars filled with black men and searched for imported guns. Hundreds of black people were arrested, but a few were able to shuttle back and forth to Saint Louis with supplies of guns and ammunition.[17] Meanwhile, unsearched cars of white men loaded with guns filed into the city.[18] Many black persons clung to the pathetic hope that if they were armed, their little minority in the city could defend itself.

On 30 May, National Guardsmen arrived, but their time was spent primarily in searching the homes of black people for weapons.[19] Several of the guardsmen were later arrested for leading attacks on the minority community.

In June 1917, mobs of whites systematically attacked blacks, particularly laborers who were entering struck plants. The *East Saint Louis Journal,* however, chose to ignore these incidents, instead, headlining stories of holdups by blacks.[20] On 1 July a car filled with white men fired random shots into the homes of black persons. When the car raced through the area again, the black residents returned the fire, hitting the automobile.

The police apparently held back and did nothing about the clashes between whites and blacks.[21] Further, the mayor's office failed to take any action whatsoever. The political machine of that time counted on the votes of both lower-class whites and blacks. Thus, while reassuring black delegations who protested the violence that a thorough investigation would be made of any incident, the mayor actually did nothing for fear of alienating his white labor support.[22]

Following the maraudings of white men into the black districts, a police car (identical to that used in the July incident of random shooting into black-owned homes) was dispatched to the scene. It contained the two men, Coppedge and Wadley, who previously had protected the black neighborhood. To the misfortune of all, the police car turned into a street where armed black men awaited in ambush. A spray of bullets ended the lives of the two detectives.

The slaying of the police officers led many of the white population to believe that a "Negro army" had invaded the town and was prepared to massacre the townspeople. On the morning of 2 July 1917, the police added fuel to the situation by displaying the dead detectives' bullet-riddled, blood-stained car in front of their headquarters.[23] Laborers passing the police station on their way to work vowed to avenge the detectives' deaths.

On the afternoon of 2 July, mobs of white persons gathered at the Labor Temple and were incited to gather arms. White laborers marched in military formation through the business district. They seized male and female blacks, young or old. They pulled some of their victims off streetcars and beat them. Blacks unfortunate enough to be caught held up their arms in a sign of surrender, but were beaten; white women attacked black women, and by early afternoon, shacks at the edges of the black residential district had been set afire. The residents of the burning buildings were shot down as they tried to escape the flames.

Paul Anderson, a *St. Louis Post-Dispatch* correspondent, saw several black persons killed on the street. "I think every one I saw killed had both hands above his head begging for mercy," he wrote. "One cried, 'My God, don't kill me, white man.' "[24]

Another *Post-Dispatch* reporter recorded his witnessing of a lynching. A mob of whites attempted to hang a dying black man from a telephone pole. The line they were using broke, but they quickly found a new one. The reporter, in the meantime, tried to get some National Guardsmen, who were standing idly watching the scene, to intervene; they refused. The second line held.

> I saw the most sickening incident of the evening when they got stronger rope. To put the rope around the negro's neck, one of the lynchers stuck his fingers inside the gaping scalp and lifted the negro's head by it, literally bathing his hand in the man's blood. "Get hold, and pull for East St. Louis," called the man as he seized the other end of rope. The negro was lifted to a height of about seven feet and the body was left hanging there for hours.[25]

By the night of the second day of continuous rioting, the white citizens decided to completely burn down the black quarters.

They chanted "Burn 'em out! Burn 'em out!"—tragically prophetic of the later cry of "Burn, Baby, Burn," in Watts. The marauding arsonists destroyed over two hundred houses in a sixteen-block area.[26] Black residents fled and sought refuge in white homes. At times, they were accepted, but more often they were refused. One white woman would not allow a black man to hide under her house because he would disturb the chickens that roosted there.[27]

Hundreds of blacks went to the city hall auditorium for sanctuary. The lights in the hall suddenly went out amidst the screams and wailings of wounded blacks; many believed it was a new plan to murder them in wholesale fashion. Later it was determined that there simply had been a malfunction in the electrical system.

Rumors circulated in the white community that massive Negro armies were converging on the city. Partially out of fear of the imagined threat, white rioters gave way to the power of the National Guard, which reluctantly but gradually moved into action to restore order.

The black community also overestimated their own power. Various black newspapers reported that enraged Negroes had thrown white rioters into the Cahokia Creek and that a black army was staging a campaign of military revenge. The *Chicago Defender*, a militant black newspaper, proudly announced "The younger members of the Race were not afraid to die . . . the firing of the whites was promptly returned by hot lead from the Race quarters."[28] While such reports may have worked to bolster the pride of many in the black community, they were not true. The riot was largely limited to the business district where whites far outnumbered blacks. White rioters for the most part feared to enter the predominantly black section of town. Many black persons, however, fled their homes in fear, leaving arms and ammunition behind. The militia eventually cowed the rioters.

No riot in early twentieth century history matched the East Saint Louis confrontation in the scope of its violence and brutality. During the days of mob rule, white rioters burned down a good section of the black ghetto, killed, burned, or maimed hundreds of black persons, and escaped with almost complete impunity for their acts.[29]

DISCUSSION: REACTIONS TO THE RIOT

Responsible members of various groups throughout America condemned the atrocities of the 1917 East Saint Louis riots. Cartoonists in prestigious newspapers depicted dead black persons lying in front of the burned-out ghetto; the caption in the *New York Evening Post* read "Speaking of Atrocities,"[30] a cryptic reference to Allied charges of German barbarity. Another cartoon in the *New York Evening Mail*[31] showed a grim President Wilson facing a black woman on her knees. "Mr. President," she said, "Why not make America safe for democracy?" Editorialists condemned the barbarism of the East Saint Louis white population and demanded that safeguards be established so that such a situation would never again occur. Southern newspapers condemned Northern hypocrisy and sardonically noted the apparent fact that no single part of the nation could be held solely responsible for barbarism against the black population.[32] Black leaders and newspapers reacted in disbelief, and the *Cleveland Gazette* asserted that the story of East Saint Louis must have been planted by Southern bigots.[33]

President Wilson remained silent, and no affirmative action was taken by the executive branch of the federal government. Theodore Roosevelt, who at the time was the retired ex-President, condemned the "appalling brutality" in East Saint Louis. At a meeting at Carnegie Hall, Roosevelt clashed with Samuel Gompers, the founder of the trade labor movement. Gompers attempted to set the blame for the riots upon the industrialists who had imported the black laborers. Angered by his response, Roosevelt shook his first in Gompers' face, refusing to accept any "apology" for the infamy imposed on the black community in East Saint Louis. He demanded a full investigation.[34]

Indeed, Congress did appoint a special investigating committee that spent months hearing witnesses to the riot. The committee diligently listened to many segments of the East Saint Louis community. They heard accounts of cruelty, graft, race prejudice, murder, and the apathy of bystanders to the riot. Nonetheless, the committee's report[35] did not result in one indictment or court-martial. While the congressional report detailed the way in which the machinations of employers, labor leaders, and local politicians paved the way for the riot, it did not make any tangible or constructive suggestions.

The Illinois state's attorney conducted some court trials, but the results were disappointing to anyone who sought justice. The great majority of whites involved in lynchings, arson, and murder were freed on the basis of lack of evidence. In some instances the activities of many had been witnessed by thousands of persons.[36] Only two white defendants were convicted of lynching and sentenced to fourteen years in prison.[37] Even in this instance, a colonel of the National Guard testified that he had witnessed the men dragging the victim to his hanging; two infantrymen corroborated the story. The widow of the murdered man positively identified the two lynchers, but the defendants received relatively light sentences.

Blacks who had been trapped in the riot suffered a worse fate than whites who were prosecuted. Twenty-one blacks were brought to trial on charges of killing the two white detectives. Since the prosecution realized the impossibility of proving that any one of the black defendants had actually fired the fatal shots, they sought to convict them on charges of a conspiracy to provoke a race riot.[38] Witnesses testified to seeing some of the defendants carrying guns. They said they heard the pealing of church bells in the black district, which was the supposed signal that a "war" between blacks and whites was to begin. One witness, a black man, was given immunity from prosecution and asked to identify the defendants as the killers of the detectives. He did, contradicting his earlier testimony before a coroner.[39] Ten of the black men were sent to prison.

In effect, nothing had changed in East Saint Louis: more black than white persons went to prison, the burned-out ghetto was slowly rebuilt within the confines of its previous boundaries,[40] labor unions continued to discriminate against blacks, and employers continued to use black labor as strikebreakers until the late 1930s.[41] The congressional report was buried in the usual files, and President Wilson remained silent.

Despite the later outbreaks of violence in other cities during World Wars I and II (particularly the Detroit riot of 1943),[42] many otherwise astute, perceptive observers hoped that the era of direct ethnic conflict ended when the Supreme Court and other federal institutions eroded some of the bastions of segregation. Writing in 1964, sociologist Elliot Rudwick felt sufficiently optimistic to make the following comment: "The Negro protest for equal status . . . has thus far occurred without a major race riot. This is itself a landmark of significance in American race relations."[43] Alas, his optimism and confidence in the American creed was not fulfilled. Building from the social movement that began in the mid-1950s, ethnic riots sputtered in 1964 and again erupted in 1965. These situations were to serve as the symbol of an age of American domestic conflict: the 1960s.

Case 5
Watts, California, 1965

The area known as Watts encompasses forty-six square miles of south-central Los Angeles. The assessed value of the area in 1965 was approximately 201 million.[44] On the surface Watts appeared to be a relatively prosperous community of small homes surrounded by gardens and shrubs. Unlike that of East Saint Louis, however, the outward facade of California living hid the poverty that existed. Like the pockets of poverty described by Michael Harrington,[45] Watts was enclosed by freeways that bypassed and isolated it from contact with the white world.

THE SETTING: CALIFORNIA, SEEKING TO FULFILL A DREAM

Fifty years ago, Watts was an orchard of orange trees tended by a handful of "Anglos," then Mexican-Americans, and finally black farmers. As people moved from the Los Angeles city center, small houses styled in the 1930 stucco manner sprouted among the farms in the area. By the late 1930s, blacks, drawn by the myth of California and her riches, gradually infiltrated the area until it became the waystation for black migrants. Hundreds of thousands of black persons moved gradually outward. As the census maps of 1950 and 1960 show, Watts gradually became a spreading inkblot on the map of central Los Angeles. The area had long been known as a center of crime. In the 1920s, organized crime got its start in the area, and succeeding generations of the various ethnic groups (Italians, Mexicans, and blacks) who moved there inherited a criminal atmosphere.[46] Nonetheless, its paved streets and neatly clipped lawns hid the undercurrents of illegal activities.

By 1965 approximately 95 percent of the population of Watts was black,[47] living in the superficially antiseptic ghetto created in part by white discrimination, realtors' actions, and eventually by California law.[48] The majority of blacks who had migrated to Watts already were urbanized. Unlike the black peasants who moved to East Saint Louis from the poor, red ground of southern farms, the black migrant to California was acclimated to city life in southern towns and then "border cities." The conditions they met in migrating to Watts hardly fulfilled their dream of a sunshine-filled, trouble-free California.

The area of Watts was three times as crowded with human beings as any other quarter of Los Angeles. Many men were unemployed wanderers, and more than 40 percent of the families were broken by divorce or desertion.[49] The breakdown of the family had predictable results: many children saw their fathers, if at all, drinking beer with buddies on the street corner while mothers worked.[50]

White merchants and police were the visible oppressors. The area was policed by 272 policemen (90 percent white). White landlords owned 70 percent of the homes and apartments. White businessmen controlled all but a handful of the stores, bars, and gas stations.[51]

Many of the black men in Watts sought escape in drugs and crime.[52] There were few, if any, ways out for the population.

Housing

Watts was the port of entry for blacks into Los Angeles. As other urban migrants, they sought the social support and aid of friends and relatives who had moved before them. Between 1950 and 1960, a total of 151,410 black migrants moved into Watts. About 206,509 whites moved out of Los Angeles to the suburbs.[53] Communities adjacent to Watts dramatically increased their white population. Torrance, a town southwest of Watts, increased over 350 percent in a decade but remained devoid of nonwhites. The population of Fullerton, to the southeast of Watts, went up by over 300 percent; Newport Beach, to the south of Watts, increased in population by over 100 percent; and Culver City, to the northeast of Watts, increased in population by over 60 percent. Only 2 percent of the populations of these areas was nonwhite in 1960.[54] In essence, a black island was created in the midst of a sprawling, otherwise nondescript city. Except for merchants in the area, the majority of white people caught only a fleeting glimpse of Watts as they sped across the Harbor Freeway. The people of Watts, except for those who worked, saw only the white policemen, teachers, and businessmen.

Employment

Between 1959 and 1965 employment in Watts dropped by 8 percent. This was a time when the rest of the American economy was burgeoning. Labor unions systematically excluded young blacks from apprenticeships. By 1965, 41 percent of the black men between 18 and 25 years of age were not working.[55]

Many Watts residents lived on welfare payments. Robert Conot, in *Rivers of Blood, Years of Darkness,* has described a typical welfare case:

A woman with nine children lived in a public housing project. She had been receiving $371 per month, the maximum possible amount, even though her needs, according to the schedule, were about $100 greater. The woman went to work at $333 a month as an aid in the Anti-Poverty War Neighborhood Adult Participation Project. Her salary, however, except for a $25 allowance for on-the-job expenses and a small additional work incentive allowance were deducted from the check. The public housing authority promptly raised the rent from $56 to $114, absorbing all the additional money, and in effect punishing her for going to work.[56]

Education

Segregated schools produced students who consistently fell behind citywide and national norms of achievement.[57]

Given these conditions, it is surprising that there were as few incidents of violence in the community as there were. In April 1962 Black Muslims exchanged gunfire with police when the officers searched the Muslim Temple for a suspected burglar. In 1964 there were small-scale riots at Jefferson High School, at the Central Receiving Hospital, and on Avalon Boulevard. Although these incidents might have served as warnings, most Americans ignored them.[58]

To the casual observer, Watts seemed a most unlikely place for violence to erupt. Its residents technically had benefited from most of the civil rights advances of the decade. The neighborhood was composed of clean, spruce, if modest, dwellings enclosed by lawns, far from the diseased alleys of Harlem in New York. Children attended legally integrated schools, albeit 99 percent black. Parents had the right to vote. Public accommodations were open to all, but the hospital closest to Watts was twelve miles away. From the public's point of view, to a man from Mississippi, Watts should have seemed a haven of freedom.

There were a few perceptive people, like the astute Assistant Attorney General Howard H. Jewel, who explicitly warned in 1964 that demonstrations in Los Angeles could escalate into major violence:

> if demonstrators [in Los Angeles] are joined by the Negro community at large, the policing will no longer be done by the Los Angeles Police Department, but by the State Militia.[59]

PRECIPITANTS: CLOSING THE DOOR

In 1964, California passed a law (Proposition 14) that in effect legalized housing discrimination and helped to ensure that black people would be kept within the boundaries of their ghetto.[60] This perceived demonstration of white contempt helped set the stage for reaction. A black man later told us, "They told us last year that they don't want no niggers living near them. Now, we done showed them that we don't want them sucking our blood."[61]

For anyone who talked with the people of Watts during the tragic days following August 1965, the mood of the black community should have been readily apparent. However imperfectly expressed, the people repeatedly explained their rebellion on three grounds: to protest against police brutality, to get all the material goods that "whitey" had, and to demonstrate manhood and dignity.

Police brutality

"Never again," said Marquette Frye, whose arrest helped trigger the riot. "Never again in this neighborhood will any young man, like my brother and me, stand by and take abuse from an officer."[62] Rightly or wrongly, almost every black person who participated in the riot echoed this sentiment. "Police brutality is like when they arrest you where it can't be seen and whip you," a 22-year-old black explained to reporters Jerry Cohen and William Murphy. "They grab you when you walk down the street. They pull you over and beat on you. That ain't right, Man, I was born in California—in Long Beach. But I'm a Negro, so I been arrested."[63]

This testimony must be tempered by two qualifications: First, the Los Angeles police admittedly participated in sweeps of "duck ponds" (i.e., areas of high criminality) before the riots of 1965. During the raids, police randomly selected people, interrogated them, and checked to see if they had failed to pay for relatively trivial offenses, like traffic penalties. These "field investigations" were conducted regularly in Watts, but never in the suburbs of Los Angeles.[64] At the minimum, therefore, the Los Angeles police submitted the people of Watts to a continuing surveillance any American would consider an insult to dignity and personhood.

Second, during the riot itself, individual policemen may have acted in a brutal fashion. There is conflicting testimony on this issue, so no final conclusion may be drawn. However, in the midst of flames and snipers it is not unreasonable to assume that some police officers reacted with a fear and hatred that might normally have been more controlled.[65]

The story of Laurence Jacques, which was contradicted by the testimony of the police officers involved, typified the type of rumors that circulated and what many black persons, with or without reason, believed.

Jacques witnessed the shooting of one looter and the arrest of another. He, too, was arrested, although he claimed he had done nothing. He was forced to lie on the ground with another black person. Jacques reported during the trial that one policeman had asked another, "How many did you kill?"

The second policeman allegedly answered, "I killed two niggers. Why don't you kill those two lying on the ground?"

According to Jacques, the first officer said, "They won't run."

"One officer came up to me and put a shotgun at the back of my head," said Jacques. "Nigger, how fast can you run the fifty-yard dash?"

"I said, 'I can't run it at all.' He kicked me in the side two times, and the other officer put his foot on the back of my head."[66]

Stories such as Jacques' circulated through the black community, even if they were complete fabrications, and added fuel to the already inflamed situation.[67]

THE NATURE OF THE RIOT

"If they come after you, just run to this house," an elderly black said to us on 15 August 1965. He pointed to a trim cottage on one of the attractive side streets in the Watts area. "Don't forget now, it's the pink one with the white shutters." We welcomed this act of hospitality and honored the courage that prompted it. To aid people of white skin during the August days of madness in Los Angeles required unusual kindness, even valor.[68]

We had disobeyed the police injunction to stay out of the ghetto. The riots in Los Angeles were not just an explosion of hoodlumism. They followed on the heels of what we felt to be a social movement. As sociologists, we felt compelled to witness this confrontation of blacks and whites.

On 15 August, after dodging the various

obstacles set up by the army reserves, we found ourselves deep in an already devastated section of Los Angeles. Jeeps, armed with machine guns, patrolled the streets, and police moved in small groups in order to protect themselves from snipers. Around them, on the main streets, the hulls of stores smoked, letting out an occasional burst of flames. Burned automobiles lined the streets. Young black men, stripped to the waist, slipped from building to building. They signaled each other by holding up one, two, or three fingers, indicating the section (and gang headquarters) to which they belonged. They obviously felt a joyous release in the fighting. They joked, drank, looted, and burned—asserting what they defined as a sense of manhood that had heretofore been denied them.

We moved to locate people who would not mistakenly regard our white faces as symbols of tyranny, and we found them. Even in the midst of the destruction, we discovered black persons—some terrified, others aiding the wounded, some in a jubilant mood, others trying to calm the mob—who would talk with white people and even offer to help them.

A black man we encountered claimed to have seen the incident that triggered the riots. By a devious route, he took us to the spot on Avalon Boulevard, which by then was spattered with glass and charred remnants. Three days before, police had arrested two black men there for drunken driving. The two men, Marquette and Ronald Frye, had resisted arrest. Their mother joined them, swearing at the police. "Those cops and their reinforcements called us dirty niggers," our informant reported.

In the sweltering heat of that Wednesday evening the conflagration began. "My husband and I saw ten cops beating a man," a black woman later testified.[69] "My husband told the officers, 'You done got him handcuffed.' One of the officers said 'Get out of here, nigger. Get out of here, all you niggers.' " Hundreds of people had gathered at the scene. After the Fryes had been dragged off, the mob broke loose. "I threw bricks and rocks and anything I could get my hands on to hurt them," an 18-year-old girl later said. "We were throwing at anything white." This initial passionate hatred of the white man, contrary to original, lurid press reports, appears to have abated after a short while.

On Thursday, 12 August 1965, seven thousand blacks rioted in the Watts ghetto. Their antagonism was directed mainly against white merchants who controlled the business in the area and against white policemen. The rioters smashed cars and looted the district of clothes, food, liquor, and guns; the victims were almost invariably businessmen regarded as parasites in Watts. Signs stating "Colored-owned" saved the smaller establishments. A Chinese merchant even erected a sign proclaiming: "I am colored too!" Black businessmen had received warnings that a riot would begin on their street, and it was suggested they board up their stores.[70]

The few white people who lived in the district and had earned a favorable reputation were not molested. One white woman with whom we talked had lived in Watts for twenty-one years. "On the thirteenth, mobs ran up and down my street," she said, "with the police coming after them in droves. But my neighbors, who are all colored, made sure that no one disturbed me."

The astonishing element in the Watts riots, then, was not the pillage and passion, but the selective nature of the attacks and respect shown different merchants. Moreover, during the early days of the riot, a festival spirit pervaded the air: people appeared almost to be celebrating rather than attacking. Black looters obeyed the usual rules of civility. One of our group bumped into a black woman carrying goods from a store and both said, "Excuse me," before hurrying on. Cars loaded with stolen goods stopped at red light signs, even though police cars may have been overtaking them from some blocks behind.

On 14 August, as the battle gained in intensity, black middle-class and lower-class workers joined in the fray. "There was a lot more 'outsiders' here than regular people," one oldtimer in Watts remarked. "People came from all over—some for profit, I guess, but a lot came because they thought we was really accomplishing something."

The rioters had, in fact, forced the police to admit defeat: eighteen thousand National Guardsmen moved into the twenty-one square-mile area, declared a curfew, and opened fire with machine guns. Thirty-five persons were killed, hundreds wounded, four thousand arrested, and property damage ran into millions of dollars.[71]

As we saw the area on Sunday, 15 August, southeastern Los Angeles, ravaged by hundreds of blazes, resembled an embattled city. Tooting the slogan on their car horns, groups of young blacks cruised the neighborhood chanting "Burn, Baby, Burn!"—a phrase made popular by a local disc jockey. Even black reporters, trying to infiltrate the area, joined in beating out the rhythm.

On Monday the Guard spokesman announced that the riots were controlled. Yet, as news reports came in, one wondered whether the end had come; in Long Beach, a few miles south of Los Angeles, riots resulted in the death of another policeman; in Orange County, to the south and east of Los Angeles, roving cars of blacks attacked some white persons; and in San Diego, 120 miles south of Los Angeles, the Logan Heights ghetto exploded in its own riot. Watts also proved to be a curtain-raiser to more demonstrated discontent in cities such as Detroit and Newark.

Printed pamphlets, mysteriously distributed in Los Angeles, correctly declared on 16 August 1965: "The song has ended, but the melody lingers." And Marquette Frye, whose arrest ignited the violence, told a Black Muslim rally on the same day: "The troops don't mean a thing. They haven't seen anything yet."[72]

His prediction came true. We witnessed only the beginning of an armed black insurrection in Northern cities that plagued the 1960s. All of the ingredients of a classic riot situation were there:[73] an objective lessening of white oppression; a consequent spiraling of black aspirations; and, as reality dashed the short-lived hopes, the heightening of frustration.

DISCUSSION: MANHOOD AND REACTION

The restraint and continuation of social amenities shown by many rioters suggest that the riots had an aim beyond revenge against white people. Many interpretations have been proffered. Dr. Harold Jones, a black psychiatrist in charge of a Watts clinic, suggested that "the rioters shared a common motivation for their action—a determination to show their strength by using violence." Further, Jones believed that the riots were "an attempt to give Negro leadership a bargaining position with white authorities." Neither of these explanations agrees fully with our analysis of the occurrence.[74] Although a latent effect of riots may be to increase the bargaining position of the community, it is doubtful that riot participants are aware of this during the actual event.

Get what whitey has

In our opinion, objective social conditions prompted a desire for goods that were visible but unattainable to most in Watts. There had been repeated promises in 1964 and 1965 that the War on Poverty funds would soon be forthcoming. These promises were not fulfilled. The Federal Office of Economic Opportunity stipulated that representatives from poor areas should participate in the handling of poverty funds, but city officials had not changed the composition of the responsible boards.[75]

The looting of liquor, appliance, grocery, and furniture stores ran into millions of dollars. One unemployed man on welfare told us: "We want everything the whites have, including color TV. The stores were open. If you are hungry and don't have no money, you want anything and everything. Having no job is no fun. With store windows broken and police doin' other things, what would you do?"

Most of the looters had never before been known as criminals; 75 percent of the adult rioters[76] did have police records, but the typical adolescent looter never had been previously arrested. Much of the looting, however, was irrational. Women would strip dress racks of anything they could find. Looters stole bags of shoes—of different sizes and colors. One man collected fifteen TV sets and stored them in his cellar, without having a plan to dispose of them. What apparently occurred was a spiraling of aspirations that had been frustrated by the economic reality of Watts. Much of the looting was, therefore, a way of getting back at society and venting hostilities rather than a rational desire to acquire useful goods.

The search for dignity

Further, it is possible that another intangible but pervasive impulse guided many of the rioters: a simple desire to prove their manhood. Many men viewed the riot as an insurrection against the white establishment, as a way of bringing attention to them and to their area. Indeed, until the riot, many blacks who had somehow escaped the confines of the ghetto refused to admit that they came from Watts. After the riot, signs surrounding the area proudly proclaimed, "You are now entering Watts."

An articulate black college graduate summarized the search for dignity and autonomy in this way:

> You can stand on 103rd, on the edge of Will Rogers Park, and look up and see the big silver and gray jetliners pass overhead. Watts is on one of the approach routes to Los Angeles International Airport. If you fly over and look down you cannot tell Watts is there. It does not look any different from any other part of the city. The things that make it Watts are invisible. Watts is a state of mind as well as a place. Part of what it is is symbolized by the low, speeding passage of planes overhead. Standing in the heart of Watts, you can look up and see the big world, the expensive and expansive world, but the people in that world cannot see you. Your existence is not visible to them. You can see them but they cannot see you. You can never reach them. You can shout but they won't hear you. Waving or running or jumping will not make them see you.
>
> There was only one time when the people up in the sky saw the people down on the ground. . . .
>
> That was when the flames of Watts riots leaped and spiraled into the air, lighting up the approach route to Los Angeles International Airport.[77]

For many people in Watts the feeling of "being recognized" and of achieving a sense—however illusory—that they had finally asserted their autonomy against society served as the major reason to riot. The importance of this feeling as instigating elements in the riot can be illustrated by a comparison between Watts and Compton, California.

The city of Compton directly borders the Watts riot area, and 50 percent of its population was black; yet, it escaped a black-white conflagration. A few abortive attempts were made to start a riot,[78] and over 150 people were arrested there. Half of those arrested, however, came from outside the city.

Many explanations can be offered for this anomaly. In 1965 Compton was still an integrated area. While the black proportion of the population rose rapidly from 4 percent in 1950 to 50 percent in 1960, the persuasive work of Compton's Human Relations Commission had stemmed the outflow of whites by the time of the riot. Living conditions were better in Compton than in Watts: median income ($5,523) was higher, people had achieved more education (a median of 10.2 years), and fewer houses were considered to be deteriorated and dilapidated (about 8 percent) in Compton.[79]

Clearly, Compton had developed (or absorbed) a black middle class with economic stakes in the community and on relatively amicable terms with the white establishment and the police. A different spirit prevailed there: a sense of integration and a belief that the economic gains achieved by blacks should be defended by blacks themselves against hoodlums.

"I think it would be naive to say that problems are all solved—they're not all solved," a white Compton policeman, Captain Harold Lindemuller, commented, "but I think the community as a whole is trying to face up to them and solve them."[80] Not only did the blacks and whites in the community talk about human relations, but when it came to protecting their community, they jointly mounted guard.

In contrast to Compton, H. Edward Ransford found that Watts residents who participated in the violence described themselves as powerless to change society, isolated from social contact, and abused by racial discrimination. Black rioters felt that they were cut off from the larger society and unable to affect it. In general, 65 percent of the violence-prone black persons in Ransford's sample felt isolated, powerless, and particularly subject to racial prejudice, while only 12 percent of those who said they eschewed violence exhibited the same feelings."[81]

A variety of factors—objective ghettoization, a feeling of isolation, a lack of economic roots in the community, a belief in police brutality—led thousands of blacks to attempt to assert their dignity for one brief moment in history.

Reactions to the riot

The most immediate reactions to the Watts riot were ominous. The widely circulated *Los Angeles Times* carried crude cartoons depicting thick-lipped, drooling blacks rampaging under the banner, "We Shall Overwhelm," and articles about the Watts situation. Religious white persons passed out a supposed Biblical verse proclaiming that "men of color" would take over at the end of the world. Gun stores in Los Angeles sold out their weapons. Rumors of sighting of paramilitary white "minutemen" were circulated. Wearing green berets and military uniforms with pants tucked into paratrooper boots, the minutemen reputedly invaded the Watts area to display their force.

On the other hand, a California state commission issued a lengthy report detailing the sources of violence, but few of its recommendations were implemented. Many agencies, particularly on the federal level, attempted to change some of the basic conditions in Watts. Federal aid, in the form of antipoverty funds, was poured into the area. New programs including credit unions, Head Start training, even an art festival, were created. Proposition 14, one of the precipitants to the riots, was declared unconstitutional by the state supreme court.

Within the Watts community itself, numerous organizations sprang up. Indigenous groups espousing a black power ideology or emphasizing the African cultural heritage of American blacks emerged. The Sons of Watts, composed in part of former rioters, attempted to build community spirit through such acts as distributing litter cans to help clean up the debris. In 1966, during the Watts Festival, this same group policed a large parade so effectively that Mayor Sam Yorty rode in an open car and the parade was unmarred by incidents. Another group, the Citizen's Alert Patrol armed itself with tape recorders and cameras and followed police to the scene of every arrest as a guard against police brutality.

All these movements may have wrought a psychological change in Watts. Indeed, many former rioters made up the majority of their membership. In 1967, we detected more hope, more dignity, and a greater sense of importance in Watts residents than before the riot.

Without denigrating the possible change in the spiritual climate of the central district, however, it must be recognized that the basic problems of Watts remained unsolved. Some groups, while well-meaning, were totally ineffectual. The Los Angeles

County Commission on Human Relations, for example, advised its "big brothers" to furnish Thanksgiving meals for deprived children. Reasonably, one could hardly expect a turkey dinner to cure the basic, year-round problems of Watts.

Economically, the area did not recuperate. Indeed, unemployment remained high, many potential industries were not introduced, and many stores did not attempt to rejuvenate themselves (partially because insurance companies refused to issue policies on them). A random sample of Watts males in 1967 indicated that 81 percent favored the use of violence in defense of civil rights.[82] Another riot in March of 1966 confronted black and Chicano gangs. This time, all of the rioters were well armed. Two men were killed. Police mobilized quickly and the adult black community succeeded in quieting the youths.

Despite these sobering facts, many black migrants continued to arrive in Los Angeles, lured by the promise of a better life. Almost all of them settled in the central district, but only a few had the technical qualifications demanded by Los Angeles industry. In the central district the rate of black population growth was about four times that of the city as a whole.

By 1976 many blacks could look forward to major, if symbolic, victories: a black mayor had been elected for the first time and housing discrimination was no longer a legal activity. Yet, high unemployment rates continued, de facto ghettoization had not changed, and Watts itself was devoid of industrial activity. As it had for decades, Watts absorbed waves of unskilled black migrants.

The ultimate effect of this trend has been prophesied by urbanologist Victor Palmieri. "This is the city of the future—the very near future. A black island spreading like a giant ink blot over the heart of a metropolis which is bankrupt financially and paralyzed politically."[83]

Case 6
Houston's police riot, 1967

A third type of urban violence appeared in the United States during the twentieth century. Unlike the East Saint Louis debacle, the violence in Houston, Texas, during the 1960s was not initiated by an attack of white citizens upon black citizens.[84] Nor did it resemble the black expression of discontent in Watts. Rather, police and military authorities were ordered to maintain control in Houston. Dissenters were subjected to firm, at times harsh, control.[85] A variety of different events ranging from the Chicago Democratic Convention in 1968 to the civil war in Beirut, Lebanon, in 1976 illustrate the new forms of violence that emasculate our cities. In America the confrontation at the University of California at Berkeley, the Kent State shooting of students, and the Houston riot symbolize this situation. In chapter 1 we briefly described the immediate situation of the Houston riot. An understanding of any riot must, however, be based on a knowledge of its background.

THE SETTING: HOUSTON, TEXAS

Houston in 1967 was a city of contradictions.[86] It contained more blacks (275,000) than any other city in the South, the Confederate flag flew prominently in bars, and blacks were closely segregated in five districts. In Houston, millionaires air-conditioned outdoor garden parties, NASA housed its headquarters, and a rigidly maintained segregation caused the busing of black children twelve miles past white schools to avoid contact between black and white children during school hours.

Compared to Watts, the black population generally lived a better life in Houston. Unemployment was relatively low; only 7 percent of blacks could not find jobs. Further, the city was the cheapest of twenty urban American regions in which to live in 1967. Blacks earned an annual median income of $3,436, a modest sum when compared to the median income of $5,902 for whites,[87] yet sufficient for a livelihood in the city.

Over half of Houston's blacks had been born in the deep South or in a small town in Eastern Texas[88] (a region known for its bigotry and lynchings). Thus, a move to Houston represented a distinct improvement in life-style and a taste of new freedoms. Local black folk songs celebrated the relative virtues of Houston by labeling it "Heavenly Houston." If blacks kept in their place, life was tolerable. Probably because many of the expectations of the black masses who moved to Houston had in fact been satisfied, the black community as a whole—unlike Watts—apparently was not stirred by deep unrest. Black and white people clung to traditions of keeping their place. If blacks (such as the relatively elitist all-black Texas Southern University students) made any move to change the status quo, the whites quickly closed any possible chance of protest.

Economics

Fifty-three percent of blacks had family incomes of $4,000 a year or less as opposed to 36 percent of whites and 11 percent of Mexican-Americans.[89] An attempt was made by a few community-based volunteer groups to combat poverty in Houston with a federally funded antipoverty program. The city administration, however, openly expressed opposition to the activities of some of these groups and regarded them as agitators. Obstacles were set in the way of implementing the antipoverty program, and it virtually came to a halt by 1967.[90]

Education

The black people who hoped to achieve a decent education in quality institutions were inevitably frustrated. White adults in Houston had completed a median of 11.3 years of schooling while blacks had finished only 8.9 years.[91] A stubborn segregationist majority on the school board foiled attempts to integrate schools.

Black children entered the public schools at a handicap; they lagged behind whites of comparable age in various achievement tests. The longer they stayed in Houston's segregated schools, however, the more they fell behind the whites. When they reached college level, blacks were far behind the level of national achievement. At Texas Southern University, for example, approximately 50 percent of graduates failed to pass tests that would have allowed them to become teachers.[92]

Politics

Ward politics rewarded those who went along with the dominant, conservative Democrats. Even in overwhelmingly Negro districts, black people hardly dared to run for office. Various black preachers were rumored to have sold votes to the white establishment at twenty-five cents a head. In return, the black population received nothing. While skyscrapers were built in abundance, the typical black person had to settle for dirt streets, water drawn from a community pump, and housing that the 1960 census found to be 50 percent unsound.[93]

Perhaps the most abrasive and direct confrontation between black and white Houstonians came in the area of police relations. The Houston police had eight black officers who, rightly or wrongly, were reputed to be the biggest thieves in the ghetto. White police were thought to hold black persons in contempt. One of the major complaints of black community people was that they were searched without warrant.[94]

The "Lucky Hill" incident illustrates the nature of the type of complaint made by black people against the predominantly white policemen. A white woman who owned a store in the ghetto reported to the police that a black man, Lucky Hill, had stolen a roasted chicken. A policeman was dispatched to the scene and found Hill next door in a bar.

Hill loudly proclaimed his innocence. Further, he was known by the community residents to be the lover of the complaining store owner. The whole incident would have been ludicrous and perhaps even humorous except that the policeman took offense at some of Hill's comments. He forced Hill to go out to the sidewalk and searched him. Hill continued to loudly curse the policeman, waving his hands in the air. The police officer presumably took this as an attack, pulled his revolver, and shot Hill in the chest. A crowd of black people gathered around Hill, and a black woman in nurse's uniform offered to minister to the stricken man. The police officer refused to allow any help to be given him. After he had called his precinct for help, the police officer stood calmly smoking a cigarette. The crowd became incensed and threatened to attack him, but black ministers arrived on the scene and calmed them.[95] Lucky Hill died, and the officer did not receive a formal reprimand.

PRECIPITANT: STUDENT REBELLION

The Lucky Hill incident occurred near the Texas State University (TSU) campus. Rumors soon circulated the campus population, but there were many reasons why the TSU students became indignant. For example, at the beginning of the fall term, 1967, a group known as the "Friends of the Student Non-Violent Coordinating Committee" (SNCC) attempted to set up a branch on the black campus. They were not only refused permission, but their faculty sponsor was suspended by an administration fearful of white reprisal through a withdrawal of funds. The banishment of the group served to spark interest in a previously uncommitted student body; after a series of demonstrations, the administration finally granted permission for the chartering of the group. On 4 April 1967, the administration charged three SNCC leaders with threatening police officers. The men were jailed and placed on $24,000 bonds. Hundreds of students marched in their defense in a peaceful vigil at the courthouse.

During the week of 8 May 1967, TSU students demonstrated near the city dump, adjacent to their campus, where a child had drowned in a pool of garbage. The city had repeatedly promised to move the dump, but failed to do so. Bearing lit candles, the students maintained a vigil over the child's place of death.

Other incidents added fever to the college students' discontent. In another area of Houston, black youths had been allegedly attacked by white gangs at an integrated junior high school. TSU students demonstrated on their behalf. The police arrested sixty of the college students and jailed them.[96]

On 16 May 1967, rumors went through the TSU cafeteria concerning the shooting of a black child by a white man. At dinner time, an orator jumped on the table and proclaimed his support for civil rights. He proceeded to denigrate the city administration for its lack of action in cleaning up the dump near the campus, its failure to halt assaults on black children in white schools, and its compliance in keeping Houston's schools totally segregated.[97]

THE RIOT: LEGITIMATED VIOLENCE

Trouble, then, had been brewing on the TSU campus. Earlier in the day police had been called by college officials, and a few shots were fired. One policeman rushed into the cafeteria and arrested the young black orator on the charge of disturbing the peace. The students who had been listening responded with a rampage of food and tray throwing.[98] After the policeman carted off his young charge, additional police cars were called for added protection. The cars surrounded the men's dormitory.

The students paid little heed to the massed police cars and formed small groups of rock-and-bottle throwing groups. Any cars driven by white persons down the street that bisected the campus were stoned. For a while, as in Watts, a seemingly holiday atmosphere prevailed. Students danced in the street, as they had been taught to do several months earlier when a black preacher-guitarist convinced a rebellious mob of students that they should turn the occasion into a block party. Some students put up barricades, sealing off the campus from traffic.[99] They had been vainly proposing this action to the city for years.

University officials, for the most part black, panicked. Regarded by the students as Uncle Toms, they believed this minor event was equivalent to revolution. Most of the administrators had already left the campus, and matters were left in the hands of a junior dean (also black). Futilely, he argued with students to return to their dormitories. They refused to obey the dean's exhortation.

Unknown to the students, Houston's police chief, Herman Short, sent out emergency calls to all of his forces and to sheriff's deputies in the area. Equipped with guns, a group of eight hundred policemen gathered at one end of the campus, prepared to enter upon command. They lined four abreast on the main street leading into TSU.[100]

The police cars trapped inside the campus and the students exchanged gunfire. The party that shot first was never determined.

Meanwhile, the mayor, Louis Welch, was awakened in the early morning hours of 17 May 1967. Welch had experienced similar situations in previous years, but consistently restrained the police from using force. The mayor consulted various members of his staff about using force.

About 2:00 A.M., together with some black ministers and other colleagues, the mayor's assistants arrived on the campus just as the chief of police radioed the mayor for instructions. Various black leaders entered the dormitories and told the students of the police massing outside. They attempted to influence students into entering negotiations with the city officials.

As assistants to the mayor in charge of race relations, we tried to convince the chief of police to disperse his men and allow the negotiators a chance to work. By the time we reached the chief's car, however, he was surrounded by newsmen and TV photographers. It not only was difficult to openly talk with him because of the crowd and the noise, but also because of the public nature of the situation. The mayor maintained contact only by radio.

Our pleas to hold off were met with a mute response by Chief of Police Short. The mayor radioed consent to use police; the chief bellowed over his microphone, "Move in and get 'em out." The eight hundred police officers dutifully marched down the middle of the TSU campus, carrying rifles, pistols, shotguns, and riot guns. Without warning, they opened fire on the men's dormitory in a shattering lethal blast. The black negotiators were still inside the student residences. A few returned shots could be heard, but the major effect of the police outburst was that their own rifle bullets ricocheted against the brick building, killing at least one white policeman.[101] After a crescendo of fire, small groups of policemen dashed inside the dormitories. Smashing doors, they moved from room to room. The sound of furniture shattering could be heard. The black students possessing guns surrendered them. While there undoubtedly had been gunfire from the dormitories, no student was ever convicted of firing at the police, and not a single policeman was indicted for any crime against the students.

The facts were never made clear. Three police officers were rumored to have been killed. They were possibly only wounded—no exact figures were released by the police. Two students were killed, 488 blacks arrested. TSU was badly mauled, and the fragile relations between blacks and whites were severed in Houston. Some students were sentenced to prison on the charge of possession of marijuana, and the police rejoiced in local white barrooms over their rout of the "niggers."[102]

It was clear to us just as it would have been to any other objective observer, that the Houston incident was a clear case of a police riot. A more sophisticated police tactic would have dictated a sealing off of the area, a rescinding of the first arrest of the black student orator, a process of discussions, and a cooling off period for negotiations.[103]

DISCUSSION: REACTION

Many Houston whites shared a belief with the police that strong measures should be taken to control a rioting population. A poll of Houstonians taken by Victor Emmanuel confirmed their belief in the use of police violence: 77 percent of the white population sampled believed that the army should have been called in, that the rioters should be shot, or that some kind of force had to be used.[104] In a city reputed for its untrammeled violence, in terms of murder, this legitimation of the use of force could have been expected.

The brief confrontation between students and police basically did not change the configuration of the city. Poverty remained unchanged, the city failed to comply with the standards for a Model Cities Program, the mayor's office and police remained in the control of the same hands,[105] and the whites failed to change their pattern of discrimination.

On only one front—the political—did blacks make some gains, and it is difficult to tell whether these advances were a result of the riot or merely coincidental. For the first time in Texas history a black woman was elected to the state senate the following year. Her district, however, was gerrymandered so that later she had to face another popular, liberal black for a seat in Congress. A year later the white reactionaries lost control of the school board and a few reforms were initiated. Nonetheless, the school board fired a liberal superintendent. The conservatives again regained control.[106] In 1972 the chief of police indicated that he would like to be mayor, but he failed to stir a public response. By 1976 Houston had elected a relatively liberal mayor. The black congresswoman, Barbara Jordan, had achieved national recognition. A continuing infiltration of Northern people (scientists, engineers, and professionals) had changed the political landscape of this modern, growing city.

Yet, as with almost all riots, these positive changes in Houston were relatively meager and could hardly be credited to the riot itself. In Houston the pendulum swings from a conservative polity to temporary reform, back to reaction, and then, perhaps, to further change.

SUMMARY: VIOLENCE AND PROTEST

St. Clair Drake has suggested that during the first 180 years of urbanization the existence of a frontier saved American cities from the types of conflicts that London and Paris suffered during the early nineteenth century.[107] Riots of Irish harborworkers in New York, however, have been recorded as early as 1836. As in the instances described in this chapter, class and ethnic overtones were mingled with the Irishmen's feelings of deprivation and finding themselves the victims of contempt or economic exploitation.

The riots depicted were precipitated by some real or imagined event in which a group within an urban setting felt that its dignity was being threatened. In East Saint Louis, whites attacked blacks on the assumption that blacks were stealing jobs, thus undermining the position whites had precariously attained. Black people in Watts, although relatively well-off compared to other blacks, exploded over an ordinary traffic incident interpreted as a "last straw" in their relations with an oppressive police force. Police in Houston advanced on black students, believing that they had to crush the menace of the black reform movement.

The actions of rioters have been morally justified not only by the rioters, but also by the majority of their own community. In Watts, for example, although only 15 percent of the population claimed to have participated in the riots, 64 percent of the community claimed that the violence was justified. In Houston the majority of white persons approved police action. Although it may be a disparaging comment upon human nature, riots—whatever their cause—may be viewed as a genuine expression of the feelings of the people.

In one fashion or another, rioters have attempted to assert their dignity in what they regarded as an unjust, perhaps threatening, situation. Whether one deals with white laborers, unemployed blacks, or frustrated white policemen, the search for dignity is an obvious motive for action.

In all three riots discussed in this chapter rioters were drawn from the lower strata of the community, usually emerging from the ranks of those who felt powerless and isolated from the rest of society. White laborers in East Saint Louis believed that they were fighting for their economic security and that their newly formed labor unions would disappear under the wave of black migration. In Watts isolated and powerless people attacked the symbols of white power: store owners and the police. They were protesting economic as well as social and political exploitation. In Houston, as elsewhere, policemen generally were drawn from a working-class background. Their social background and the very nature of their work isolated them from the elite of the community as well as from those with whom they worked.

However, knowledge of a generalized dissatisfaction, threat, or even objective state of oppression would appear to provide an inadequate understanding of riots. In the three examples we have described, rioters had undergone some type of experience that raised their expectations, only to come face to face again with a situation that appeared hopeless. In East Saint Louis the white laborers were just beginning to enjoy the fruits of their labor organization when the black migration occurred. Black people had journeyed to Los Angeles with the hope of finding a better life. Instead they found the same type of ghettoization and economic discrimination they had left behind. The police in Houston thought that their chief (a man who rigidly stressed law and order) and their mayor should have allowed them to carry out their job of maintaining law and order long before the 1967 incident. In quite different forms the three groups had expected more than they received.

Dissatisfaction is not, of course, a unique characteristic of cities. After all, peasants have existed for centuries in rural squalor and deprivation that make contemporary cities appear to be paradise. And yet, peasant riots and revolts rarely have occurred. Urban life attracts and concentrates people with high expectations who have abandoned the resigned fatalism of rural areas; they expect their lives to markedly improve, and yet some meet futility and frustration. Their subjective, even irrational, feelings of oppression increase. A very natural reaction for such groups is a spontaneous eruption of violence.

One further characteristic of cities contributes to riots: the lack of intimate, face-to-face social controls and, in their stead, a reliance upon anonymous formal controls. Oddly enough, the very growth of formal urban institutions such as the police force apparently can contribute to the possibilities of a riotous situation. Freed from the intimate restrictions imposed by village life, the urbanite is more prone to express violent feelings against opponents.

The specific triggering mechanisms for riots may be quite commonplace, as we have demonstrated: a traffic incident, a student oration, or an error in the judgment of a politician. When combined with a history of tension, stress, and discontent, riots may be understood in terms of any one of the theories that have been suggested by social scientists. One must first understand the particular history of events preceding the specific riot.

Ralph Turner, noted for his work dealing with collective behavior, reviewed three theories to explain riots: *convergence* theory, *emergent norm* theory, and *contagion* theory.[108] In convergence theory, crowd behavior is based on the "convergence of a number of persons who share the same predispositions. The predispositions are activated by the event or object toward which their common attention is directed."[109] In urban America, residential segregation of class and caste groups maximizes the likelihood that persons with similar predispositions (in terms of antagonisms and frustrations) will converge on the scene of any particular event. Further, because people who are similar in class and caste tend to associate with one another, the communication of a reported event (real or falsely rumored) also is understandable. Even those members of the community who are not actually on the scene of a particular incident are likely to hear of it soon after its occurrence. The telephone and the development of the electronic media puts us on the spot of an event. These factors then may feed into the process of collective behavior. Of course, we realize that mere knowledge of an event, or even of an ongoing rebellion, is insufficient in itself to stimulate rebellion. However, as Herbert Gans pointed out, such knowledge may "raise tension levels in the ghetto, outside it, and among the police, increasing the likelihood of an (additionally) inciting incident."[110]

Completely new norms for behavior may emerge among people congregated in a specific area, particularly if they are predisposed to some action and sensitized to an incident defined as "another injustice." Unique to that particular collectivity, these emergent norms provide an explanation for the apparent patterning of expressions commonly perceived as unanimity on the part of people who had no preplanned action and probably had not even met before.[111]

Contagion, or the induction of intense feelings and behavior at variance with usual behavior, in part also explains the participation of some members of the collectivity. Moreover, bystanders also provide support for the ongoing violent or otherwise variant behavior through their covert legitimation.

The results of a riot are usually grim. In East Saint Louis and Watts, whole communities were destroyed; in Houston a university was damaged and many of its students were hurt. Economically, riots may devastate a community. Politically, a riot may alert others to realities heretofore ignored; seldom, however, does violent behavior result in the general satisfaction of all people. Bruce Smith has suggested that riots may achieve limited goals if the rioters have a clear objective and their opponents have the power to change the situation. On the other hand, where the "objective and targets of action were unclear, as was likely to be the case in the Northern cities, protest seemed doomed to be ineffectual."[112]

A reform movement at times eventuates as a reaction to a riot, as in the instance of Watts. The reforms that are accomplished, however, rarely serve to abolish the real causes of the riotous situation. Martin Oppenheimer has observed that there are only two real solutions for the majority group:

> The dominant power structure can cope with paramilitary activity in a combination of two ways, similar in most respects to its strategy in any insurgency war. It can move radically to solve the problems of the population, thus cutting off . . . the base of support in the populace; or it can move to suppress military activity through counterinsurgency warfare. This seems far more typical.[113]

Since little short of a major political, social, and economic revolution would cure America's urban ills, it is highly unlikely that those in power would acquiesce in fundamental changes. Revolutions, like successful reform movements, as we shall see, are led by those who are already much more successful in dealing with the societal elite than those who participate in riots.

It must be recognized, however, that

spontaneous urban riots could—with the proper leadership, skill, and ideology—ignite into full-scale revolutions. In a highly significant article published in 1968, Colonel Robert B. Rigg pointed out the technical difficulties the United States Army would face in putting down a well-planned urban insurrection.[114] Rigg warned that "organized urban insurrection could explode to the extent that portions of large American cities could become scenes of destruction approaching those of Stalingrad in World War II."[115] The very technological advances of cities—the establishment of a water supply that could be poisoned, the building of skyscrapers that could serve as fortresses, the creation of electrical grids—turn urban areas into fragile complexes. From a military point of view, Rigg has contended:

> After all, we have seen many square blocks totally ruined in Watts. . . . Were organized insurrection to break out and military power needed to suppress it, destruction in city square miles could mount tremendously over what we have seen.[116]

The officer envisaged a situation far grimmer than Vietnam:

> Roof-tops, windows, rooms high up, streets low down, and back alleys nearby, could become a virtual jungle for patrolling police or military forces at night when hidden snipers could abound. . . .
>
> Even in the face of large-caliber artillery, the battle of Stalingrad demonstrated that a city of steel, concrete and brick offers unusual protection to its defenders and great obstacles to its assailants. . . .
>
> What tank or bull-dozer is going to flatten an old 20-story apartment or office building that is sniper-ridden by night and vacant by day? Here, urban guerrillas could shoot down into the streets, drop fire bombs, and not even need mortars.[117]

Whether the streets of American cities will be turned into the holocaust that Colonel Rigg has prophesied depends basically on man's ability to eliminate the social and political ills of urban areas. In such a crucial matter the time is short, since from a purely military viewpoint "the finest 'jungle' for insurrection was not created by Nature; it has been built by man."[118]

Perhaps the most important positive benefit to accrue from most violent, riotous behavior is that it allows a catharsis for some group in the community. This psychological benefit hardly seems worth the toll in lives usually involved. The uselessness of riots, as such, has long been recognized. In his introduction to Marx's *Class Struggles in France,* Engels, for example, pointed out that "In the future, street fighting can be victorious only if this disadvantageous situation is compensated by other factors." Recent studies reviewing riots throughout the world indicate that a riot by a group that does not have military supremacy can succeed only with outside support, or in times of immense social distress such as a great depression or an international defeat. Only in these instances, perhaps, can riots be viewed as signaling profound changes in societal reorganization.

Issues for further discussion

1. What pattern of common causation links together the East Saint Louis, Watts, and Houston riots?
2. What elements in the urban experience contributed to these uprisings?
3. What measures might have been undertaken that would have prevented the urban riots discussed in the chapter?
4. Under what conditions could a riot escalate into a revolution?
5. Do urban riots serve a social function?
6. Why does urbanization promote the incidence of riots?
7. Examine a riotous situation other than those cited in this chapter (e.g., linguistic riots in Calcutta) and explain its nature, origins, and outcomes.

FOOTNOTES

1. We gratefully acknowledge the meticulous historical research done by Elliot M. Rudwick, *Race Riot at East St. Louis* (Carbon-

dale, Ill.: Southern Illinois University Press, 1964).
2. R. H. Leavell, *Negro Migration in 1916–17,* (Washington, D.C.: U.S. Department of
3. "Select Committee to Investigate Conditions in Illinois and Missouri Interfering with Interstate Commerce Between the States," U.S. Congressional Hearings (1918), p. 1478.
3. U.S. Congressional Hearings, p. 1478.
4. *St. Louis Republic,* 10 May 1917.
5. Rudwick, *Race Riot,* p. 26.
6. Cited in the *Chicago Daily Tribune,* 6 November 1916.
7. See *Belleville Daily Advocate,* 17 November 1916.
8. Rudwick, *Race Riot.*
9. See Norval D. Glenn and Charles M. Bonjean, *Blacks in the United States* (San Francisco: Chandler Publishing Co., 1969), pp. 38–42, 386–388, and Ray Marshall, "The Negro and Organized Labor," *Journal of Negro Education* (Fall 1963).
10. Norman Thomas, *Proceedings of the Socialist Party Convention, 1919,* p. 45.
11. Rudwick, *Race Riot,* p. 146.
12. See "Select Committee," pp. 3156, 3164, 3182.
13. *East St. Louis Journal,* 25 May 1917.
14. Alexander Flannigan, quoted in Rudwick, *Race Riot,* p. 28.
15. "Select Committee," pp. 546–547, 557–562.
16. Ibid.
17. *St. Louis Post-Dispatch,* 2 July 1917, and *St. Louis Globe-Democrat,* 2 July 1917, 8 July 1917.
18. See "Select Committee," p. 3164.
19. *St. Louis Republic,* 30 May, 1917, and *St. Louis Argus,* 1 June 1917.
20. *East St. Louis Daily Journal,* 22 May 1917, 24 May 1917, 25 May 1917.
21. See "Select Committee," pp. 1078, 1350.
22. Mayor Mollman, cited in "Select Committee," p. 1354.
23. "Select Committee," p. 2039.
24. People v. Evanhoff, Circuit Court, Sept. Term, 1917, pp. 8–9.
25. Cited in Rudwick, *Race Riot,* p. 47.
26. *Belleville Daily Advocate,* 3 July 1917.
27. W. E. B. Du Bois and Martha Gruening, "The Massacre of East Saint Louis," *Crisis,* no. 14 (1917).
28. Cited in Chandler Owen and A. Philip Randolph, "The Cause and Remedy for Race Riots," *Messenger* (Sept. 1919), pp. 14–17.
29. Rudwick, *Race Riot,* chap. 6.
30. *The New York Evening Post,* 10 July 1917, p. 48.
31. *The New York Evening Mail,* 11 July 1917, p. 13.
32. *Atlanta Constitution,* 4 July 1917.
33. *Cleveland Gazette,* 7 July 1917, 14 July 1917.
34. Theodore Roosevelt, speech at Carnegie Hall, quoted in the *New York Times,* 7 July 1917.
35. House Resolution #128, 65th Congress, 1st Session, 1917.
36. People v. Bundy, No 13366, Reports of Cases at Law, *Illinois Reports,* CCVC, 1921, p. 323.
37. Ibid.
38. Ibid.
39. Ibid.
40. Rudwick, *Race Riot,* p. 219.
41. Whether or not blacks were used as "scab" labor, they have been perceived as a threat to the economic position of other laborers in Northern cities. See *Racial Violence in the United States,* ed. Allen D. Grimshaw (Chicago: Aldine Publishing, 1969).
42. See J. J. Rushton et al., "Factual Report of the Committee to Investigate the Riot Occurring in Detroit on June 21, 1943," and Thurgood Marshall, "The Gestapo in Detroit," in Grimshaw, *Racial Violence,* p. 137.
43. Rudwick, *Race Riot.*
44. Jerry Cohen and William S. Murphy, *Burn, Baby, Burn* (New York: E. P. Dutton & Co., 1966).
45. Michael Harrington, *The Other America: Poverty in the United States* (New York: The MacMillan Co., 1962).
46. Cohen and Murphy, *Burn, Baby, Burn.*
47. 1970 U.S. Census.
48. See Robert Conot, *Rivers of Blood, Years of Darkness* (New York: Bantam Books, 1967). See discussions of the Rumford Act and Proposition 14, which was an attempt to legalize the restriction of buying and selling through the choice of the landlord.
49. Conot, *Rivers of Blood.*
50. See, for example, Elliot Liebow, *Tally's Corner* (Boston: Little, Brown and Co., 1967).
51. See Captain Howard Lindemuller, "Why No Fire Next Time," Pacifica Foundation Broadcast, KPFK, Los Angeles (30 May 1966).
52. Ibid.
53. 1950 and 1960 U.S. Census.
54. Ibid.
55. Conot, *Rivers of Blood.*
56. Ibid., p. 12.
57. See William McCord et al., *Life Styles in the Black Ghetto* (New York: W. W. Norton & Co., 1969).

58. Conot, *Rivers of Blood.*
59. Howard J. Jewel, personal communication with Attorney General Stanley Mosk, 25 May 1964.
60. Proposition 14 would have allowed landlords to choose their tenants and buyers of property.
61. Personal interview, 15 August 1965.
62. Personal interview, 16 August 1965.
63. Cohen and Murphy, *Burn, Baby, Burn,* p. 47.
64. Conot, *Rivers of Blood.*
65. See Joseph Lohman, "Law Enforcement and the Police," and Burton Levey, "Cops in the Ghetto: A Problem of the Police System," in *Riots and Rebellion,* ed. Louis Masotti and D. R. Bowen (Beverly Hills, Calif.: Sage Publications, 1968). Also see Seymour M. Lipset, "Why Cops Hate Liberals and Vice Versa," *Atlantic Monthly* 223 (March 1969): 76–83.
66. Cohen and Murphy, *Burn, Baby, Burn,* p. 204.
67. The role of rumor in collective behavior has been documented many times. See Ralph H. Turner and Lewis M. Killian, *Collective Behavior* (Englewood Cliffs, N.J.: Prentice-Hall, 1957).
68. Although open to criticism concerning the selective nature of the sample, this represents one of the contingencies of research in a conflict situation. Interviews of the more militant, hostile population must await cessation of the event and may be subject to criticism on the basis of retrospection.
69. Personal interview, 15 August 1965.
70. Cohen and Murphy, *Burn, Baby, Burn.*
71. See Cohen and Murphy, *Burn, Baby, Burn;* Conot, *Rivers of Blood;* and McCord, *Life Styles;* based on hearings of the McCone Commission, a board appointed by the Governor to investigate the riots.
72. Quoted in the *Los Angeles Times,* 17 August 1965.
73. For example, see Masotti and Bowen, *Riots and Rebellion.*
74. Quoted in the *Los Angeles Times,* 16 August 1965.
75. Personal interview with Mayor Sam Yorty, 20 August 1965. Yorty believed that the board already represented the leadership of the black community.
76. See report of the McCone Commission, quoted in Conot, *Rivers of Blood.*
77. Personal interview, 16 August 1965. Also quoted in the *Los Angeles Times,* 20 August 1965.
78. See Lindemuller, "Why No Fire Next Time."
79. Ibid.
80. Ibid.
81. H. Edward Ransford, "Isolation, Powerlessness and Violence," *American Journal of Sociology* (1968), pp. 581–591.
82. John Howard, "Watts: The Revolt and After," in McCord, *Life Styles,* chap. 3.
83. Victor H. Palmieri, "Hard Facts About the Future of Our Cities," Los Angeles County Commission on Human Relations (1967), p. 3.
84. See Allen D. Grimshaw, "Lawlessness and Violence in America and their Special Manifestations in Changing Negro-White Relationships," in Grimshaw, *Racial Violence.*
85. See Lohman, "Law Enforcement and the Police," and Levey, "Cops in the Ghetto," in Massotti and Bowen, *Riots and Rebellion.* Also see Lipset, "Why Cops Hate Liberals."
86. Bernard Friedberg, "Houston and the TSU Riot," in McCord, *Life Styles,* chap. 2.
87. "Dimensions of Poverty," Houston-Harris County Economic Opportunity Organization (1965).
88. "Nowhere to Go," Episcopal Society for Cultural and Racial Unity, Houston (1965).
89. See "Dimensions of Poverty."
90. One of the requisites to obtain federal aid was the establishment of residential/commercial zoning laws. The city officials could not be moved together to do so by representatives of such organizations as the B'nai B'rith, the National Council of Churches, as well as individuals prominent in the Houston community who were working to this end.
91. See "Dimensions of Poverty."
92. Ibid.
93. 1960 U.S. Census.
94. See surveys of opinion in Houston, "Negro Opinions," in McCord, *Life Styles,* chap. 5.
95. Personal observation, August 1967.
96. *Houston Post,* 14 May 1967.
97. Personal interview conducted on the night of 16 May 1967 with ten students who had been in the cafeteria.
98. Ibid.
99. Personal observation, 16 May 1967.
100. Ibid.
101. Ibid. Also see, *Houston Post* and the *Houston Chronicle,* 17 May 1967.
102. Personal observation, 17 May 1967.
103. See, for example, R. S. Shellow and D. V. Roemer, "The Riot That Did Not Happen," *Social Problems* 14 (1966): 221–233, and Robert Shellow, "The Training of Police Officers to Control Civil Rights Demonstrations," in *Minority Problems,* ed. Arnold

Rose and Caroline Rose (New York: Harper & Row, Publishers, 1965), pp. 425–430.
104. Victor Emmanuel, "Houston Citizen Survey," University of Houston (1967).
105. Friedberg, "Houston and the TSU Riot," in McCord, *Life Styles,* chap. 2.
106. See *Houston Chronicle,* education series (1968–70).
107. St. Clair Drake, "Urban Violence and American Social Movements," in *Urban Riots,* ed. Robert H. Connery (New York: Vintage Books, 1969).
108. Ralph Turner, "Collective Behavior," in *Handbook of Modern Sociology,* ed. R. E. L. Faris (Chicago: Rand McNally & Co., 1964).
109. Ibid, p. 394.
110. Herbert Gans, "The Ghetto Rebellions and Urban Class Conflict," in Connery, *Urban Riots,* p. 49.
111. Turner, "Collective Behavior," in Faris, *Handbook of Modern Sociology,* p. 293.
112. Bruce Smith, "The Politics of Protest: How Effective is Violence," in Connery, *Urban Riots,* p. 49.
113. Martin Oppenheimer, "Para-military Activities in Urban Areas," in Masotti and Bowen, *Riots and Rebellion,* pp. 436–437.
114. Col. Robert B. Rigg, "Made in U.S.A.," *Army* 18, no. 1 (January 1968): 24–28, 30–31.
115. Ibid., p. 24.
116. Ibid., p. 24.
117. Ibid., p. 26.
118. Ibid., p. 26.

SUGGESTED READINGS

Elliot M. Rudwick, *Race Riot at East St. Louis* (Carbondale, Ill: Southern Illinois University Press, 1964) has written the finest description of the East Saint Louis riot.

Writing with the finesse of a novelist, Robert Conot pieces together a variety of descriptions of the Watts riot in his *Rivers of Blood, Years of Darkness* (New York: Bantam Books, 1967).

One of the best descriptions of the Houston riot is provided by Bernard Friedberg, "Houston and the TSU Riot," in *Life Styles in the Black Ghetto,* ed. William McCord, John Howard, Bernard Friedberg and Edwin Harwood (New York: W. W. Norton & Co., 1969).

For an excellent anthology on the problem of riots, see Robert H. Connery, *Urban Riots* (New York: Vintage Books, 1969). Part II of Louis Masotti and Don R. Bowen, *Civil Violence in the Urban Community* (Beverly Hills, Calif.: Sage Publications, 1968) presents a variety of empirical studies of incidences of civil disorder and the attitudinal structure that supported the violence. Cases are drawn from Houston, Oakland, Los Angeles, Cleveland, Omaha, Rochester, and Buffalo. Documents and some analysis of *Racial Violence in the United States* is presented in a volume of that title edited by Allen D. Grimshaw (Chicago: Aldine Publishing Co., 1969).

For a portrayal of conditions that lead to urban riots in a non-American context, see Selig S. Harrison, *India: The Most Dangerous Decades* (Princeton, N.J.: Princeton University Press, 1960).

The nature of police riots is explicated by Rodney Stark in *Police Riot* (Belmont, Calif.: Wadsworth Publishing Co., 1972).

chapter 7

Revolution

Revolutions break out when opposite parties, the rich and the poor, are equally balanced, and there is little or nothing between them.

Aristotle

The past three hundred years can rightfully be labeled the age of revolution. Triggered by the advent of the French Enlightenment, the dawn of slogans such as "fraternity, equality, and liberty," and the spread of urbanization, profound revolutions have spread across the globe from France to China. Indeed, revolutions seem to keep step with the spread of industrialization throughout the world.

In contrast to military coups and reform movements, revolutions aim at securing total change: political, economic, and social. In their more exalted moods, revolutionary leaders foresee the dawning of a new way of life in every aspect of human activity.

Three contemporary revolutions are described in this chapter. Because of their recency, only future historians can judge the full extent to which each of these diverse revolutions changed their societies. The three events took place in separate geographical and cultural areas:

- The Cuban revolution of 1959 brought Fidel Castro to power and, theoretically at least, changed the nation from a military dictatorship into a Marxist-Leninist example for its neighbors in Latin America.
- The Northern Ireland (or Ulster) conflict first stirred into action at the turn of the century, but burst into overt violence in 1969 as a convoluted civil war.
- The successful revolt by Neguib and Nasser in 1952 dethroned King Faruk in Egypt, but was followed by a less successful program to transform Egyptian society.

Each of these revolutions embodied changes far beyond the more specific aims of particular reform movements or the diffuse discontent of riots. They all have proclaimed a nationalistic ideology and aimed against imperialism of one variety or another. Despite claims that the revolutions represented peasant or "people's" uprisings, they were essentially urban in origin and leadership. The three examples were chosen for inclusion in this chapter because they represent diverse outcomes: success in Cuba, failure in Egypt, and an uncertain outcome for at least the next generation of Irish.

At the outset, each of these revolutions was signaled by riots, attempted reform movements, or limited shifts in power. The question remaining is why did they escalate into full blown revolution?

Case 7
Cuba: An urban bourgeois revolution

Violence has marked Cuba from its inception as a Spanish colony through every period of its history, from the earliest extermination of indigenous Indians, periodic slave uprisings, and invasions, through the emergence of the last of three revolutions beginning in 1898 and ending in the 1950s. The general tactics and guerrilla warfare that characterized the most recent revolution (culminating in the triumphant entry of Fidel Castro into Havana in 1959) represent no sharp break with the past.

SETTING: THE PARADOX OF THE ISLAND PARADISE

Even a cursory review of Cuban history clearly indicates the particular set of developments that encouraged the transformation of the island country since 1959.

Politics

Political instabilities, for example, were in evidence soon after the establishment of Cuba's independence from Spain in 1902. The first and reputedly least corrupt president—popularly known as the "Honest President"—Don Tomás Estrada Palma, was faced with revolt and accusations of fraud after a little more than four years in office. Palma resigned in 1906 and was replaced in 1909 by General José Miguel Gómez, who set the precedent of personal aggrandizement and extravagance, which was to be a consistent pattern for most of the five decades preceding the rise of Castro. Each administration, beginning with Gomez (1909–13), General Mario García Menocal (1913–21), Alfredo Zayas y Alfonso (1921–25), through Gerardo Machado y Morales (1925–33), was characterized by graft and corruption.[1] These precedents hindered the development of a stable, efficient political structure.

Between 1933 and 1959 the political history of Cuba can be outlined in terms of the rise of Fulgencio Batista y Zaldívar to power. Summarily, this climb was marked by the following events:

- September 1933: *Sergeant* Fulgencio Batista, headquarters stenographer, occupied official posts and assumed command of the army.
- October 1933: *Colonel* Fulgencio Batista personally led an attack of former army commanders who barricaded themselves in the House National. Colonel Batista appointed Chief of Staff of the Cuban Army.
- December 1939: Fulgencio Batista announced his decision to run for the presidency. By maintaining army loyalty, rewarding labor unions and leaders, and playing to the desires of businessmen and professionals to maintain the status quo, Batista was elected and inaugurated on 10 October 1940.[2]
- In 1944 Batista stepped down and allowed the election of a former rival, Dr. Ramón Grau San Martín. Remaining behind the scenes between 1944 and 1952, Batista watched as Grau and his successor, Dr. Carlos Prío Socarrás, assumed leadership. The political wars between the Autenticos (formerly a party demanding reform) and their rivals broke out almost immediately. Yielding to the temptations wrought by wartime prosperity, Grau and Prío betrayed their stated principles, leading to eventual deposition. On 10 March 1952 *Senator* Fulgencio Batista reassumed control of the Cuban government.[3]

The years paralleling Batista's rise to total power and the coup of 1952 that established him in the position of dictator were marked by multiple sources of strain and frustration for the Cuban people. Aside from the ineffective Grau and Prío administrations, World War II meant a loss of tourism, a scarcity of goods, and the sinking of two Cuban ships (August 1942). The conclusion of the war did not seem to improve the lot of most persons, particularly those who remained in rural areas.

Life-style and the economy

According to a report of the International Bank for Reconstruction and Development (IBRD) in 1950,[4] an estimated 60 percent of the rural population suffered from malnutrition. Children were subject to intestinal parasites. More than 75 percent of the rural dwellings were described as "thatched huts"; electricity was found in approximately 9 percent and piped water in 2.3 percent. Over 54 percent of the dwellings had no sanitary facilities whatsoever.

Urban dwellers, though decidedly better off than their rural cousins, also were affected by the nature of the economy and the unstable political system. By 1958, one in five Cuban laborers was a skilled worker. Cuba ranked third in Latin American countries in number of physicians and first in the number of television sets and receiving stations. The IBRD report noted that 87 percent of urban dwellings were supplied with electricity and 55 percent with running water. Yet, ironically, the report also pointed out that fully 30 to 40 percent of urbanites also suffered from malnutrition. Further, although Cuba had for some time been credited with one of the highest literacy rates in Central America, the 1953 census[5] disclosed that among the 10–14 age group the illiteracy rate was 31.8 percent compared to 23.6 percent of the population as a whole. The higher illiteracy rate in this age group is indicative *not* of progress but educational retrogression.[6]

To add to the Cuban paradox, the standard of living in Cuba was relatively high by Latin American standards. Only Venezuela, Argentina, and Chile ranked higher.[7] Sugar, of course, dominated the Cuban economy. Upper-class Cubans and foreigners held a tight grip on this industry.

Because of world sugar market trends the income of all groups in Cuba declined: based on 1945 prices, per capita income fell from 228 pesos to 129.9 in 1956.[8] A few of the upper-class members could survive the downward trend in prices, but the depressed peasant group sank to a subsistence level. The lower-class refinery workers, seasonal farm laborers, and peasants, after all, were subject not only to spiraling prices but to unpredictable work seasons. The economic progress of the 1940s encouraged the growth of a sizable middle class in urban areas. Most observers agree that the middle classes suffered from the most *subjective* deprivation. "Economically, the middle sector was the most frustrated of the groups in Cuba," Ramón Ruiz commented. "It was well off, but not sufficiently so to satisfy its appetite for a greater share of the economic and political benefits of Cuban progress."[9]

Moreover, under Batista the urban middle classes had many complaints beyond the state of the economy. Students and intellectuals particularly objected to Batista's suppression of freedom of thought and his enforcement of rule by imprisonment of dissenters. While this particular segment of the middle classes took a major role in the actual fighting, other factors within Cuba led to the disaffection of the middle classes.

The virtual monopoly of wealth held by the upper class and foreigners forced even the most ambitious middle-class individual to remain on the periphery of control. The middle class was well off, but not sufficiently so to satisfy its growing appetite for a larger share of the benefits of progress. Understandably, under these conditions various segments of the urban middle class turned to politics as a means of expressing their interests. The Autenticos represented one middle-class interest in the election of Ramón Grau San Martín and Carlos Prío Socarrás.

Unfortunately, however, for Cuba and its people, public office had always been coveted more for personal gain than for public good. Improvements were started, but due to inefficiency, waste, and a lack of funds were never completed. During the Prío term in office, for example, Hart Phillips, a *New York Times* journalist, described Havana in the following manner:

> Havana looked like a bombed out city in Europe. Streets are torn up. Low lying sections of the city are flooded every time it rains due to lack of drainage. Mosquitoes and flies swarm over the city and suburbs. Public works projects are started and stopped leaving Havana more ugly and more in ruin than before the project had been undertaken. The Grau administration spent four years

on one mile of the important highway stretching between Havana and José Martí International Airport.[10]

In view of these politico-economic-social conditions it is not surprising that the 1952 Batista bloodless coup was met with little real resistance. The explanation for the revolution which was to follow Batista, however, must be sought in the specific mechanisms whereby the public grievances reached a point sufficient to establish consensus among the people. After all, following the 1952 coup the economic report indicates that sugar sales were high, and agriculture and industry were expanding. That something was wrong was indicated in the high unemployment figures, the suppression of intellectuals, and the discomforts and inconveniences of day-to-day life in Cuba. Unemployment, however, was always high in Cuba. Political corruption and graft were almost expected by the public.

THE PRECIPITANTS: SYMPTOMS OF REVOLUTION

Rumors of conspiracy were circulating throughout Cuba almost from the beginning of the Batista regime. Five days after the coup, Fidel Castro reputedly wrote a letter to Batista warning him that the latter's actions, if not changed, would lead to his downfall.[11]

Castro: a hero in the making

Fidel Alejandro Castro Ruz, one of seven children, was born on 13 August 1927. Although not immensely wealthy, Fidel's father, an immigrant from Spain, had built a comfortable fortune by growing sugar and harvesting the timber on his farm. The junior Castro's interest and immersion in politics paralleled his years of study at the Havana University Law School where he developed his talents as an orator. Fellow students have since commented that they were even then somewhat in awe of Fidel's remarkable rhetorical ability. He could silence the opposition with almost inexhaustible discourse.[12]

Castro's first brush with revolution occurred during his second year at the university when an expeditionary force was organized for the purpose of invading the Dominican Republic. Some three thousand men were trained and set sail, only to be intercepted by frigates of the Cuban navy. Reverberations from the Inter-American Conference meeting in Brazil forced the Cuban president, who had up to this point tacitly encouraged the project, to intervene. Castro and three companions escaped capture by jumping overboard and swimming to shore.[13]

Some months after this frustrated expedition to the Dominican Republic, Castro began a tour of Venezuela, Panama, and Colombia, proceeding to Bogata where he was to serve as a delegate to a newly formed Latin American Student Congress. Before the Congress convened, however, Castro was caught up in civil disorders that broke out because of the assassination of a popular Liberal party leader, Jorge Eliecer Gaitán. Castro then returned to Cuba, resumed his studies at the university, married, and within a year had a son. Despite the numerous distractions, Castro graduated with honors from the University of Havana in 1950 and entered a law partnership with two associates.[14]

On 26 July 1953, although it was not recognized at the time, the Cuban people were to witness, if only for a brief moment, the birth of the new movement destined to change their lives and their country. It was on this date that Castro, a 27-year-old lawyer of Havana, and 165 young revolutionists attacked the Moncada army post. The uprising was minor and soon under control. Within a short time the rebels were tried in the Urgency Court of Santiago de Cuba, whose jurisdiction covered criminal cases. Speaking in his own defense, Castro (the leader of the uprising) outlined his plans for social and governmental reform in Cuba.

He was sentenced to fifteen years in prison. Raoul Castro, his brother, and others received lesser sentences.[15]

The 26 July movement

After nineteen months in prison, amnesty was granted to political prisoners by Batista. Whether this action was a ploy to demonstrate the security and solidarity of his position or the result of public pressures on the Batista regime is unknown. In May 1955, Castro, his brother, and others returned to Havana to be greeted by family and a crowd of supporters. Undaunted in his determination to obtain an honest election in Cuba, Castro journeyed to Mexico to organize various segments of revolutionary groups gathering there. They dubbed their group the "26 July movement" and raised the cry "liberty or death in 1956." Batista was sent a proclamation to form a national unitary government or to expect revolution.[16] Batista ignored the proclamation, labeling the movement "just another student uprising" and "another harebrained scheme."

On 25 November 1956 the revolutionary expedition, consisting of eighty-two men under Castro's leadership, boarded an ancient, leaking yacht that might comfortably have accommodated eight persons and headed for Cuba. Early on the morning of the eighth day (two days behind schedule) they arrived off the southern coast of Cuba near Cabo Cruz. An inland uprising, scheduled to coincide with the landing, had taken place *on time* two days before the ill-fated landing. Batista's forces, forewarned of the invasion, hit with land and air forces. Most of the eighty-two would-be invaders were killed, or captured and shot. Twelve men managed to slip through the lines and lose themselves in the virtually impenetrable jungles of the Sierra Maestra: Castro, his brother Raoul, and Ernesto ("el Che") Guevara were among the group.[17] Speculation abounded among the people and in the press as to the fate of the revolutionaries who were known to have escaped to the hills. It was not until Herbert L. Mathews, a *New York Times* reporter, talked to Castro in the Sierra Maestra mountains two months later that the rumors of Castro's death were proven false.[18] The interview and subsequent publication of facts must have been the cause of much consternation to the Batista government. By the time of the circulation of the news the Batista releases had convinced many that Castro was dead.

Although the invasion and the attack on the Batista forces had been a thorough failure in almost all regards, it had one important consequence. The 26 July movement was underway and served as a means of focusing public attention, even for a little while, on the issues underlying rebel discontent. A student attack on 30 November 1956 on the army garrison at Moncada led President Batista to suspend constitutional guarantees; police and soldiers guarded public buildings, strategic streets, and harbor tunnels. These actions no doubt caused some public irritation; yet, the public did not appear ready to begin a full-scale assault on the Batista regime. Commerce and industry were prospering, the tourist season was good, and the government began pouring money into public works and new industry. Businessmen hoped that the government would soon crush the tiny rebellion. Only the youth of the island appeared behind Castro and his intention of overthrowing the Batista regime.[19]

Terrorism: molding a consensus

Late in 1957 terrorism spread throughout the island. Young men were found dead on streets and roads. The official explanation claimed that the causes of the deaths were undetermined. Stories of brutality on the part of the Batista police circulated among the population. The stories, at times, were even confirmed by Batista supporters. Hart Phillips reported the following incident:

> Relatives came to my office to tell me of boys disappearing. One young lawyer was arrested because he was defending revolutionists in court. He hap-

pened to be a good friend of a man who had connections with Batista. The man went to Batista and demanded that the young lawyer be released. Batista gave the order, but by the time they got him out of the police station, where Ventura, a professional killer in a police uniform had been "interrogating" him, it was too late. He died a few days later.[20]

Terrorism was the mode of trying to control the guerrilla warfare used by the rebels. Rebel bombings, police shootings, and the spread of propaganda had to be stopped to maintain some semblance of Batista's authority. Yet because of Batista's actions, a change in the attitude of the public was discernible in the following types of news release: "Many Havana citizens, once angry at the bombing terrorist actions of the rebel group seem now to almost enjoy seeing the strong man's [Batista's] authority flouted."[21] The *New York Times* headlines reported:

Two Cuban Rebels Killed in Clash

Army Reports Arms Seized

Ex-President's Nephew Tells of Being Kidnapped and Inflicted with Serious Burns[22]

Batista was proving to be his own worst enemy. A snowballing effect was soon evident. The increase in terrorism and retaliation could not have had any but an agitating effect on the public. The middle class, which had reacted indifferently to Batista up to this point, began to withdraw and reassess its position. Beyond this, Batista suspected a revolt of the entire Navy after an outbreak in Cienfuegos in late 1957. He was able to maintain his power because of the presumed loyalty of his military forces. The infiltration of the navy caused him to become suspicious of some of his soldiers who had served as the main source of his ability to retain power. The crisis of revolution had arrived.

REVOLUTION

Castro was making headway. Batista's regime was shaky, and although reports from Cuba indicated that leadership of the revolutionary movement was split between Castro, Havana plotters, and a shadowy group of sympathetic exiles in Miami, it was clear that an apparent consolidation of leadership was imminent. As an admirer of Castro reported: "They [referring to the more conservative elements of the revolutionary movement] have to worry whether Castro is a socialist, and yet they can't help but admire him. He acts like a king, before the Magna Carta, sitting under a tree and dispensing justice."[23]

The shaping of a revolution depends on the manipulation of many elements. Beyond the definition of the objects of hostility provided by Batista's own action there must be a definition of the general and specific goals of the movement. Further, there also must be a definition of the preliminary plans of attack and a definition of the "we" group.[24]

Early in 1957 Castro made his bid at gaining outside support and sympathy for his cause in the form of a bulletin published in *Cuba Libre* (a Costa Rican publication).[25] Copies of the bulletin were distributed in Cuba. The scope of the grievances outlined by Castro encompassed a wide variety of salient issues: the land situation, living standards, unemployment, public health, civil liberties, and "political democracy." The article, in part, stated: "There are 200,000 rural families without a square foot of land, yet Cuba has ten million acres of untouchable land. Most of the best arable land is in foreign hands. Cuba's problem will only be solved if we Cubans dedicate ourselves to fight for the solution to our problem with the same energy, integrity and patriotism our liberators invested in the country's foundations."[26]

Other publications circulated in the United States and Cuba outlined both long- and short-term goals. For example, in "Why We Fight," published by *Coronet*,[27] Castro stated his goals in the following terms: the establishment of a representative government, creation of a free mass communication system, promotion of land, social, and educational reform, stabilization of the economy, and reestablishment of personal and political rights for all citizens. More specifically, in this publication, Castro promised that as soon as Batista was ousted there would be a special convention (composed of various civic organizations) to prepare and conduct a general election. In addition, he guaranteed the release of all political, civil, and military prisoners. He wrote: "We will gain the decisive victory with comparatively little bloodshed and by expending this year's [sugar] crop. . . . My family's crop must be the first to burn as an example to the rest of the nation."[28] Indeed, Castro and his rebels moved to burn their land and crops. As Batista was losing his hold on the middle class, Castro acted in part out of the necessity to survive as a guerrilla to gain the allegiance of the rural population. Lines of "we and they" were slow, but sure, to form. The exploits of Castro and the men in the mountains seeped through the population. The mysticism surrounding the leader of the mountain rebels increased.

On 12 March 1958 Castro issued a manifesto to the people, calling for intensified revolutionary action, rebellion of the armed forces, and a general strike. Batista responded to the threats by posting double guards at the public buildings, installing machine guns at the presidential palace door, and frightening workers. He issued an order for a 35 percent increase in army personnel. He was, however, increasingly plagued by army desertions, control of transport routes by rebels, and the growing restiveness of labor unions.[29] As 1958 progressed, Havana underwent a state of seige. Transportation was paralyzed and rebels blew up railroads and tracks.

The successful removal of Faustino Pérez (head of the revolutionary movement in Havana) from under the noses of the Havana police and the barrage of propaganda from the Castro forces through pamphlets and the radio also contributed to the lowering of morale of the Batista forces. Further, as casualties increased supplies diminished, and the country sank into anarchy, the middle classes increasingly deserted Batista. Even the enlisted men who admired Batista began to question the wisdom of his policies.[30] On Christmas Day the decisive battle of the revolutionary movement was fought at Santa Clara. President Batista prepared to leave the island. On New Year's Eve, 1958, Batista and a party of a "select few" departed in four planes for the Dominican Republic.

Convalescence and reform

On New Year's morning in Havana, news of Batista's flight was quickly circulated by word of mouth. Castro supporters were reported to have entered the sunlit streets with a holiday spirit that lasted only a few minutes.[31] Their élan soon turned to bitterness. The first symptom of mob action was the destruction of parking meters, which were symbolic of one of the changes instituted by Batista. Urban mobs formed to focus on the brutality of Batista's police. Raiding and killing began.

In a short time the "26 July" militia moved in and looters were shot. For the first time in Cuban history a volunteer group kept law and order and protected property.[32] Rebels arrived in Havana from Santa Clara on 2 January 1959. The public was awed by the presence of these bearded young men who did not drink liquor, but, instead, sipped coffee and soft drinks. They spake with "courtesy and friendliness." They so impressed the people of Havana that even the pickpockets and petty thieves reportedly took a holiday from their accustomed activities.[33]

On 2 January Castro proclaimed Manuel Urrutia Lleo "Provisional President of the Cuban Republic."[34] The prime minister appointed by Castro was José Miro Cardona, head of the Havana Bar Association. All important positions were occupied by active anti-Batista people.[35] A numerical estimate of the number of executions of pro-Batista people conflicted, but American reaction to the reports was threatening and negative.[36]

Carlton Beal, in Havana at the time of the executions, wrote: "Nothing has done more to solidify the Cuban people behind the revolutionary government than the bath of blood statements by our Congressmen, the veiled threats of intervention, the possible cutting off of trade, the imposition of sanctions, the proposal that American tourists be prevented from going to Cuba. The cry is 'UNIDAD.' "[37] The executions served two purposes: (1) they helped eliminate portions of the remaining opposition; and (2) they aided in the unification of the people.

The early provisional government of the "new" Cuban Republic included many businessmen and industrial leaders who had sided with Castro.[38] *Life* magazine reported, however, "that the principal short-coming of the first provisional government seems to be a lack of proven political savvy."[39] The government acted quickly with many small reforms and an arbitrary 50 percent cut in rents. The revolutionary leaders could hardly fail to do so in order to retain control of the situation.

The legalization of the new government rested mainly on the shoulders of the first provisional president. Urrutia was right for this task. As a judge during Batista's regime he had legitimated the rebels. "The tyranny of Batista," he said, "is illegitimate. Therefore, the insurrection is legitimate."[40]

In an apartment of the Havana Hilton Hotel the commander of the rebel army, Fidel Castro, sat, seemingly removed from the situation. In the government buildings a rigid man of law presided over the council of ministers. Urrutia, during his brief presidency, was legality itself.

In spite of the fact that Castro vehemently denied that he would rule the country,[41] evidence suggests that he did not intend to allow political affairs to get out of hand. He remained aloof, yet strove to create an image as "a figure of peace." While Castro spoke before a crowd of forty thousand early after his victory over Batista, his supporters released three white doves from just below the platform. Two alighted on Castro, one on his shoulder. For symbolism nothing could beat it. All of Cuba saw the image of an athletic, yet mystical, leader surrounded by doves of peace.[42]

Further, Castro, in his tireless oratory, kept the limelight by providing ideas that were used as the bases for the early legislation of reforms instituted by the provisional government. The first council of ministers appointed by Urrutia represented the many groups that had fought Batista, but it was soon apparent that Castro was the supreme leader. Urrutia had ruled only six weeks when Castro took official power as premier (February 1959). Castro ran his government under the "Fundamental Law," a slightly revised version of the Constitution of 1940.

The revolution betrayed?

When Castro assumed power in early 1959 he took the reins of government with the announced intention of creating a land of "humanism" that combined "liberty with bread without terror." The turning point came with the Agrarian Land Reform Law in May 1959. "Whereas," it begins, "the progress of Cuba involves both the growth and diversification of industry . . ."[43]

His admirers in the Western world—C. Wright Mills, Jean-Paul Sartre, Simone de Beauvoir—contended that Castro had no intention of transforming Cuba into a socialist or totalitarian state and that he had no desire to affiliate with the Eastern bloc. It was perhaps this vaguely liberal ideology that drew him overwhelming support from the urban middle classes. As we have pointed out, Castro's original revolution was neither a peasant's nor a worker's revolt.

Once Castro was in power, his original cabinet (and succeeding ones) was overwhelmingly drawn from the urban middle class. In describing Castro's first set of ministers, Theodore Draper observed: "Every one attended a university (some in the United States), came from an upper- or middle-class home, and became or aspired to become a professional or intellectual. Not a single one represented in any conceivable sense the peasantry or proletariat."[44]

Moreover, as we have stated, the original revolution of 1959 occurred in a relatively rich society. It was not *absolute* poverty that brought the revolution to a head but a subtle "relative deprivation" of the middle classes. There were, of course, glaring inequalities in the country: the rural segment of Cuba was almost invariably poor (47 percent of the population and Cubans of African descent were at the lowest level of the socioeconomic ladder). Yet, the fact remains that these groups did not initially lend active support to the revolution. "It was the desertion of the middle class—on which Batista's power was based—that caused his regime to disintegrate from within and his army to evaporate."[45]

Of course, the urban middle classes were not a monolithic group. They had diverse interests and goals and were splintered in a variety of political groups. The workers perceived no more benefit from (often corrupt) middle-class rulers than from dictators. The middle classes, however, held two common beliefs. First, the middle classes—due to the tutelage of Americans after Spain's defeat and the very nearness of America—underwent a revolution in expectations. They consciously accepted the American belief in progress but found in the economy of the 1950s an apparent block to their hopes. Second, middle-sector Cubans shared Castro's abhorrence of the island's almost total dependence upon America and particularly the American sugar quota. Until 1959 they could easily share the sentiments of Castro expressed in his famous speech: "History Will Absolve Me." A strict return to constitutional rule, an appeal for land reform, an end to dictatorship; these slogans coincided with their interests and their own vague ideologies.

The unique historical circumstances of Cuba cannot be ignored: its total dependence on America, its tradition of violence, and its dependence upon one-man rule. Perhaps the greatest of Cuban heroes was José Martí, whose background, charismatic oratory, and *caudilloism* closely resembled Castro's. In a nation whose greatest national hero, Martí, is considered immortal, it is not surprising that his "reincarnation" appeared on Cuban land.

As Castro proclaimed, "I carry in my heart the teachings of the Maestro. Martí is the instigator of the 26th of July Movement."[46] This cry echoed in the hearts of the middle class, particularly the students. Early in Castro's regime, government officials referred to Martí as the mainspring of their ideas on humanism, of the identity of country and humanity, and as the epitome of mankind. Thus, Castro was following in the mainstream of Cuban thought in his own glorification of Martí. In remarkable ways their lives ran parallel. Martí was born in Havana in 1853 and was—like Castro—the son of a landholder. He took part in the first revolution against Spain and, like Castro, served a few months in prison. Both Castro and Martí had studied the lives of North American patriots, and both were entranced with the words of the United States Declaration of Independence. Both Castro and Martí considered themselves romantic dreamers. Both turned against America and espoused a pugnacious brand of Cuban nationalism. Martí was fond of proclaiming "I will stake my fate on the poor of the earth." Castro's original speeches noted the same dedication: "When we speak of struggle, 'the people' means the vast unredeemed masses, to whom all make promises and whom all deceive."[47] Castro, like Martí, believed that he spoke for all of Latin America against the colossus of the north.

Whether by planning or merely because he accepted the common adulation of

Cubans for Martí, Castro first put himself forward as the logical successor to Cuba's most admired man: "Castro and the 26th of July Movement stepped out of the mold created by the independence struggle that Martí led more than a half a century before."[48]

Thus, Castro emerged as the newest idol of Cuba's urban middle classes in 1959. Temporarily, he shared their deepest humanistic beliefs, he apparently stood for a return to a liberal model of government, he had a distaste for American domination, and he espoused economic and political reforms the middle classes believed would benefit them. They soon learned differently.

The transition to socialism

Many words, including Castro's, have been wasted over the issue of whether he was really a Communist before 1959. Probably he was vaguely Marxist as a student and came increasingly to proclaim communism as his own creed only when events showed him that alliance with the Eastern bloc was the most expedient way to achieve his goals. Clearly, however, Castro's Cuba changed rapidly from a revolution oriented to the middle class (and, to a lesser degree, to peasant interests) to a totalitarian socialist regime. "The Cuban revolution ironically was essentially a middle-class revolution, that has been used to destroy the middle class,"[49] as Theodore Draper has cogently observed.

The steps through which the transformation passed can be briefly chronicled:

Originally, Castro proclaimed simply that he wished to give land to landless peasants and establish cooperatives that would help get their products to market.[50] Most of his advisers took his announced goals literally. In 1959, however, when the first agrarian reform law was announced, it became apparent that Castro had decided to establish state farms where the title of ownership would pass from the old landholders directly to the government. The peasants were mobilized as they had been during the disastrous agricultural policies of the Stalinism era.

The first signs that Castro had betrayed his own movement and sought a single party united with the Communists came on 20 October 1959, long before the United States took any overt actions against his regime. On that date, one of Castro's leading comrades, Major Hubert Matos, resigned from the 26 July movement, was arrested, and sentenced to twenty years for treason. The court did not even attempt to adduce evidence of treason except for a "crime" the prisoner freely admitted: he had opposed the appointment of a growing number of Communists to various official posts throughout the government and army. Various cabinet officers and other old colleagues of Castro had voiced similar complaints. But after Matos's conviction it became clear that Castro tolerated only a one-party system oriented to Communism with him as the supreme leader.[51]

At this time he was negotiating abroad for economic and military support from Russia. Domestically he made every gesture to encourage the melding of the official Communist party (which had strong support among trade unions) into a single party. This policy was in direct contrast to his statement of April 1959 in which he denied strict adherence to either capitalism or communism. The former because it "killed people with hunger" and the latter because it suppressed "the liberties which are so dear to man."[52]

On 15 October 1960 a large number of foreign and Cuban owned industries were nationalized. On 16 April 1961 Castro officially announced the birth of "a patriotic democratic and socialist revolution." The information was given at the end of a long funeral oratory of persons killed during bombing raids on Cuban air bases.[53]

In January 1961 Castro announced that it would be necessary to "annihilate" counterrevolutionaries if the revolution was to succeed. His government issued a law condemning "terrorists and saboteurs" to sentences ranging from a minimum of twenty years to a maximum of death. On 29 November 1961 Castro officially introduced "revolutionary terror" into Cuba. The regime, perhaps, had entered its "Robespierre" stage and began gobbling up many of its previous leaders such as David Salvador. Once the leader of the anti-Batista movement and head of the Confederation of Labor during the first year of Castro's rule, Salvador was arrested for "conspiring" against the government when in fact he was simply one among many of the original leaders who opposed the growing influence of Communism within the regime.[54]

By 1962 Cuba entered a period of forced industrialization. Workers were urged to higher productivity, an official plan was introduced, and that generation was told that it must sacrifice for future generations.

In the brief span of three years Cuba had established all of the basic forms of a totalitarian socialist society.

Why did Cuba make the jump so swiftly from an essentially bourgeois revolution into Communism? Some writers have claimed that pressure from the United States was the primary reason for the move into socialism and terror. There can be little doubt that the Eisenhower administration's suspension of the sugar quota, the Bay of Pigs fiasco, and the eventual Cuban missile crisis hardened the hatred of many Cubans for North America. Yet, this interpretation overlooks several crucial facts: the United States had suspended all military aid to Batista during the revolution, the American government was neutral and wary during the first months of Castro's regime, Castro refused various offers of American economic aid, and the contours of socialism were already well established by April 1961.[55] All of these events occurred *before* the futile Bay of Pigs invasion. Other factors then must be sought to explain the change:

First, as soon as Castro took power, he inherited a drastic agricultural crisis that had serious consequences in the cities. The 1961 sugar crop failed to meet previous standards, standard consumer foods such as bananas, sweet potatoes, and other plants had to be rationed, and meat disappeared from markets. The crisis occurred because of a lack of understanding by the new politicians. Forced state farms took away incentive from the producers, and new governmental controls were naturally met with resistance from small landholders.[56] Since Cuba's economy depended upon the production of sugar, Castro turned to the Soviet bloc for assistance. Although even Che Guevara admitted that Russia produced abundant crops of sugar cane itself, the Soviet Union signed a pact to purchase Cuban sugar and thus redress the balance of trade. While this one action did not entirely solve the Cuban economic crisis, it solidly established Cuba's dependence on Russia and erased American influence.

Second, Castro realized that only an alliance with the Eastern bloc would save Cuba from continuing economic dependence on the United States and the threat of invasion.[57] For the first time in its history Cuba did not *have* to depend solely upon the United States. A second alternative—Russia—had appeared on the horizon. Thus, for both economic and military reasons Castro sought the aid of socialist nations.

As Russian arms poured into Cuba, United States President John F. Kennedy authorized the abortive attack on the Bay of Pigs. Aided by the United States Central Intelligence Agency, a handful of exiled Cubans were trained and prepared for an attack on the island. For unknown reasons the Cubans were encouraged in their desperate effort by Americans and then were assigned to attack a military beachhead rather than allowing for a political infiltration. Thus, Castro concentrated all of his weapons at a single spot. Deprived of promised American air support, the Cuban counter-revolutionists went down to ignominious defeat. While the American invasion did not determine Castro's move to the political left and his embrace with Russia, it did speed up the pace toward totalitarian rule by offering Castro the legitimate excuse of an imminent attack by a foreign government.

In turn, the aggressive action by America gave Khrushchev a rationale for introducing missiles into Cuba. The resulting Cuban missile crisis of 1962 brought the world to a confrontation that easily could have resulted in nuclear devastation. Although interpretation of the events differs, it is clear that the precipitate actions of Khrushchev, Kennedy, and Castro might have brought about the end of the world through nuclear destruction.

After learning that nuclear missiles had been implanted in Cuba, Kennedy ordered the United States armed forces to "Defcon 3" (war alert) and the Strategic Air Command to "Defcon 2" (full war footing). The Army Strategic Reserve went on alert and various regiments and divisions moved to their posts in Florida, ready for an invasion of Cuba. American nuclear submarines were ordered to sail from their base in Scotland and then to submerge near Russia ready for a nuclear attack. Most of the Strategic Air Command's nuclear bombers were kept in the air ready to attack. For six days the world waited while Kennedy imposed a blockade and Khrushchev continued assembling missiles in Cuba. At the climax, both sides backed down and both claimed victory.[58]

For ten years after the crisis Russia refrained from aiding Cuba in aggressive overtures toward the United States. The United States, in turn, gave up alternative invasion plans, and Cuba under Castro settled into relative peace. Castro had won a revolution—even if he had betrayed his original purpose and condemned his closest comrades.

DISCUSSION: SUCCESS

Why did Cuba undergo a revolution in 1959? The reasons would appear to be clear:

First, Cuba was not a poor country. It had undergone urbanization and experienced a period of prosperity. This trend was partially reversed in the period immediately preceding the revolution and gave rise to a disgruntled urban middle class that had little control over the economy but contributed to chaos through misuse of the political structure.

Second, class divisions marked Cuba long before the revolution and gave rise to bitterness and discontent. In this case the urban middle classes were most drastically affected, particularly because they subjectively compared themselves to the models of a nearby rich neighbor—the United States.

The history of Cuba has long been intertwined with that of the United States. Debate over the future status of Cuba in relationship to the United States began almost from the beginning of American independence. The United States sent arms to insurgents, occupied Cuban territory, and finally imposed the Platt Amendment. The Platt Amendment, drawn up in 1902, "limited the authority of the Cuban government to negotiate internal treaties or borrow funds from abroad."[59] Although the Platt Amendment was abrogated in 1934, scores of Cuban intellectuals apparently did not forget the humiliation of the second-class citizenship status it implied. Paradoxically, then, the salience of American influence was dually enforced.

The fact that Cubans looked to the United States rather than other Latin American countries is significant, for it suggests that urban social upheaval does not spring from the depths of poverty and despair, but more probably from the degree of social injustice subjectively experienced by the people. In spite of a relatively higher standard of living compared to that of many Latin American, Asian, or African countries, it is important to note that in 1956 Cuba's per capita income was 336 pesos in comparison with $829 in the state of Mississippi. (Mississippi had the lowest per capita income in the United States.)[60] Moreover, the distribution of income in Cuba was grossly uneven. Vast differences existed between urban and rural populations, black and white populations, and the upper, middle, and lower classes.

Third, urban intellectuals had long since deserted the regime and turned toward revolutionary ideology. The old institutions of Cuban society, such as the Cuban Catholic Church, offered little refuge for discontent.

Fourth, the elite (such as Batista, his allies, and the sugar-owning crowd) no longer could control the government machinery. When even the navy openly rebelled and the army failed to support the regime in an active fashion, it was evident that Batista no longer governed their actions.

Fifth, factors unique to Cuban history also played their part. Cuba had a long revolutionary heritage. In the tradition of José Martí, Castro and his myth personified all the virtues worshiped in Cuban society. In its "special relation" to the United States—a situation that involved nationalistic passions—Cuba was also ripe for a leader who could exploit the situation.[61] Further, since the Soviet Union acted as a powerful third force, Castro's actions were undoubtedly affected.

The continuing nature of revolutionary change is demonstrated in the fact that in 1970 the revolution was described as having taken "still another turn."[62] Castro admitted that Cuba was not yet ready to live in true Communism and had settled for the pre-Communist phase of "each according to his own work." Workers were mobilized and rewarded for contributing to the nation's welfare; children were meticulously indoctrinated in the ideology of the welfare of the collective; and regimentation ruled almost all phases of life.[63] All of this was done in spite of Cuba's continued dependence on her single most important crop—sugar.

Cuba has prospered, however, and since Castro and the revolution the gap between rural and urban existence has been closed; the dire poverty and flagrant contrasts between unlimited private wealth and urban poor have been eliminated. Further, Castro mobilized a literacy campaign that reduced illiteracy to 3.9 percent of the population. The literacy campaign of 1961 (originally an example of what teachers could do if they worked together) set the conditions for even greater mobilization of all people, for now the masses could read the propaganda materials delivered to them.[64]

By 1976 every observer of Cuba agreed that the lot of the masses had vastly improved: education flourished, sugar production went up because of world market prices, and the most drab urban sections had been replaced with new housing. Although Castro failed to export his revolution to the rest of Latin America, he had established six military missions in Arab and African countries. Some ten thousand Cuban troops had participated in the pro-Communist victory in Angola. With disarray spreading through Southern Africa, it appeared that Castro had established himself as a world rather than merely a Cuban leader of revolution.

Case 8
The fighting Irish

The "Irish problem" has existed for at least three hundred years. Most recently, since 1969, all of the intertwined conflicts of Ulster—religious, political, economic, and social—have erupted into a civil war. From the point of view of the Catholics, the Ulster torment represents a genuine urban revolution designed to unite this British province with the rest of Ireland and to effect a vast socioeconomic change throughout the country. It is, however, a continuing revolution since no solution has been reached that can satisfy all parties involved in the conflict.

THE SETTING

As long as history has been recorded, the Irish have been fighting—foreign invaders, each other, or the misty darkness that envelops the island. Today's "troubles" are hardly new; Ireland has always been a land of tragedy and sadness. Perhaps this is why they have produced that melancholy group of men who compose the romantic ballads still sung in the cafes. Generation after generation of poets and authors, satirists like Jonathan Swift who cut the human race down to Lilliputian size, two hundred thousand brave men who climbed over the trenches in World War I to the sound of an English whistle to face the withering fire of German machine guns, the rag-tag battalion that marched up O'Connell Street in the midst of a world war to confront the might of the British army, and contemporary romantics, alone in the modern world, who destroy each other in the name of Jesus Christ.

Although in 1921 Ireland was technically declared an independent state, Northern Ireland continued its existence as a province of the United Kingdom. For the past fifty years, however, British secretaries of state have been politely excused from even visiting that part of the United Kingdom. Perhaps from the British point of view that was acceptable. As long as England has recognized Ireland's existence (some eight hundred years), the perennial "Irish problem" has bothered the nation.

In the 1970s the British found themselves again entangled, and not a single statesman could clearly see the way out of the quagmire. Northern Irish prime ministers (in fact, three between 1969 and 1972) undoubtedly had done their best; yet, the situation continued. The events that preceded the entry of the British are easily chronicled. The spiraling of animosities as well as the solutions to the problems are complex.

To understand fully the Irish problem, one must examine an apparently sectarian revolution on a variety of levels: the religious, to be sure, but also the social, economic, and political. Further, in the light of Ireland's peculiar history, another factor—Irish romanticism—may also be considered.

Religion: "Tis the only modern land where Christians kill each other in the name of Christ"

"We're not fighting to convert those Fenian scum," one Ulster Vanguard man assured us during an informal interview. "They are lost in Popery." And, on the other side, an Irish Republican Army (IRA) provisional commented: "They can have their own religion, however pagan it may be, if they only let us alone." He manufactured petrol bombs as we talked.

Obviously, religion clearly marked the geographical lines of battle. Certain Catholic areas were "no go" to British troops and the (predominantly) Protestant policemen. The IRA fully governed these sections, imposing rent and rate strikes and dispensing justice.

The roots of the sectarian conflict go back to Oliver Cromwell's barbarously established Protestant Ascendancy in 1649, an event that alienated even the most moderate Catholics. In 1689 James II, seeking to gain control of England by first conquering Protestant Ireland, landed on Irish soil and besieged the town of Londonderry (Derry). He failed, and his antagonist, Protestant William of Orange, came to Derry's rescue. Protestants still celebrate William's victory by staging an annual celebration.

During our stay in Northern Ireland, we discovered that the Protestants believed they were defending themselves against absorption into the theocracy of a united Ireland Republic—a condition they believed would lead to censorship, a ban on contraceptives and divorces, and a total loss of freedom to the church. The Protestants elaborated a set of stereotypes about Catholics that sounded all too familiar to Americans acquainted with the shibboleths concerning American blacks: the Catholics were lazy, shiftless, dirty, violent, propagated like rabbits, and lived off the dole. Thus, the Protestant slogan—pregnant with memories of their ancestors' defense of Derry—"No surrender!"

The Catholics contended that continued Protestant Ascendancy involved subordination of their schools, discrimination in housing, a lack of employment opportunities, and the literal destruction of their places of worship.[65] (This latter fear came true in 1972 as Protestant groups used firebombs to burn down churches.)

Clearly, religion permeates Irish life. The 4,700 churches in Ulster exceed even the number of ubiquitous pubs.[66] The Catholic church's membership works to build bigger and better edifices.[67] The Protestants posted signs announcing that they had found the way to salvation and urged "the benighted" to join them on the road to heaven.[68] In addition, hundreds of thousands of Protestants annually celebrated their moral superiority by marching through the streets.

Since there was virtually no intermarriage, a distinct caste system (like that in India or the United States) emerged. Except for actual emigration, it was virtually impossible to escape its effects. Emigration had always been a paramount Irish issue in both the North and the South. In the North the Protestant control of the economy and politics has driven out the Catholics. In the south the economic pressures (particularly "the Great Famine") forced millions to leave the country.[69]

Economics

Probably the most vicious, self-perpetuating effects of the Irish caste system lay in the economic realm. Some Marxists like Bernadette Devlin claimed that the Ulster conflict could be traced solely to economic reasons.[70] This is no doubt an oversimplification.

In an economy marred by an overall 8 percent unemployment rate, Catholics were most likely to join the ranks of the jobless. In some sections of Ulster's Catholic community unemployment had reached the astounding level of 40 percent to 50 percent. Consequently, Catholics deferred marriage until an average age of 33. Some Catholics migrated abroad (primarily to England) to make their fortune in a foreign land. If a Catholic remained in Ulster he married and sired children, seeking solace at the local pub; the pattern reproduced itself.[71]

By 1974 a doctrinaire Marxist interpretation—based on the "slave" conception of the Ulster Catholic worker—failed to explain the confrontation of the Ulster drama. Most Northern capitalists, for example, fearing the withdrawal of foreign investment, sought some strategy of reconciliation with the Catholic worker.[72] Their long-lived policy, however, already had borne evil fruits even for them. Catholics suffered from the appalling rate of joblessness and remained, in large part, unskilled in a modern economy that demanded technicians. Further, Protestant workers fiercely opposed any encroachment of Catholics on "their" jobs, and as a result, Belfast's major industry, shipbuilding, employed only six hundred Catholics out of twelve thousand workers.[73]

From the Marxian point of view the most disastrous development of the last fifty years was the actions of trade unions. Seeking to preserve their hegemony, the unions systematically excluded Catholic apprentices.[74]

Ulster walked step-by-step with England in economic development. However, the new welfare state created by the labor government in 1945 initiated special problems for Ulstermen. The Protestants had a number of objections to the program.[75] First, the welfare legislation provided no room for religious discrimination. Second, Northern Ireland had to contribute to the welfare payments, thus decreasing the pressure on Catholics to emigrate. Third, the Protestants feared that the coming of a welfare state would increase the Catholic birthrate.

These apprehensions on the part of many Protestants were heightened by the fact that Catholic children attending school (approximately 50 percent) eventually would have outnumbered Protestants. The proportion of Catholic adults was maintained through economic discrimination and emigration of adults. In 1911, 34.4 percent of the population was composed of Catholics; in 1974 it was almost the same.[76] Therefore, despite the higher birthrate among Catholics, systematic economic discrimination prevented the Catholic adult population from becoming numerically more powerful.

Education

By far the most significant effect of the introduction of a welfare state was the opening of universities at virtually no cost to the Catholic population. This one action created a new group of intellectuals who soon took the lead in opposing Protestant domination.

Higher education suddenly became free for Catholics who had been economically forced and even legally proscribed from attending universities. In 1905, Queen's University in Belfast enrolled only 5 percent Catholics. By 1960 this figure had risen to 22 percent and by 1974 to approximately 30 percent.[77] The social repercussions of this transformation can hardly be overemphasized: by the 1970s education had produced many liberal Catholics who were aware of their prior deprivations. They soon led the attack on the foundations of Protestant political power.

Politics

Perhaps the greatest symbol of political discrimination was Stormont Castle, a magnificent gray edifice rising majestically above Belfast. From its chambers the Protestant aristocracy ruled Ulster for fifty years. From its balcony two Protestant enemies—Brian Faulkner and William Craig—shook hands and then petulantly announced their opposition to British direct rule before a crowd of one hundred thousand Orangemen on 25 March 1972. Ulster Vanguard (Protestant) partisans later claimed that Faulkner (a man with a keen sense for political winds) had forced himself into the scene without invitation; the next day Faulkner dissociated himself from Craig's Ulster Vanguard. The balcony episode was symbolic in ways that escaped the Protestant leaders:

- The great castle stood for the ultimate power of land in Northern Irish politics. Until 1972 no man could enter the Stormont parliament unless he was a householder. A person's vote depended utterly upon his ownership of land. Thus, great landholders and corporations commanded as many as six votes in local elections, while those who rented homes (some two hundred fifty thousand in all) had no voice in their own governance.[78] Naturally, Catholics suffered most gravely from this eighteenth century anachronism.
- Stormont also epitomized the absolute predominance of Protestant aristocrats in Ulster politics. The names sounded a familiar litany: Craig (commander of the Ulster Vanguard), Faulkner (ex-prime minister), Chichester-Clark (who had spent the previous year as prime year as prime minister), and O'Neill (present only in the wings, a former prime minister and a descendant of the Viking who had cut off his own "red hand" to claim sovereignty over Ireland). These same Protestant families, representative of the landed aristocracy, have ruled Northern Ireland for centuries. Catholics were not, of course, allowed to enter their names on the privileged roster.[79]
- The civil service, previously ruled by Stormont, systematically kept out Catholics. Aided by the Catholic church's original resistance to political participation, the Orangemen succeeded in keeping all branches of the civil service as exclusively Protestant domains. The civil service roles revealed that only 10 percent of the government employees called themselves Catholic, when in 1972 Catholics comprised over 35 percent of the population. Moreover,

at the highest administrative levels, only one person out of thirty-one was Catholic in 1972.[80]

To ensure their dominance in Derry, the Protestants carved out districts that would vote solidly for their candidates in parliament and left one tiny overcrowded district to the Catholics. Although Derry (however gerrymandered) had over twenty thousand Catholic voters and some ten thousand Protestants, the Unionists (Protestant) decisively won two-thirds of the available government seats.[81] Gerrymandering, coupled with subterfuges that forbade Catholics from buying homes in Protestant wards, successfully ensured the dominance of a one-party state.

One other intangible yet real element in the Northern Irish tragedy was sheer romanticism. In a dreary, rainy, dark environment the "fighting Irish" destroyed each other with a vigor usually reserved for only four other events: marriage, funerals, drinking, and conversation. Aside from the objective issues, the Irish fought each other simply because of a long romantic tradition that glorified the warrior (particularly the heroic underdog who *loses*) as the most gallant of men.

We can document this assertion with only the vaguest of evidence. At best, we can offer illustrations of the quixotic strain woven into the Irish skein:

- In 1972 a group of IRA (Catholic) revolutionaries entertained no hope of winning a battle against the English army. Yet, when trapped in a Bogside bar, they refused to accept an offer to escape by a secret exit. The English troops surrounded them, and they had no chance of a successful way of getting around the soldiers except by the artful hatch. The IRA men, like their ancestors in 1916, refused to leave. They *wanted* to become martyrs in the cause of Irish union. In their case, ironically, they failed. The English withdrew their troops to another position and no one was killed.
- In 1972, together with a French journalist, we questioned an IRA bomb expert. Because gelignite is bulky and heavy, the Frenchman asked why the revolutionaries did not use "plastique" (an adhesive lump of explosives widely used during the Algerian crisis, which anyone can easily attach to a car or a building). "It's just tradition," the IRA man, after thinking for a moment, replied. "The lads of 1916 found it useful and we go on."
- Proclaiming "we must bury our own," IRA men, conspicuously outfitted in black berets and dark glasses, left their hideouts to attend funerals. They knew well that British intelligence compiled its dossiers largely on the basis of photographs taken at funerals. Yet, the IRA marched with the casket, even though the same men were picked up the next day.

We would argue, therefore, that this strange admixture of romanticism vastly complicated any strictly rational theory of the Ulster revolution. Both the Protestants celebrating the Battle of the Boyne and the Catholics bemoaning an IRA funeral still proclaimed the same message: we are men and we wish attention to be paid. Unfortunately, their exaggerated masculinity led them into follies even the most conceited peacock wisely avoids.

THE PRECIPITANT: A USUAL EVENT

The beatings, burnings, bombings, and murders began with an outwardly innocent event in County Tyrone in February 1968. Miss Emily Beattie, unmarried and 19 years old, was given a council (public-owned) house in the village of Caledon. She had served as secretary to the local councillor's solicitor, who was a Unionist (Protestant) candidate for Parliament. She took possession of 9 Kinnard Park and evicted some Catholic squatters, the McKenna family. By all accounts, Miss Beattie was a charming, pretty girl and supposedly had plans to marry and eventually raise a family. She moved to the house by herself on 13 June 1968. The McKenna family departed for parts unknown.

Until this point, events proceeded without unusual commotion. After all, the Unionist (Protestant) councillor for years had controlled the allocation of houses. An eviction of a Catholic family was hardly out of the ordinary. In fact, the McKenna family and their neighbors next door at 11 Kinnard Park were all squatters. By any legal definition, the Protestant councillor, his solicitor, and Miss Beattie had every right (under the Ulster law) to displace the tenants.

But the girl and her patrons overlooked a new situation that had developed in Ulster. First, many Catholic families living in urban filth and squalor had waited years to find a house like Miss Beauttie's. Not only were the majority of their abodes in miserable condition, but the very fact of being segregated in a Catholic ghetto had proved politically discriminatory.[82] This was a fact Catholic residents had suddenly begun to realize. Second, "squatting" on buildings deserted by Protestants had become standard practice. In 1972 more than ten thousand ramshackle buildings were occupied by families who had no other place to call home.[83] Third, according to the Cameron Report, "by no stretch of the imagination could Miss Beattie be regarded as a priority tenant."[84] Fourth, television had suddenly come to Northern Ireland, and people throughout the world knew of her actions. In addition, they soon learned of the eviction (with full television coverage) of the Goodfellow family, who had been squatting next door at 11 Kinnard Park.

It seems unlikely that Miss Beattie—whose inadvertent actions provoked the first full-scale Catholic protests since the founding of Ulster in 1921—had even the remotest knowledge of why her action should have triggered such a reaction. She may have known, in some abstract fashion, of the economic, social, political, and religious discrimination by Protestants of Ulster Catholics. Many of the events preceding this seemingly incidental one probably escaped her attention.

Protestant oppression

Early in 1966 newspapers announced a Protestant campaign of action against Catholics. A statement signed by the anonymous Adjutant of the First Belfast Battalion of the Ulster Volunteer Force (Protestant) declared war on the IRA (Catholic Irish Republican Army) and announced that IRA men would be "executed mercilessly and without hesitation."[85]

In June the promises were kept: unknown assassins shot John Patrick Scullion, a Catholic student. On 27 June three Protestants shot four Catholics as they left a pub.[86] On 28 June Mrs. Matilda Gould, a 70-year-old Protestant widow died of burns: a result of a petrol bomb explosion. The bomb had been aimed at a Catholic pub next to her house.[87]

The Protestants, led by a heretofore unknown Presbyterian preacher, Rev. Ian Paisley, were fighting a battle of attrition against their Catholic neighbors. The Catholics, on the other hand, had begun their fight to obtain a "fair share" of economic and political power with a strategy and demands familiar to those aware of events on the United States scene in the 1960s.

THE BATTLE: A CONTINUING SAGA October 1968

Derry has always been a Catholic city. In 1688 the Apprentice Boys closed the gates of the city against the onslaught of William of Orange and his Protestant troops. The city survived a sustained seige and some of the original walls still stand.

In 1968, some two hundred eighty years later, the walls of Derry were breached—not by armed soldiers but by civil rights marchers. On 5 October 1968 a circumspect, nonviolent, largely middle-class group marched through the streets of Derry demanding the most modest of requests: freedom of speech, freedom of assembly, "one man, one vote"

(Derry, like all of Ulster, based its electorate on householding rules), fair dispensation of public housing, and an improvement of economic conditions.

Initially, although short-lived, the movement was nonsectarian. The leaders, both Catholic and liberal Protestant, planned a march route partially through a Protestant area (long off limits to Catholics) to demonstrate their unity.[88]

William Craig, then minister of home affairs (later prime minister) banned the march on 3 March. For the civil rights demonstrators the line was clearly drawn. Did they have or have not the right of peaceful assembly? And, in the Irish context, did they have the right to show the nonsectarian nature of their movement by moving peacefully through Protestant sections?

Craig's response was "No!" but on 5 October the march proceeded. A cordon of police stopped the marchers in a Protestant quarter of the city and battered them with batons. Pressed by the police, the crowd sang "We Shall Overcome." They eventually dispersed, but 5 October signaled two events: (1) the fact that sectarian feeling had not marred the protest and (2) that the lower-class people of Derry had the courage to confront directly the powers of Stormont, the Protestant government.[89] The government had won the physical battle, but it was a Pyrrhic victory.

The forays by civil rights defenders escalated during October. On 7 October one thousand students at Queen's University in Belfast announced that they would march to the city hall on Wednesday, 9 October, in support of the Derry group.[90] Ian Paisley, the Protestant firebrand, promptly proclaimed that he would gather his men to deflect the protesters. He succeeded. On 9 October police stopped the students from entering Shaftesbury Square: Paisley had formed his blockade.

On 8 November a civil rights group formed to hold a march in Armagh later in the month. Paisley again appeared and had his followers distribute pamphlets[91] printed in red ink that proclaimed:

> "For God and Ulster"
> S.O.S.
> To all Protestant religions.
> Don't let the Republicans, I.R.A. and C.R.A. make Armagh another Londonderry
> Assemble in Armagh on Saturday, 30th November.

Assemble they did. The night before, Paisley and his assistant, Major Ronald Bunting, arrived in Armagh. Backed by hundreds of Protestants, they placed a road block across the route the marchers would have taken. The police later found revolvers, picks, scythes, lead pipes, and billhooks on the Paisleyites.

The police stopped the unarmed civil rights marchers but failed to disband Paisley's group. Later in the day, however, the police charged a group of Catholics in another part of the city and beat them with batons.[92]

January 1969: the long march

Paisleyites were at first triumphant over their victory, which had been duly recorded over national television. The Protestant extremists had—at least temporarily—reached the height of their power. The "People's Democracy," a Marxist, more Catholic-oriented organization of students and workers, announced that they would stage a protest march from Belfast to Derry on 1 January. Protestants proclaimed they would stop the trek.[93]

On 1 January 1969 thousands of people (mostly students) assembled at the city hall in Belfast to prepare for the cross-country march to Derry. Among the leaders of the march was a pert young girl, Bernadette Devlin, who was later to become the symbol of Catholic opposition in Ulster. Along the way of the march, Bunting and other Protestants harassed the marchers. As Devlin recalled it, the march began in good spirits:

> Outside Belfast Major Bunting dropped out the procession—just at the entrance to Bellevue Zoo, made everybody feel pretty witty. . . . New recruits were joining us all the time; passing drivers threw us cigarettes and encouragement; the weather was far from bad.[94]

The protesters proceeded through a variety of towns. Some (like Randalstown) were hostile and showered stones on the procession. The accompanying police claimed they could not interfere. In others (like Toome) the largely Catholic population welcomed the marchers.

In Derry, Paisley and Bunting addressed a large crowd of their supporters in the guildhall. They urged the men to assemble the next morning to prevent the entrance of the civil rights marchers into the city of the "Apprentice Boys."[95] The marchers held their own planning meetings. Speakers urged nonviolence. They hoped also to attract Protestant workers as their "natural" allies.

Alas, this hope proved naive. As the marchers approached the outskirts of Derry, Protestant workers brought in truckloads of newly quarried stones, clubs, and cudgels with nails driven through them.[96] Each man in the Protestant mob received a sack of bricks and stones. The Protestant "B Specials," a paramilitary group out of uniform but armed, moved into position to face the column of marchers.

Again, civil rights leaders such as Eammon McCann and Michael Farrell appealed to the marchers to avoid violence as they entered Derry, the last step of their procession. McCann, in particular, attempted to stress that the Protestant workers were the allies of the Catholic marchers:

> Remember the nature of those who have hindered us during the last few days. They are not our enemies in any sense. They are not exploiters dressed in thirty-guinea suits. They are the dupes of the system, the victims of landed and industrial Unionists. They are the men in overalls who are on our side, *though they do not know it yet* [emphasis added].[97]

Trained in a Marxist logic that may well have described objective conditions in Ulster, the civil rights and People's Democracy orators believed that the Protestant workers were aware of their situation. They were, however, wrong. A Protestant who participated in the attack on the Catholic marchers later told us, "People were tired of all the marching, they wanted to be done with the mess. We thought if it's all to wind up in a battle, let's get it over. Sure, we have it almost as bad as those Catholic scum—but at least we have jobs and wanted to keep them. The more Fenians there are, the more they try to get in."

The Protestants were waiting in ambush for the Catholic marchers about seven miles outside of Derry at the Burntollet Bridge. A screening force of police moved ahead of the marchers, while another police cordon separated the Protestants. The marchers agreed to link arms, to carry any of the injured with them, and to push ahead into Derry.

The marchers advanced three hundred, then six hundred yards without a threat of violence. Then they arrived at Burntollet Bridge. As Bernadette Devlin (who was in the front ranks) recalled the incident:

> From lanes at each side of the road a curtain of bricks and boulders and bottles brought the march to a halt. From the lanes burst hordes of screening people wielding planks of wood, bottles, lathes, iron bars, crowbars, cudgels studded with nails and they waded into the march beating hell out of everybody.[98]

The attackers threw people into the river, attempted to drown them, and stoned them when they crawled up the bank. Some of the Protestants threw girls off the bridge into the stream, attacked with the nailed clubs, and threatened rape.[99]

When a remnant of the bloody and battered marchers finally arrived in Derry, a large crowd of Catholics welcomed them. But by late afternoon of Saturday, 4 January 1969, the Protestant attackers had regathered. Drunk and triumphal, they climbed the walls surrounding the city and showered sticks, stones, and bottles down on the marchers.

In the small hours of the morning of 5 January, after a night of drinking, the police themselves entered the fracas, acting as uninhibited supporters of the Protestants. They invaded the Catholic Bogside area of Derry, clamping their batons to their shields and shouting invectives at the residents. They smashed the windows of Catholic houses and banged on their doorways.[100] As brutal as this initial series of events was, it was merely a prelude to subsequent events.

August 1969

In April 1969 Ulster was in flames once again. On 19 April, Protestant militants invaded the Catholic dominated Bogside area of Derry and fought a pitched battle with residents. Aided by the Royal Ulster Constabulary and the B Specials, Protestant mobs wrecked Bogside homes.[101]

In the eastern part of Ulster, explosions ripped apart vital utilities. Electricity failed in Belfast, a number of post offices (technically owned by the British) were blown apart, and explosions wrecked the sources of Belfast's water supply. Government announcements proclaimed the destruction as the work of the IRA, but—and this is crucially important in understanding the psychosis that overcame Ireland—*the sabotage was actually committed by the Protestant Ulster Volunteer Force.*[102]

The goal of the Protestant extremists was to bring about the fall of Captain O'Neill's relatively moderate government and to force a state of emergency that would involve the full recall of all Protestant B Specials.[103] The Ulster Volunteer Force succeeded. O'Neill called for a reform of the voting process in Ulster and was opposed by one of his own ministers, the minister for agriculture, Major Chichester-Clark. The prime minister resigned and Chichester-Clark took over for one year as prime minister of Northern Ireland.

One of Chichester-Clark's few actions while in office was to declare an amnesty that allowed both Catholics and the ubiquitous Paisley and Bunting out of jail. For a short while a false calm pervaded the little nation.

Then, on 12 July—the occasion of traditional Orange (Protestant) marches—looting, fighting, and bombings broke out in Derry. Mobs of Catholic youth rampaged through the city center committing acts the Protestant government later described as vandalism and hooliganism.[104] The Catholic Bogside area, following the usual pattern of anarchic riots, tore its own area apart. In Dungiven the Catholics burned down the Orange Hall and tried, with seared fingers, to throw the hot stones of the building into the surrounding bush.

Everyone in Derry waited for 12 August 1969, the anniversary of the Apprentice Boys' Procession in the city. Every year approximately twenty thousand Protestants marched around the city's walls, banging drums and playing the pipes celebrating—in a fascinating but now ironic pageant—Ulster's struggle for religious and civil liberty. Leaders on both sides urged that the march be postponed, but Chichester-Clark, fearing that he was losing the only populist base that supported the Stormont government, declared that the Apprentice Boys' Procession would proceed as usual.

When 12 August dawned, contingents of Protestants from all over Northern Ireland convened to participate in the demonstration. The thirty thousand Catholic residents of the Bogside vowed to keep within their own territory and to avoid provocation. At first the singing and marching proceeded peacefully. Soon, however, rocks were thrown by both sides and fighting broke out. Large units of riot police equipped with armored cars, water cannons, and canisters of Cs gas moved toward the Bogside. This time they were backed by thousands of Protestant marchers. The Catholics erected makeshift barricades against the marchers and pelted them with rocks and then petrol bombs. The police moved steadily forward, however, and cleared the barricades.

"We drove them back," one of the participants told us, "all the little kids and the women made the bombs. The Orangemen didn't have the guts to stand up against us."[105] On their side, the Orangemen shouted slogans about keeping the Fenian rabbits in their pens. By nightfall the Catholics had regained control of their ghetto borders, and the police were reduced to heaving cans of Cs gas indiscriminately into the Bogside. Southern Ireland's government mobilized troops on the border and threatened to intervene if the Bogside battle did not subside. It was, however, a mere gesture, since such action probably would have provoked British intervention.[106] Ireland could neither risk losing an essential economic agreement with England nor could it match its army against that of England. At best, after refusing to send in gasmasks to protect the Bogside people from tear gas, the Irish government set up field ambulances at the nearby border and secretly forwarded medical supplies.[107]

Meanwhile, in response to urgent pleas from Derry, the Belfast Catholics surged into the streets. B Specials, dispatched by Chichester-Clark, attacked the demonstrators with machine guns and armored cars. They burned down row after row of houses in the Belfast Catholic areas.[108]

By 14 August the British government realized that Stormont could not control the situation. By that point the Catholics—having whipped the B Specials in their own game—had established "Free Derry" and "Free Belfast" areas behind formidable barricades. In an exercise of constitutional power the English army took over the maintenance of safety in Northern Ireland. Free Derry and Free Belfast welcomed the British troops as their protectors. Later, their representatives negotiated openly with representatives of the British Home Office. England intervened with decisive force and persuasive promises of reform. The following reforms were proposed:

1. The abolition of householding restrictions on elections, so that each man would receive one vote
2. The disbanding of the now notorious B Specials
3. A relaxation in brutal police methods
4. On paper, a dismemberment of the entire system of discrimination in the economic, housing, and educational system

The barricades gradually came down, and the Catholics waited for the expected reforms to materialize. Yet, Stormont refused to accept the English proposal.[109] The B Specials were, for example, dismantled but only to be replaced with an Ulster Defense Regiment recruited largely from members of the old B Specials. The reform of the electoral provisions were postponed as the elections themselves were suspended.[110]

November and December of 1969 began with a series of bank robberies—a sign that the IRA was gathering the funds necessary for a full-scale attack to bring down the Protestant government.[111]

1970: the rebirth of the IRA

Since 1916 the Irish Republican Army had enjoyed a romantic position in Irish politics. In the original Easter Rising in Dublin in 1916 it had failed as a military force. Yet the British made the incredible political mistake of executing its most prominent leaders, thus insuring the hostility of the Catholic Irish. In the North, during the glorious days of 1916, the IRA had performed badly.[112] Orders were jumbled, supplies did not arrive, and in a stupidly open fashion a letter appeared in the Northern press announcing that the rebellion had been postponed. Northerners believed it and failed to take to their guns when the actual fighting did begin.[113]

For decades the IRA languished in a legend of hopeless heroism. At times, as in the mid-1950s, a handful of its soldiers launched attacks on border regions in Ulster—only to be ignominously routed by the British army. Even by 1970 one leader of the Northern IRA confided that he could count on only thirty active fighters in the area.

Yet the decisions made by Westminster and Stormont in 1969 revived the dormant organization. It hardly makes sense to argue, as some do, that the IRA intimidated the Catholic population.[114] That contention ignores the problem of how the IRA can succeed in finding enough men to keep a half million people under their control.

No doubt the sometimes inadvertent storm trooper tactics of both the Protestant majority and the British army united the ghetto Catholics behind the IRA. In addition, the government in Dublin followed a policy that can, at a minimum, be described as incomprehensible. The exact history of all the dealings that occurred between the Southern Irish government and the IRA leadership will have to be detailed by future historians; however, Northern IRA men were convinced, for example, that the Dublin government had promised them two hundred thousand pounds to buy arms.[115] Their sole assurance was a deposit of five pounds in a Dundalk Bank. The Southern Irish government, however, probably did donate arms, and some money under various disguises to the IRA. For example, one hundred thousand pounds went to the Irish Red Cross. Since they do not operate in Ulster, the money was given to a committee of Ulster Catholics who banked it in the name of the Belfast Fund for the Relief of Distress. The money was later transferred to accounts in Dublin under fictitious names.[116] The account of a "George Dixon" was used for arms purchases.

Equipped with money, support from the Catholic community, and guns (reportedly smuggled in by Scotsmen), the IRA soon became a potent force initiating a series of bombings and battles.

By 29 June 1970 squads of English soldiers roared through the Catholic ghettos confiscating arms. Their haul was pitiful. They discovered twelve pistols, a Schmiesser submachine gun (minus a magazine), and a few explosives. In an area that six days before had experienced a Protestant attack, the army's search could not have been more ill-timed, provocative, and futile. The English raids did, however, accomplish one purpose —a magnificent increase in IRA morale as the dependable protectors of the Catholic minority. As the writers of the London *Sunday Times* Insight Team reported:

> In the months that followed, recruitment to the Provisionals was dizzily fast: the movement grew from fewer than a hundred activists in May-June to nearly 800 by December. Time was running out.[117]

By late June of 1970 the Protestants were scared, and their government turned to harsh penal laws to curb the surging Catholic dissent. In panic the Stormont government passed a law that provided for imprisonment of anyone who had engaged in riotous behavior, disorderly behavior, or behavior likely to cause a breach of the peace. Equipped with such vague legal terminology the Ulster police and the British troops moved into the Catholic ghettos with unusual dispatch. Stormont rushed the bill through, giving extraordinary powers to the military and paramilitary forces. The military obliged and promptly arrested over one thousand people on a variety of charges.

London Times reporters have recorded one such arrest:

> On August 1, 1970, in a disturbance in Belfast, the former chairman of the Civil Rights Association, a dentist, Frank Gogarty, was recording the sounds with a microphone and tape. He was stopped by an Army patrol, bundled against a wall and searched, being thrown against the wall twice in the process. When he protested, he was cursed, kicked and thrown into a jeep—at which he said: "Stop kicking me, you British bastard."[118]

Gogarty received two years imprisonment for his "crime."

Another man, a Belfast docker, John Benson, wrote on a wall, "No Tea Here"—a reference to the previous practice of Catholic women to give relief to British troops whom they thought were there to protect them. For this offense—"an obvious attempt to intimidate people"—the court sent Benson to an internment camp for six months as his reprimand for a breach of the peace.[119]

Policies such as this tended to polarize even those who remained apolitical in the Catholic community and sent the moderates into a more militant camp.

1971: internment

By 23 March a white-haired man named Brian Faulkner replaced Chichester-Clark as prime minister of Ulster. He had served in the Stormont parliament as a young man, but it took him twenty-two years (after service as minister for home affairs, commerce and development) to arrive at the height of his power. Like all the rulers of Stormont, he came from a wealthy Protestant family, but was disdained by the Protestant aristocracy. Lord Brookeborough, a leader of the traditional elite, once called him "the little shirt-maker from Comber."[120]

Faulkner was an eminently flexible man. On one day he could be photographed beside Eamon de Valera, the arch-Republican of Ireland; on the next (once he was safely across the border into the North) he could condemn the Roman Catholic Church. On 26 March he made a symbolic visit to the headquarters of the Orange movement.[121] In essence, Faulkner was an extremely able man, adept enough to assume the prime ministership of Ulster after two predecessors had fallen from favor in two years.

Yet Faulkner, like his predecessors, experienced difficulty in handling the situation. Riots in Ballymurphy (a Catholic "estate" in west Belfast) sprung up as the work of teenaged gangs who attacked British soldiers. Rioting in Derry proceeded for four days beginning on 2 July 1972. English troops stood their ground and, on the whole, refused to fire against the Catholics. Indiscriminate bombings continued throughout Ulster.[122]

For more than six months after taking office the frustrated Faulkner had argued for the internment of suspected terrorists. On 9 August the British army was dispatched, and on the first night more than one hundred fifty people were arrested. Their names were added to the list of potential terrorists or disturbers of the peace.

A typical case of the indiscriminate use of internment has been documented by *London Times* writers in an incident involving Kevin Duffy.

As described by the *Times* reporters, Kevin Duffy had been a moderate, neither a member of the IRA nor even of the Republican party.[123] His sole qualification as a disturber of the peace was that he belonged to the Gaelic Association—a group that promotes the study of the Gaelic language, literature, and football. His father had been well-known as a promoter of Catholic-Protestant peace in Moy, a village approximately forty miles from Belfast. Catholics had poured steadily into the Duffy house because it provided a base for the sharing of interests in sports and social affairs. No other charges were brought against him—indeed, the baffling aspect of the internment policy was that no charges needed to be provided against anyone.[124]

Duffy emerged from internment a different man. "I really was a moderate before all this," *Times* reporters quoted him. "I had no interest in politics and didn't like the methods the IRA used. Living in my house, you saw that Catholics and Protestants *could* live together peacefully. Everything has changed now. . . . "[125] Duffy lost his job because of his internment.

The internment policies inflamed much of the Catholic population. Men were popped in and out of prison with little apparent justification and without trial. The army lamely argued that it did not have sufficient time to gather evidence to bring people to court.[126] The Stormont government contended that the conflict would have worsened if an internment policy had not been indicated. Raw statistics belie this assertion:

In the four months before internment—April to July 1971—four soldiers were killed, no police and four civilians. In the four months after it—August to November—thirty soldiers were killed, eleven members of the RUC and the Ulster Defence Regiment, and seventy-three civilians.[127]

1972: Bloody Sunday

By this point the Catholic ghettos controlled their own communities, patrolling at night and allowing British patrols to pass through during the day. IRA men guarded the remnants of buildings that previously had been burned to the ground by Protestants. Few people entered the Catholic ghettos without being thoroughly searched. Informers were shot in the legs before being tied to a flagpole and tarred.[128]

The explosive emotions of Northern Ireland erupted again on 30 January 1972. Thousands of Catholics—in defiance of a ban on marching—paraded in the tense city. On this Sunday, thousands of Catholics took to the streets under banners of "united or we shall die." The British troops were ready. As Gail Sheehy recorded the instance:

> We saw the paratroopers. The lids of their Trojan tanks were open and the old no-necked toads kept popping up and down in their red berets, giving us looks as mean as sub. . . . Abruptly, the grim military barricades were just ahead. . . . For the next quarter hour we were all occupied with vomiting up Cs gas (two large volleys had been thrown plus red dye sprayed by a water cannon), and dragging those wounded by rubber bullets into the flats for treatment.[129]

Witnesses later disagreed on what happened, but thirteen Catholics had been killed. Major General Robert Ford, the British commandant, said later that there had been no plan to force a confrontation between British forces and the IRA.

General Ford claimed that a common tactic of the IRA was to use unarmed civilians, particularly women, as their cover. He had expected the Sunday march to be taken over by "hooligans," and had ordered his men (paratroopers) to "respond in the lowest possible key." When he saw the Catholics advancing, however, General Ford observed that they were equipped with weapons—sticks, canes, and iron bars.[130] The troopers responded and fired their weapons. The general thought it was only "right and proper."

Other observers thought the army response excessive. The chief superintendent of police, Frank Lagan, for example, tried to restrain the British troops from entering the Bogside area. He failed.

On 14 March Lagan testified before the Widgery investigation (a one man commission led by the Lord Chief Justice of England). Lagan testified that he had argued with Brig. Patrick McClellan, the British army commander in Derry, to forbid the paratroopers from marching into the area. "For heaven's sake," Lagan was quoted as saying, "hold them until we are satisfied that the marchers and the rioters are separated." The Brigadier responded, "I'm sorry, the paras have gone in." The police chief added, "From his tone, I gathered he was not responsible for their going in."[131]

Another witness, James Chapman, a former regimental sergeant major from the British army testified before the same commission that he had seen troops "opening up at almost point-blank range at about 150 to 300 people filing through a barrier."[132] Mr. Chapman had not heard any firing before the British troops entered Rossville Street, where most of the deaths occurred.

A priest, the Reverend Edward Daly recountered, "I heard a fusillade of gunfire. A huge number of shots were fired. There was tremendous panic, women screaming. I kept on running and looking behind. The Saracens [armored cars] kept coming on very fast, overtaking the crowd. I saw a body thrown up in the air and I don't know whether it was a man or woman who had been hit by one of the vehicles."[133]

Eventually, Lord Widgery reached his conclusions after hours of testimony. On 19 April 1972 he declared that the events of "Bloody Sunday" were due to "those who had organized the illegal march" and that he was "entirely satisfied" that the initial firing had come from a sniper.[134]

Catholics in Ulster immediately denounced the inquiry as a whitewash. And indeed, the evidence supporting Widgery's conclusions was circumstantial. For example, Lord Widgery could find no actual evidence that a sniper had first fired at the troops. Rather, he said, he reached the conclusion not from the testimony of any single witness but from "watching the demeanor of witnesses under cross-examination."[135] Further, he found no evidence to support the army contention that civilians carrying firearms or bombs actually existed. Lord Widgery admitted that no weapons were recovered by the army and that "none of the many photographs shows a civilian holding an object that can with certainty be identified as a firearm or bomb."[136] The army did not suffer any casualties from firearms or bombs. Finally, not a single person of the thirteen killed had actually been discovered holding any kind of weapon. From paraffin tests, however, Lord Widgery concluded there was a "strong suspicion" that some of those killed might have been handling firearms or had been close to those who did (a somewhat strained conclusion since the town of Derry was infiltrated with gunfire that day—including English bullets). The world will probably never know what exactly happened on Bloody Sunday, but one fact is certain: the nonviolent marchers who were there will never forget.

1972–1974: the IRA takes the offensive

If Stormont or the British army had even the faintest hopes that a show of force on Bloody Sunday would avert further violence, they were sadly wrong. Indeed, the toll of violence and disruption in Ulster increased during February and March of 1972. In the belief that the British army had turned against them, both the official and provisional wings of the IRA escalated their attacks.

The violence in Ulster continued through 1975. The British increased their troops, the Protestants mobilized, and the IRA struck back. As the toll of dead British soldiers rose, the British public became incensed at the investment of blood and money in the conflict. In a hope to squash the revolution the British proposed a "White Paper" in March of 1973. This paper offered each side minor compromises: for the Protestants, Ulster was to remain part of the United Kingdom; for the Catholics, more political representation; and for all, economic aid.

However, this solution failed to satisfy any side, and the conflict continues—sputtering, abating, and erupting again. A moderate coalition of Protestants and Catholics managed to form a government that lasted little more than a year; it fell in the spring of 1974. The British increased their troops, the Protestants tried to maintain their supremacy, and the IRA took the battle to England. In the winter of 1974 IRA terrorists bombed crowded areas of English cities; the English reacted with increased antagonism toward the revolutionaries. In December 1974 the conflict dragged on with an almost monotonous repetition of violence. And yet, on 31 December 1974 (in recognition of a Christmas truce called by the IRA) Britain decided to release a portion of the six hundred political prisoners they had taken. Optimists hoped this gesture toward reconciliation might calm the situation; pessimists contended that basic economic and social problems had not been eradicated.

By 1976 Ulster's economy had seriously deteriorated: unemployment rose to 12 percent, emigration had tripled since the 1960s, and fifty major factories had closed their doors. The Protestant majority, led by the paramilitary Ulster Defense Association, vowed that Catholics should not be allowed political power and that Ulster would never be united with the rest of Ireland. With a collapse of political initiatives the British reintroduced direct military rule over the province. Some Protestants talked of secession, the IRA continued to bomb

London, and the British subtly and quietly reduced their investments in Northern Ireland. All agreed that the Irish problem, cresting and flagging, would continue into the unforeseeable future just as it has for the hundreds of years since Cromwell's brutality, through William's massacre, and even through the conciliatory efforts of statesmen such as Winston Churchill.

DISCUSSION: THE ONGOING ULSTER AGONY

Any Irishman will tell you that Ireland's troubles are unique. In some ways this is true. Ireland has been at war with others or with itself as far back as recorded history; its sectarian divisions are seldom replicated in the modern world. Particular solutions to its problems, such as the partition between North and South, have not often been successfully attempted; and, as is true of other events in history, the personalities of individual leaders have played an important role in the drama. Yet, to view the Ulster agony as an exceptional case in human experience beclouds the issues and perhaps precludes the search for a solution.

We should recognize, on the one hand, that Ulster has its own peculiar history and that the island's unique experiences continue to influence events. Even today the particular memories of the Protestants are reflected in the ancient toast of the Orange Order:

> Here's to the pious and immortal memory of King Billy, who saved us from knaves and knavery, slaves and salvery, Popes and Popery, brass money and wooden shoes.

On the other hand, one can see some obvious similarities between the Ulster conflict and other battles in history and in the present world. Like Northern Ireland, the Nigerian-Biafran conflict involved religious, caste, and economic differences. The United States Civil War offers analogous differences in ideology, territorial divisions, and economic conflicts, which bear some resemblance to the Irish conflict. Battles for colonial independence in Cuba, Africa, and Asia could also be cited for comparative reasons.

Perhaps an apt analogy to conflict in Ulster is the situation of American blacks versus whites. Both Irish Catholics and American blacks have suffered from slavery or serfdom. A caste system has developed which, in the United States, divides blacks and whites by color. In Ireland the distinctions (based on name, address, school) are equally powerful in separating Catholics from Protestants. Both American blacks and Irish Catholics suffer from economic and political discrimination, high unemployment rates, and the indignities of life in a ghetto.

Both groups have chosen similar means for improving their situation. Both groups have used migration as a way of fleeing oppression. Both groups have used passive resistance and guerrilla warfare as means of freeing themselves (although the Irish Catholics have developed the latter technique with greater ferocity).

The social-psychological effect of this position has also been similar. The Irish Catholics and the American blacks have moved in the direction of a matri-focal family. Both groups have elaborated a cult of masculinity.[137] Even roughly similar personalities have emerged to cope with a situation of powerlessness. Both groups have produced their crop of militants. Expectedly, each has a high share of "escapists." Among Irish Catholics, for example, the rate of alcoholism is notoriously high, as is the incidence of drug addiction among urban black youth.[138] In any situation of extended deprivation people develop lifestyles that allow them to cope with their anxieties.

Perhaps the most significant difference between the Irish Catholic and American black is that the former theoretically could depend upon the influence of a neutral third force—the English. Even this generalization was suspect, however, since English troops have hardly proved to be the protectors of Irish Catholics, and the federal government in the United States has—at such times as

Mississippi in 1964—acted as an arbiter between blacks and whites.

As in the Cuban case, a new middle class (university intellectuals) led the Irish revolt. Again, revolution occurred under conditions of urbanization when, in fact, the economic and social position of the deprived group (in this case, Catholics) had improved. And, as in Cuba, the Irish revolutionaries had other models (for example, Catholic rule in the South and economic prosperity in England) that taught them through the media or by migration that revolution might bring a true improvement in their lives. Sadly, as with so many revolutions, violent urban insurrections have not produced solutions to social ills.

Thousands of miles away and vastly different in religion, Egyptian revolutionaries learned a similar lession.

Case 9
Egypt: A revolution in search of a hero

The revolt by "free officers" in Egypt offers a classic example of a military coup that succeeded in accomplishing its initial aims but failed to bring about more extensive social change.

In 1965 we stood on a balcony overlooking one of the main streets of Cairo. A tall man, standing erect in an open convertible, passed by. He waved to the crowds, smiled broadly, and seemed totally unmindful that an assassin might gun him down in the alleys of the sprawling city. Gamal Abdel Nasser, at that time, was truly the hero of Egypt and, to a lesser degree, of the Arab world. He had overthrown a king, established a socialist regime, built the Aswan Dam, and opened a flood of aspirations among the Egyptian masses, He stood at the height of his power and like de Gaulle in France (whom he had recently defeated in a series of diplomatic gambits placing France and Britain in a humiliating role) he appeared invincible. No man could accuse him of corruption, self-seeking, or personal incompetence. His convertible passed by, and although we happened to be visiting a group of people who disagreed with Nasser's politics, no one refrained from cheering his majestic presence. The almost unanimous praise of Nasser took place despite the fact that most persons, particularly urbanites, felt that their lot had not improved since his ascendance to power; that most people realized Israel could, and probably would, defeat him in a real show of power; and that members of the government knew that all attempts at economic progress had been hindered by favoritism, bureaucracy, and corruption at lower ranks.

THE SETTING: MODERNIZATION AND CORRUPTION

Nasser, this extraordinary leader, came to dominance in July 1952 through a revolution against Egypt's King Faruk.

Faruk, the descendant of an Albanian revolutionary, ruled Egypt, a feudal corrupt domain, in 1952. The corpulent king, hated for his own corruption, had allied himself with remnants of the Turkish nobility and, to a lesser degree, with the British who retained colonial control over the Suez Canal. Politically, Faruk juggled the *Wafd* (the ruling party at the time of his overthrow), the Moslem Brotherhood (a group of religious fanatics who wished to establish a theocratic state), and newly formed urban groups such as trade unions, the Communist party, and the officer corps (who generally represented a secondary elite drawn from urban middle classes rather than the traditional landowning nobility).[139]

Faruk appeared not to realize that Egypt no longer could be treated as a rural fiefdom. Under British colonial rule and, inadvertently, during Faruk's reign, Egypt had undergone an intense period of modernization. The English had established an educational system, rationalized agriculture, introduced electricity and water supplies to cities such as Cairo and Alexandria, and laid down the infrastructure for industrialization. Faruk inherited these benefits as well as two other results of modernization that spelled his doom: urbanization and an enlarged middle class.

Urbanization

In an unplanned way, Egypt had entered the path of rapid urbanization. From 1900 until the collapse in 1952, Cairo had been growing at an average rate of 50 percent a decade. The city, little more than a rural outpost in 1900, absorbed millions of migrants, exposed them to new life-styles, educated them, and spewed them into some of the most densely populated ghettos in the world.[140]

Other cities we have discussed—Houston, Los Angeles, and Belfast—had grown at equally astonishing rates at different periods of history. The very rapidity of growth in itself seems to intensify problems of social conflict. It leaves people without traditional social supports and puts an enormous strain upon a city's economy. One may reasonably speculate that violent social conflicts, as in Cairo, will erupt at those historical points where urbanization is most rapid.

The growth of the middle class

Urbanization emerged with the growth of new social classes that eventually turned against Faruk as a symbol of the old order, imperialism, and corruption. The new educational system of Cairo and Alexandria produced classes of intellectuals with no place in the old regime; industrialization led to the emergence of merchants and workers who also were considered second-class citizens; the need of the British for an efficient support army created an officer class drawn from urban-educated groups. Each of these urban groups, often in secrecy from the others, planned the overthrow of Faruk.[141]

The king might possibly have retained his throne beyond 1952 if Egypt had not suffered from a series of disastrous reversals that totally undermined whatever prestige the old ruling class possessed.

The economy

Immediately preceding Faruk's downfall, Egypt reeled under the impact of economic shocks. Temporarily, during World War II, Egyptian cities enjoyed a high rate of employment. With the Allied victory, however, the Egyptian economy collapsed, unemployment jumped, and the inflation created by the war continued. A series of urban riots ensued (although the peasantry, as it almost always does, remained passive).[142]

The riots ended partially because of repression by Faruk's forces; more probably they ended because of the increases in the world demand for cotton, which was Egypt's main export. Temporarily both the cities and the countryside boomed. Unfortunately, however, Faruk and his cronies had rigged the world cotton market to an artificially high price. When the Korean War sputtered to an end, the demand for cotton subsided, and as a result, Egypt was virtually unable to sell its 1951 and 1952 crop. The Egyptian people had been riding an economic roller coaster: their hopes and expectations rose dramatically only to be dashed by the latest economic disaster.

Military weakness

In addition to economic problems, Egypt suffered from a humiliating defeat from Israel during the 1948 war. At first the Egyptian army advanced as far as Bethlehem, but they were surrounded by Israelis. Supplies did not arrive and those that did were often defective;[143] Nasser and the other officers never forgave the Faruk administration for what they believed was corrupt profiteering on defective ammunition and guns. They believed, as did Hitler after World War I, that they had been "stabbed in the back" by traitors on the home front.[144] By early 1949 all that remained of the Egyptian advance was a small enclave of troops at Faluja headed by Gamal Abdel Nasser. Futilely, if bravely, they held a sand pocket by the sea until 7 January 1947 when Egypt was forced to succumb to Israel.

This military disaster further confirmed the belief of Egyptian officers and other urban radicals that the Faruk regime had betrayed them. It led to urban riots and the assassination of the minister of the interior. It also cemented together men like Nasser, Anwar el-Sadat, and other young officers in their pledge to modernize Egypt and avenge the defeat.

As in the Meiji Japan instance, military humiliation fanned the emotions of nationalism. In Egypt, however, class divisions, rapid urbanization, economic disasters, and the corruption of the Faruk regime prohibited a nonviolent reform movement.

PRECIPITANT: REVOLT

Since 1938 Nasser had contended that three evils possessed the Egyptian world: the rule of a degenerate monarchy, imperialism, and the poverty of the Egyptian peasant. As a young man he had dedicated himself to overcoming these problems.[145]

His first success came in July 1952 when he masterminded the overthrow of King Faruk. On the night of 22 July Nasser ordered his free officer corps—nominally headed by General Neguib, the chief of staff—to seize control of Cairo, Alexandria, Suez, and other Egyptian cities. Tanks moved through the night almost unnoticed by civilians. The rebel units took key positions in the city, occupying the telegraph offices, the radio stations, and police offices.[146] Peasants took no part in the revolt, although it was conducted in their name; it was an urban uprising led by men imbued with an urbane ideology. King Faruk's High Command had advance knowledge of the coup, but they had so little power that they sent a mere captain and a squad to stop the revolt: the captain almost immediately joined the conspirators.[147]

Other cities capitulated easily. British forces (which then occupied the Suez Canal zone) did not intervene. Nasser believed this was because he had thrown a cordon of his own men around the area. In reality, the British had consciously decided not to use their army because of their contempt for the Faruk regime.[148] Six years later, when they did intervene, Nasser's forces collapsed.

General Neguib, as Nasser's figurehead, submitted a demand to King Faruk to abdicate his throne. The proclamation condemned the king for creating "anarchy" in the country, violating the constitution, allowing "corrupt people to amass shameful fortunes and waste public funds while the people continued prey to hunger and want, and furnishing defective arms to the soldiers who fought in Palestine." "Thus," the document continued, "the king should abdicate in favor of his Heir Apparent, His Highness Prince Ahmed Fuad."[149]

King Faruk followed the instructions when he found that he could not rally the armed forces to his defense. Nasser's officers allowed him to board the royal yacht, *Mahroussa,* announcing the occasion with a twenty-one gun salute. The king and his family sailed out of the harbor at six P.M. (Nasser's deadline).[150] The three hundred pound ex-monarch died soon after in his Italian exile.

Politics

At first the Nasserites were careful to preserve the remnants of monarchy and the old order, for they did not have the power to challenge either the old aristocracy in Egypt or the new radicals such as the Moslem Brotherhood. Further, they had not obtained the legitimation of the people in the countryside.[151]

In fact, the revolt did little to change the country. Prince Abdel Moneim was appointed to a regency council to preserve the rights of the infant king, and Cheral Neguib, a supporter of the regime until the last few months before its overthrow, became the real ruler.[152] The poor and hungry peasants felt no change in their situation. A handful of industrial workers at Kafir el-Dawar, near Alexandria, attempted to seize the ownership of their textile factory. They were promptly put down by members of Neguib's army. Their two leaders were hanged. Ironically, they were the first victims of the revolution.[153]

The only concrete move by the officers was to abolish the title of "pasha" on 30 July. As one observer put it, "malish [no matter]—one knew who was a pasha in Egypt!"[154]

The original policy of the new rulers, sometimes called the free officers, was to collaborate with the old regime. At first they did not touch the issue of land reform. General Neguib appointed various conservatives from the old regime to his council.[155] In accord with nationalist beliefs the free officers eventually rid Egypt of the old monarchy, but they did little to change the facts of poverty in Egypt.

The economy: land reform

The basic problem the new government confronted was that Egypt's population far outstripped its productivity. The British invasion in the nineteenth century, bringing with it modern methods of medicine, vastly increased the problem. At the end of the nineteenth century Egypt had three million people; by 1952 there were twenty-two million.[156] Cultivable land, however, had increased by only 50 percent. In fact, the Egyptian population was growing hungrier and hungrier. At first the free officers believed there should be a more just distribution of land.[157] About 65 percent of the land was owned by 6 percent of the people; 10 percent was owned by only two hundred seventy families.[158] In the conviction that land reform would help the agricultural problem, the new regime limited ownership to two hundred acres per person in September 1952. This land distribution did not help the peasants. Clever landlords simply gave out the land to their subordinates. When the land was really divided, it was parceled out in acreage that was too small to produce profitable crops. Moreover, only about 8 percent of the land was actually held by people who had over two hundred acres. Thus, the redistribution of land—although it gave farms to two hundred forty thousand families—was a negligible factor in increasing production.[159]

The new government embarked on a disastrous agrarian policy, most notably the creation of "Victory Province." This area, originally a desert, was guided by a free officer who knew little about agriculture.[160] In an area that encompassed roughly two hundred thousand acres of desert, for example, the officer built new villages, fertilized the land, and installed expensive sprinkling systems to irrigate crops. Each village was equipped with a medical clinic, a school, and an agricultural extension service. But the project met with two problems: first, the peasants from the Nile valley would not move to the desert. They already grew productive crops (at about twice the rate of American farmers); they did not want to leave their fields for the unproven ground of the desert. Second, attempts at cultivating Victory Province, although successful, proved costly. Sheer irrigation alone cost twenty times the average for acreage near the Nile.[161]

Tradition

The officers in charge of the Victory Province believed they could reclaim people as well as land. A cadre of peasants was picked who would be transformed into productive agricultural people. They had to meet the following criteria: one wife, no property, and a willingness to undergo extensive psychological training. They also had to substitute traditional gowns for a Western farmer's clothing. Their children were to be educated in Kibbutzim-like schools and imbued with civic virtues.[162] Needless to say, as an elementary knowledge of peasant life would dictate, these "new men" did not materialize, and Victory Province was left to fester. The officers were fired.

The free officers, somewhat embarrassed by their inexperience in economics and politics, originally made great efforts to co-opt the knowledge of the old elite. They encouraged old guard politicians to join the regime, courted foreign capitals, and restored good relations with the British.[163] The economy, nevertheless, remained stagnant. At the same time, Neguib tried to conciliate the Moslem Brotherhood, a radical group bent on turning Egypt into a truly Islamic state.

Those who participated in the original revolt hoped to enlighten the masses and spur them to action. Alas, the fatalism of the peasant, the conviction that any change was a change for the worse, prevailed even in the 1960s. In one study we interviewed approximately five thousand Arabs and asked them questions pertaining to their beliefs.

In response to the question "Will you have any influence in the changes that are taking place in the world nowadays, in daily life and society?" 59 percent of the peasants felt they would have no influence. Similarly, when asked "Can man change his destiny?" 74 percent of the traditional rural dwellers felt that their fate had already been preordained. Even among urban people only 56 percent believed they could effectively change their destiny.[164] Faced with such attitudes, the free officers could hardly be expected to change the society easily.

FROM REVOLT TO REVOLUTION

Politics

Frustrated in their attempts to change the society, the free officers altered their tactics and more energetically attacked the structure of Egyptian society itself.[165] In 1953 General Neguib, for example, attempted to introduce democracy to Egypt. He demanded the demilitarization of the government, the election of a parliament, and a popular vote on his own position as head of state. The rest of the free officers, led behind the scenes by Nasser, opposed his movement toward democratization on grounds that it would dissolve their attempted social and economic revolution.[166] During February 1954 Nasser experienced second thoughts about supporting Neguib. On his left, Nasser had to consider the urban-based Moslem Brotherhood, the Communists, and the Wafd (a vaguely socialist party). On his right, he still had to deal with the landowners and other rural, conservative groups within Egypt; his (or Neguib's) temporary alliance with them brought no tangible benefits. Nasser at first dismissed Neguib from his more important posts, then restored him, and then locked him up under house arrest. These various maneuvers were prompted by Nasser's concern with public opinion, which at that time overwhelmingly backed Neguib. Nasser soon realized that his control over urban military forces was far more important than Egypt's changeable public opinion.[167]

In fact, Nasser had decided to implement his revolution in the summer of 1954. In this case "revolution" is a difficult word to define since little had changed in the political, social, or economic institutions of Egypt. Nasser consolidated his military control of the nation; Faruk's successors disappeared from public view; the miniscule landowning class had already lost its property; and dissident groups (such as some officers in the police and the editors of *Al-Misr*) had been subdued. Nasser's only opponents were composed of urban leftists who demanded further decentralization of the control over the economy. Nasser complied.[168]

As in most revolutions, Nasser's rule entered its "Robespierre stage." He hung the more adamant of his right wing opponents and began a socialist transformation of Egyptian society. *He moved to the left politically, for the simple reason that he could eliminate a despised old order with relative ease and offer vast promises for a new society without having to fulfill them immediately.*[169]

The Aswan Dam project

The most ambitious project of the rebels was the creation of the Aswan High Dam, a massive structure designed to hold back the waters of the Nile, prevent floods, and provide water for both irrigation and the production of electrical power. After America refused aid, Egypt turned to Russia for assistance. Both money and technical advisers poured into the country. In addition, Nasser planned to reconstruct the Aswan province and called in a variety of social scientists to help in the transformation. We were assigned three tasks: (1) to rebuild the city of Aswan, (2) to transfer thousands of Nubians who would be flooded by the new waters of the dam to a safe area, and (3) to establish fourteen factories that would absorb skilled workers from the dam once the project was completed.

The group of social scientists could not anticipate the convoluted bureaucracy, Byzantine politics, the fear that permeated the rebel camp, and the fact that the urbanite rulers in Cairo knew little of peasant life.[170] Therefore we failed miserably. We succeeded only in convincing Nubians that they should leave their traditional land for a safer plateau. At first, all went smoothly until it was discovered that one minister in Cairo had canceled a crucial order for pumps submitted by another minister. The machinery was necessary for transferring water from the Nile to unirrigated areas where the Nubians had settled. When the water did not arrive, the transplanted people sparked a minor revolt and martial law had to be established.

Further, as indicated in chapter 1, it was found that the major occupation of the city dwellers was smuggling. To move them would have totally disrupted their trade route and left many bereft of income. Yet, it was difficult to report this fact to the rebel government in Cairo.

The Aswan Dam was completed, but it brought little surcease to the Egyptian population. Because of bureaucratic disputes, no one could decide just what to do with the accumulated water. The irrigation ministry wanted to use it in August (the most propitious time to water crops), while the electricity ministry wanted to peak the water in the winter months to generate the most power for Cairo's plants. Neither side won, and as a result the dam worked inefficiently as both a source of irrigation and of electric power.[171]

Economic strain

After his turn to the urban-based political left, Nasser had to face an accumulation of neglected problems, including the dam. His first five-year plan ended in June 1965; Egypt had run up some three billion dollars in foreign debts, and the economy showed signs of severe strain.[172]

Almost simultaneously, Egypt struggled with the problem of Israel. The devastating "six-day war" broke down Egypt's armed forces, destroyed much of its territory, and left it without many internal resources for development.[173]

In 1968 many of these problems came to a head. Egypt was finding itself involved with great internal difficulties while simultaneously engaged abroad in Yemen, Southern Arabia, Nigeria, the Congo, and Israel. Moreover, Western creditors called in their loans, and Egypt's relation with America, England, West Germany, and eventually Russia became problematic. If the Egyptian revolt was to succeed, three goals had to be accomplished:

1. Egypt could not succumb to its own propaganda about Israel, but instead had to follow a policy of moderation. In fact, Nasser sought cooperation with Israel. His immediate successor, Anwar el-Sadat, attempted to regain Arab territories without using the instrument of war.[174]

2. Neither Neguib, nor Nasser, nor el-Sadat actually faced the real sources of the nation's economic difficulties, its bureaucratic waste, and its population explosion.[175] Each man, tied to his urban background and

resultant mentality, tried to keep population growth to a minimal level, and engaged in grandiose projects to industrialize the nation by means such as building the Aswan Dam, steel plants, and a Fiat factory. Nonetheless, the population grew, and waste within the bureaucracy continued while Egyptian leaders privately admitted their helplessness.[176]

3. The new Egyptian leaders extended efforts to establish a democracy. Without an effective system of checks and balances, however, the old pashas continued to bleed the economic system.

Many factors worked against attempts to fulfill these goals. Israel, for example, destroyed Egypt's air force and much of its armored power in 1968. El-Sadat could no more solve the population problem than could Nasser: therefore, the economic problems of Egypt continued. In 1974, despite the supposed "opening of the society," the only visible result was a revolt of the students from both the left and the right wings.[177]

The most drastic and lasting failures of the regime came on the economic front. Nasser's original five-year plan (launched in 1960) was only a partial success. Agricultural production was reported to have increased by 40 percent in five years. Textile, chemical, petroleum, metallic, vehicle, and electrical industries also benefited.[178] Through nationalization of British, French, and Belgian interests after the Suez invasion, Egypt received a new influx of interest-free capital.

Life in Egypt: people and the bureaucracy

With the implementation of the five-year plan the people benefited from an extension of welfare services. Between 1960 and 1970 educational facilities grew at a rapid pace and some 80 percent of school children under the age of twelve attended school in 1973. Bilharziasis and trachoma, diseases ending in death or blindness, were virtually eliminated in people under the age of fifteen.[179]

Nevertheless, the government's lack of a coherent policy drastically hindered the fulfillment of its aims. In 1964, economic planners hoped that the national income would have increased by 50 percent. The average Egyptian family in 1974, however, still earned approximately the same income as it had earned a decade earlier.[180]

Bureaucratic rule

Essentially, as in so many developing nations, socialism in Egypt entailed the centralization of power in the hands of an urban bureaucracy. This was too often characterized by mismanagement, corruption, patronage, and apathy. For example:

1. The government bureaucracy, unchecked by public scrutiny or by market mechanisms, at times committed gross errors in judgment. In Cairo (1965) a newly approved twenty-story building leaned in the wind. Drastic architectural surgery removed the top nine floors and saved the structure from total collapse.[181] Coke ovens at the Helwan steel and iron factory were burned out by inexperienced engineers.[182] The Fiat plant, originally a government automobile monopoly, had to close its doors.[183]

In other words, no matter how noble its motives, the rebel government was not equipped to run modern industrial concerns. After eliminating the political right wing (which included many experienced Egyptian managers) the rebels had few persons to turn to for help. Thus, one lesson to be gleaned from this rebellion is that one should not eliminate the businessmen and technicians of an economy and hope to conduct a complicated system in an efficient manner.

2. Despite the honesty of Neguib, Nasser, and their major followers, corruption proceeded unchecked in Egypt. Depending upon one's position in the society, the corruption could be regarded as highly functional. That is, for privileged people at the

top of the economic scale it was always useful to get small favors granted—the buying of a visa, the selling of an automobile, the purchase of imported goods—if one paid off the right people. Indeed, after the revolt, Egypt had an entire group of people known as "accommodators" whose only function in life was to bribe the right persons. In 1975 el-Sadat continued to try to root out corruption.[184]

3. Centralization also often led to a paralysis of decision making. As already noted, the government could not decide what to do with its most majestic project, the Aswan Dam.

4. In an attempt to enforce egalitarianism, the government tried absolute control over the wages and movement of labor. On paper, in 1965, a college graduate received forty pounds a month, while even the prime minister received only three hundred sixty pounds.[185] In fact, however, a clever person in the Egyptian economy, particularly the professional man, found that he could hold three or more jobs simultaneously. His efficiency may be low, but his income remained relatively high. The wealthy, far from being eliminated, just scrambled more assiduously for their income and hid it more effectively from the tax inspector.

In addition, the government directed each person into a particular place of work; once there, the employee could be dismissed only with the greatest of difficulty. When this policy worked well, it had the obvious merit of channeling labor where it was most needed. Unfortunately, political "pull" and internal pressures within the bureaucracy really directed the flow of labor. Thus the ministry of land reform regularly hired four hundred college graduates a year even though the level of urbanization had rendered them useless.[186]

5. Perhaps one part of the failure of the Egyptian government was its inability to escape from its overwhelmingly urban mentality. The population problem serves as one example, since in this crucial area urban planners used methods (such as TV propaganda) that were totally inappropriate in those village regions where the problem lay—and where few homes possessed a television set. Thus, population growth proceeded unabated. Approximately eight hundred thousand children were born each year. Between 1913 and 1957 national income rose by 65 percent, but population increased by 100 percent. Between 1957 and 1970 national income went up by approximately 40 percent, and population increased by about 30 percent.[187] Thus, the average Egyptian of 1974 was in almost the same situation as his grandfather in 1913.

By 1976 Egypt had radically changed its political course and looked to the United States for economic and military aid. In spite of help from oil-rich nations, Egypt's economy was still faltering and the rate of urbanization continued unabated. Its unpaid foreign debts had risen to an astronomical level; its middle class prospered while the peasants continued to suffer; and the benefits of the Aswan Dam had been exhausted by population growth.

DISCUSSION: A REVOLUTION THAT FAILED?

In viewing the Egyptian revolt some years after its inception, one finds it difficult to reach a balanced judgment as to its impact. In some ways Egypt was changed drastically; in many other ways the country was little affected.

A great deal of convincing evidence could be amassed that proves the Egyptian revolt succeeded. The prime political goal of the free officers of 1952 was accomplished effortlessly, that is, the dethroning of King Faruk. A second explicit goal, ridding Egypt of imperialism, also was fulfilled in that the British did, however reluctantly, withdraw from control of the Suez Canal zone. Further, most British, French, and Belgian business interests were expropriated in 1956. Neguib and Nasser's third goal, a basic social and economic revitalization of the country leading to an eventual democracy, was continuously subverted by events, mistaken policies, and perhaps by the urban nature of the Egyptian leaders.

The objective faults in the regime should not be regarded as derogatory comments on Nasser's skill as a creative leader of the rebellion. For many years he carefully built a cadre of loyal free officers, he convinced a wavering national hero (General Neguib) to assume symbolic leadership, he maneuvered the traditionally oriented religious leaders to support his policies and, once he assumed power, became a powerful influence on world affairs. Just as other creative people, Nasser's own inner drives and abilities led him to become a hero in search of a role. Tragically, the vast problems of Egypt and the Arab world did not succumb so easily to his personal greatness as did the feeble political regime of King Faruk.

Thus, it would appear that Nasser's revolt was a tactical victory, but has thus far resulted in the loss, or continuation, of the strife involved in a successful revolution.

REVOLUTIONS IN PERSPECTIVE

Crane Brinton's classic study of the English, American, French, and Russian revolutions, *The Anatomy of Revolution,* clearly delineated the uniformity in their development in spite of historical idiosyncrasies. This is not to say that the peculiar circumstances of a social event such as a revolution should be ignored. Without Castro's switch to socialism the Cuban Revolution, for example, would hardly have taken the shape it did; without the resistance of Protestant leaders to creating a more equitable situation for Catholics, and the Irish Catholic spirit, Ulster might have lived in peace. Clearly those who lead revolutions do not operate in a social vacuum. Their successes or failures are conditioned by a set of historical, economic, and political circumstances.

Some of the crucial elements in a revolutionary situation are as follows:

Urbanization, as we have discussed in the context of reform movements and riots, creates a volatile social environment in which conflict is extended and intensified. The cases of Cuba, Ireland, and Egypt (as do those of Russia and France)[188] further underline this fact. Before their revolutions each nation experienced extremely rapid rates of urbanization. In each case new urban groups were created—army officers in Egypt, intellectuals in Cuba, industrial workers in Ireland—that played a crucial part in leading the revolution. Each of these groups had absorbed ideologies and had witnessed the breakdown of traditional social controls. Urbanization had also led to a growth in expectations, which were sporadically frustrated in the city environment.

Both the Cuban and the Ulster revolutions ocurred during periods of *urban-economic transition.* In Cuba the emergence of a new middle class and the decline in the sugar market broke the old patterns of economic dominance by landholding interests. The transition to urbanization and industrialization in Ireland began rather late in the history of Western Europe. The major thrust of industrialization and centralization of populations in Ireland came during World War II and continues today.

In the instance of the Egyptian revolution, urbanization had spawned the group that initiated the military coup against Faruk. Once in power, the attempts of the new leaders to speed up the modernization of the total society was due in large part to the external threat they experienced. Nasser and his advisers fully realized that their survival as a nation depended on their ability to hold off the urbane Israelites.

These same elements in urban life, however, have correlated with the growth of reform movements or the eruption of riots. And, indeed, reform movements and riots preceded the explosion of revolution in Cuba, Ulster, and Egypt. The issue remains: what unique elements in the situation led to the failure of, say, reform movements and the escalation of discontent into revolution? Judged by these three cases and by other historical evidence,[189] an urban revolution occurs when certain other elements are added to the situation.

Economic growth and disaster

Revolution would seem most likely to occur when a period of extended growth in urban areas is ended by a drastic economic reversal. At times the reversal is due to factors outside the control of the ruling group. Further, contrary to the prediction of Marx, Brinton has noted that "revolutions are not started by down and outers, by starving, miserable people."[190] Rather, they occur only when a new burgeoning class feel they have been held back by the ruling elite.

Following this pattern, Cuba prospered until a sudden fall in sugar prices; revolution was initiated by members of an urbane middle class that had been ascending the socioeconomic ladder. With control of the economy out of their reach, the middle class in Cuba took to politics for their outlet. Catholics in Ulster benefited from the provisions of the English welfare state, but found advancement blocked by Protestants. Ulster's pervasive caste system, the one-party government of Stormont, and a continuing separation from coreligionists condemned Catholics to an unchanged subordinate position both politically and socially. Egyptians had enjoyed the temporary prosperity of World War II and an artificial inflation of the price of cotton during the Korean war—then the bottom fell out of the economy. Leaders of the military (largely drawn from a second level of Egyptian society) led the attack on the monarchy and then attempted to change the total society. The vicious cycle of advancement (such as economic improvement followed by a downturn) embitters the newly formed urban middle classes against the old regime.

In each of the societies we have examined, the ruling elite discriminated against the potentially revolutionary group in a variety of ways. The type of discrimination ranged from the political repression of students in the pre-Castro days to the systematic exclusion of Ulster Catholics from the higher reaches of economic and political power. In Egypt, Faruk reserved the highest echelons of the general staff for members of the upper class.

Yet, the repression of the new urban classes was never quite systematic or total: the Cuban middle class had attained the presidency, a handful of Catholics were allowed to enter the Ulster parliament, and the Egyptian middle class were the officers of the military. Thus, the incomplete repression, coupled with continuing overt disadvantages, undoubtedly gave rise to feelings of great relative, rather than absolute, deprivation.

Desertion by the intellectuals

Brinton has noted that the signaling of the alienation and discontent of the people initially can be found in the desertion of the intellectuals.[191] From French writers of comedy to Russian authors of tragedy the intellectuals of the countries he examined turned against the ruling regime before its downfall. This is in contrast to reformists and rioters who maintain some faith in the viability of the ruling group.

Similarly, university faculties and students almost unanimously opposed Batista in Cuba. Irish Catholic leaders such as Bernadette Devlin refused to cooperate with Protestant or British authorities (although in many cases, Catholic intellectuals did not go so far as to endorse the activities of the IRA). In Egypt, of course, the intellectuals had long abandoned Faruk.

Desertion by the military

Since it monopolizes physical power, the position of the military in any regime is often crucial. In most instances, the military in a revolutionary situation either supports the insurrection or passively abstains from defending the old regime. In Russia the army turned against the Tsar; in China, Chiang's armies threw away their guns rather than fight the poorly armed Communists; in Cuba the Navy participated in its own abortive revolt; and in Egypt the army led the revolt. An army would appear to desert its leaders when it believes it has been subjected to an unfair military disaster or when the officer corps, as one segment of the urban secondary elite, believes it has been unjustly excluded from the corridors of power. In a few situations, of course, the army may remain loyal (such as the Protestant B Specials in Ireland) but simply may not possess sufficient power to crush the revolutionaries. Usually, however, a successful revolution requires the army's collaboration.

A tradition of violence

In all of the major world revolutions an historical tradition of resistance to the rulers was established long before actual revolution occurred. This was true in France (after its initial great revolution), in Russia (after the 1905 rebellion), and even in China (after the first downfall of the ancient regime). A period of prolonged violence, perhaps accustoming the people to the normality of violent change, precedes revolution.

In the examples presented, revolution would appear to have been part of a long-experienced civil violence. At times violence would even seem to have become part of the cultural heritage of the nation. Cuba, for example, has been suffering social strife since the downfall of the Spanish rule; its national hero, José Martí, embodied a revolutionary tradition. Ireland has long glorified its revolutionary leaders; the use of violence is an accepted part of its tradition. Egypt too has been subject to a long line of invaders. In modern times, invaders like Napoleon and the British represented conditions of violence to Egypt's sovereignty.

Frailty of the ruling elite

Characteristics of the ruling elite should also be noted in any analysis of the revolutionary process. One part of the setting for revolution has been found in the general inefficiency of the old regime.[192] For example, the old regime usually has failed to develop new means for adopting the economy to more modern conditions and has failed to exercise its taxation powers in an equitable way. Further, as Brinton noted, "the government's hold over its own troops is poor or of a previous militia, and the old gives place to the new."[193] Cubans, Egyptians, and residents of Ulster suffered from the inefficiency of the ruling class. Moreover, Batista's army had no desire to engage the rag-taggle guerrillas in the mountains. In Ireland the Protestant B Specials could not cope with the urban revolutionaries and the English exacerbated the situation through their treatment of the Catholic rebels. Faruk's power was destroyed after the Egyptian army was beaten by the more efficient Israelites.

Other regimes faced with potential revolution have proved sufficiently flexible to abandon some of their traditions and defuse the discontent. England's gradual admission of new urban classes to the political process and even to the House of Lords during the eighteenth and nineteenth centuries serves as a prime example.

Intervention by a third force

Brinton's analysis of revolutionary form clearly emphasized internal contradictions that developed. In an era of jet travel and instantaneous communication, however, perhaps the role of outside forces also should be considered. In different ways each of the revolutions we described was decisively influenced by the intervention of outside forces: the Americans and Russians in Cuba, the British in Ulster, and Israel in the instance of Egypt. From the examples we have provided, it is suggested that third party intervention may encourage or even prolong revolutionary activity; in some cases it provides a symbolic enemy that serves to unify the revolutionary forces. In some cases—

America's failure to aid Batista or the refusal of England to defend Faruk—the *absence* of intervention may help a revolution.

Stages in the revolution

Once an old regime is overthrown, Brinton noted, the revolution proceeds through a series of four stages: the moderate, the extremist, convalescence, and a return to the status quo. Each stage carries the seeds of its own destruction and can be short-lived. The *moderate* period (such as the short-lived Kerensky regime in Russia), Brinton concluded, is an inherently precarious position because the leaders may be identified with the old system. Unwilling to use terror to introduce reform, the moderates are opposed by radicals to their left. The *extremist* period in Brinton's analysis, on the other hand, is the era of the guillotine and concentration camps. Powerful enemies, either internal or external, push the extremists to a greater centralization of power during this time, and the government intrudes itself in even the most common activities of the citizenry.

The extremist period is followed by a period of *convalescence* when people return to their daily lives. Former rebels against the new regime may achieve amnesty during this period, and a type of casual gaiety appears. Governmental pressures against the people are relaxed. Finally, the revolutionists accept many repentant members. Thus the course of revolution, as Brinton saw it, moves from right to left and then swings back again. As to the final outcome of the revolutionary process, Brinton contended that "some new and useful tracks or courses in the network of interaction that makes society have been established, some old and inconvenient ones—you may call them unjust if you like—have been eliminated."[194] Cuba, Ireland, and Egypt confirmed this generalization.

The success of a revolution can largely be attributed to whether the leaders can adapt their urban mentality to the particular conditions of their nation. Nasser's revolution, for example, partially failed because its leaders attempted to use urban solutions to problems of the countryside (such as population control). China's Mao and Chou, sons of rich families who were given a highly sophisticated urban education, wisely abandoned many of their preconceptions (such as the belief that an urban proletariat should lead a revolution) and turned instead to the peasantry for support. A variety of other factors—aid from an outside power (as in Egypt and Cuba), the stability of economic conditions, efficient propaganda—vitally affect the durability of the new regime.

SUMMARY

Urban revolutions occur because of the very processes unleashed by urbanization itself. They turn into total insurrections when a combination of several other factors are added to the volatile mixture of city life:

1. The economy spirals upward and then falls disastrously and abruptly.
2. The ruling elite discriminates against a large, but new, rising urban group—but fails to do so with full suppression.
3. The intellectuals and the military both abandon the old regime.
4. The nation suffers from a tradition of civil violence.
5. The old elite acts in an inefficient, corrupt, or irrational manner.
6. An outside force intervenes in the situation—either by aiding the revolutionaries, abstaining from helping the old regime that had counted on foreign aid, or by providing a scapegoat irrevocably linked in the public mind with the policies of the old rulers.

Revolutions, as Brinton pointed out, pass through predictable stages, usually "eating up their own children." Once a revolutionary regime is successful, its stability depends on the leaders' ability to adapt their urban mentalities to newly emerging conditions.

Revolutions, riots, and reform movements have become an ineluctable part of the urban landscape. The rich variety of their emergence, form, and outcome is, of course, conditioned by unique historical factors. One could not conceive of the Ulster conflict, for example, without considering the enduring hatred of Protestants and Catholics; one could not picture a riot such as Watts without some acquaintance with the history of slavery in the United States; one could hardly understand the relatively peaceful Meiji reformation without some characterization of the Tokugawa regime. History is complex, influenced by individuals, twisted by unforeseen events: we have tried through describing some of our own experiences and the experiences of others to illustrate the vagaries of social conflict. Yet the goal of social science is to bring some sense out of the chaos of individual events. In chapter 8 we undertake the task of linking together the seemingly inevitable progress of urbanization with the omnipresent fact of social conflict.

Issues for further discussion

1. What common pattern of causation underlies the revolutions in Cuba, Northern Ireland, and Egypt?

2. Under what conditions can revolutionaries fulfill their goals?

3. Why does a reform movement or a riot turn into a revolution?

4. If you were chief of the ruling class opposing a revolution—let us say, the British prime minister governing Northern Ireland—what measures would you undertake to defuse a potential revolution? Why?

5. How does urbanization lead to conditions that may incite a revolution?

6. What is the role of intellectuals in a revolutionary situation? In a riot? In a reform movement?

7. In a successful revolution, what is the usual role of the army? How can armies be "politicized"?

8. In what ways does the ruling elite of a particular area contribute to a revolutionary situation?

9. Considering other revolutionary situations than those discussed in this chapter, what contributed to their success or failure?

10. Is America ripe for a revolution? Why or why not?

FOOTNOTES

1. Hart L. Phillips, *Cuba: Island of Paradox* (New York: Ivan Obelensky, 1959), p. 4.
2. Ibid., p. 63.
3. See Oden Meeker, "Cuba Under Batista: More Apathy than Disaffection," *The Reporter* (September 1954).
4. Reported in Loree A. R. Wilkerson, *Fidel Castro's Political Program: From Reformism to Marxist-Leninism*, series 2, no. 1 (Fainville, Fla.: Center for Latin American Studies, University of Florida Press, 1965), p. 12.
5. Ramón Eduardo Ruiz, *Cuba: The Making of a Revolution* (Boston: The University of Massachusetts Press, 1968), p. 10.
6. Wilkerson, *Castro's Program*, p. 12.
7. Theodore Draper, *Castro's Revolution: Myths and Realities* (New York: Frederick A. Praeger, Inc., Publishers, 1962), p. 22.
8. Ruiz, *Making of a Revolution*, table on p. 11.
9. Ibid, p. 12.
10. Quoted in Phillips, *Cuba: Island of Paradox*, p. 264.
11. Jules Dubois, *Fidel Castro* (New York: Bobbs-Merrill Co., 1959), p. 26.
12. Wilkerson, *Castro's Program*, p. 18.
13. Ruiz, *Making of a Revolution*.
14. See Dubois, *Fidel Castro*.
15. Ibid.
16. Ibid., p. 94.
17. "Hit and Run Revolt," *Time* (Dec. 1956).
18. In Feb. 1957 Herbert Mathews of the *New York Times* published articles and pictures that indicated Castro's survival. See Draper, *Castro's Revolution: Myths and Realities*, p. 40.
19. Phillips, *Island of Paradox*, p. 29.
20. Ibid, p. 309.
21. "Cuba: The First Year of a Rebellion," *Time* (9 December 1957), p. 43.
22. "2 Cuban Rebels Killed in Clash," *New York Times*, 9 December 1957, p. 25.
23. Ibid., p. 43.
24. See Crane Brinton, *The Anatomy of Revolution* (New York: Vintage Books, 1962).
25. "What Cuba's Rebels Want," reprinted in *Nation* 185 (30 November 1957): 399–400.

26. Ibid.
27. "Why We Fight," *Coronet* (10 February 1958).
28. Ibid.
29. Leo Huberman and Paul M. Sweezy, *Cuba: Anatomy of a Revolution* (New York: Monthly Review Press, 1961), pp. 61–62.
30. Phillips, *Island of Paradox,* p. 39.
31. "Cuba Under Castro and the U.S.," *Newsweek* (12 January 1959), p. 42.
32. Phillips, *Island of Paradox,* p. 397.
33. "Cuba Under Castro and the U.S."
34. Ibid.
35. Leo Huberman and Paul M. Sweezy, *Cuba: Anatomy of a Revolution,* p. 84.
36. Phillips, *Cuba: Island of Paradox.*
37. Carlton Beal, "As Cuba Sees It," *Nation* (Jan. 1969).
38. "What Next for Cuba and Its Hero," *Newsweek* (19 January 1959), pp. 42–43.
39. "A Verdict, A Triumph, and Trouble," *Life* (2 February 1959), p. 24.
40. Jean Paul Sartre, *Sartre on Cuba* (New York: Ballantine Books, 1961).
41. *U.S. News and World Report,* vol. 43, no. 33 (Jan. 1959).
42. "What Next for Cuba and Its Hero."
43. Huberman and Sweezy, *Cuba: Anatomy of a Revolution,* p. 110.
44. Draper, *Castro's Revolution: Myths and Realities,* p. 43.
45. Ibid., p. 23.
46. Ruiz, *Making of a Revolution,* p. 12.
47. Ibid., p. 67.
48. Ibid., p. 75.
49. Draper, *Castro's Revolution: Myths and Realities,* p. 10.
50. *Pensamiento Politics, Economics y Social de Fidel Castro* (Havana: Editorial Lex., 1959), pp. 44–45.
51. See Draper, *Castro's Revolution: Myths and Realities.*
52. Wilkerson, *Castro's Program,* p. 55.
53. Ibid., p. 68.
54. See Draper, *Castro's Revolution: Myths and Realities.*
55. Ibid.
56. Ibid.
57. Ibid.
58. See, for example, Robert Divine, ed., *The Cuban Missile Crisis* (Chicago: Quadrangle Books, 1971).
59. Ruiz, *Making of a Revolution,* especially chap. 2.
60. See William McCord, *Mississippi: The Long Hot Summer* (New York: W. W. Norton & Co., 1965).
61. Ruiz, *Making of a Revolution,* p. 11.
62. Ted Morgan, "Cuba," *New York Times Magazine,* 1 December 1974, p. 27.
63. Ibid.
64. Ibid.
65. See Bernadette Devlin, *The Price of My Soul* (London: Pan Special, 1969).
66. The *Sunday Times* Insight Team, *Ulster* (Harmondsworth, Middlesex, England: Penguin Books, 1972), p. 23.
67. See Liam de Paor, *Divided Ulster* (Harmondsworth, Middlesex, England: Penguin Books, 1970).
68. Personal observation, William McCord, 1972.
69. *Sunday Times* Insight Team, *Ulster.*
70. See Devlin, *Price of my Soul.*
71. See Donald S. Connery, *The Irish* (New York: Simon and Schuster, 1968), chap. 5.
72. See Andrew Boyd, *Holy War in Belfast* (Dublin: Anvil Books, 1971), chap. 10.
73. Ibid.
74. Devlin, *Price of my Soul.*
75. Liam de Paor, *Divided Ulster.*
76. See Human Relations Council, *The Forum,* Belfast (Spring 1974).
77. Ibid.
78. *Sunday Times* Insight Team, *Ulster.*
79. Ibid.
80. Ibid.
81. Personal interview with Richard Walsh, *The Irish Times* (Aug. 1972).
82. Liam de Paor, *Divided Ulster.*
83. Ibid.
84. Cameron Commission, "Disturbances in Northern Ireland," Report of the commission appointed by the governor of Northern Ireland (1969), para. 22, 28.
85. Quoted in *Sunday Times* Insight Team, *Ulster,* p. 43.
86. Ibid, p. 44.
87. Ibid.
88. Personal interview with Mrs. Betty Sinclair, a leader of the march, 12 April 1972.
89. Ibid.
90. Petition, Queen's University students, 5 October 1968.
91. This was possibly printed by the Ulster Constitution Defense Committee although no acknowledgement could be found. It was distributed in Armagh.
92. See Irish Television archive pictures of the march.
93. Personal interview with Major Ronald Bunting, commander of the Ulster Protestant Volunteers, 30 November 1968.
94. Devlin, *Price of my Soul.*
95. Public speech by Major Ronald Bunting, Derry, 1 December 1968.

96. Devlin, *Price of my Soul.*
97. Eammon McCann, quoted in *Burntrolly,* pamphlet (Londonderry), p. 19.
98. Devlin, *Price of my Soul.*
99. Ibid.
100. Cited by the Cameron Commission, "Disturbances in Northern Ireland."
101. *Sunday Times* Insight Team, *Ulster,* p. 76.
102. See, Liam de Paor, *Divided Ulster.*
103. Cameron Commission, "Disturbances in Northern Ireland," p. 38.
104. Ibid.
105. Personal interview, 12 April 1972.
106. *Sunday Times* Insight Team, *Ulster,* p. 22.
107. Ibid.
108. Ibid., p. 109.
109. See *Financial Times,* London, 6 August 1969.
110. Ibid.
111. See *Irish Times,* Dublin, 10 December 1969.
112. See Andrew Boyd, *Holy War in Belfast.*
113. Ibid.
114. See, for example, Liam de Paor, *Divided Ulster.*
115. Personal interview with Belfast IRA leader August 1972.
116. *Sunday Times* Insight Team, *Ulster.*
117. Ibid., p. 270.
118. Ibid., p. 272.
119. Ibid., p. 269.
120. Ibid., p. 252.
121. Ibid., p. 253.
122. Ibid., p. 256.
123. Ibid., p. 269.
124. Ibid., p. 352.
125. Liam de Paor, *Divided Ulster,* p. 354.
126. Personal interview with General Robert Ford, 16 August 1972.
127. *Sunday Times* Insight Team, *Ulster,* p. 269.
128. Personal interview with Belfast IRA leader, 20 August 1972.
129. Gail Sheehy, "The Fighting Women of Ireland," *New York Times,* 13 March 1972, p. 50.
130. Personal interview with General Robert Ford, 16 August 1972.
131. Frank Lagan, quoted in the *New York Times,* 15 March 1972, p. 27.
132. James Chapman, quoted in the *New York Times,* 24 February 1972, p. 10.
133. Rev. Edward Daly, quoted in the *New York Times,* 24 February 1972, p. 32.
134. *The Widgery Report* (19 April 1972) cited in the *New York Times,* 25 April 1972, p. 25.
135. Ibid.
136. Lord Widgery, quoted in the *New York Times,* 25 April 1972, p. 10.
137. Donald Connery, *The Irish,* see chap. 3.
138. Ibid.
139. See Jean et Simone Lacouture, *L'Égypte en Mouvement* (Paris: Editions du Seuil, 1962).
140. See Charles Issawi, *Egypt in Revolution* (London: Oxford University Press, 1963), chap. 5.
141. Ibid.
142. Ibid.
143. See Tom Little, *Egypt* (London: Ernest Benn, 1958), chap. 12.
144. Ibid., chap. 13.
145. Ibid., chap. 14, and Gamal Abdel Nasser, *The Philosophy of the Revolution* (Cairo, Egypt: Govt. Press, 1957).
146. Lacouture, *L'Égypte en Mouvement.*
147. Little, *Egypt,* chap. 15.
148. Ibid.
149. Anwar el-Sadat, broadcast of 23 July 1952, Cairo.
150. Little, *Egypt,* p. 198.
151. Ibid., p. 217.
152. Lacouture, *L'Égypte en Mouvement.*
153. Ibid.
154. Little, *Egypt.*
155. Bernard Lewis, *The Middle East and the West* (Bloomington, Ind.: Indiana University Press, 1964) presents the social and political background that prompted this conservatism.
156. Issawi, *Egypt in Revolution.*
157. Little, *Egypt,* chap. 14.
158. Lacouture, *L'Égypte en Mouvement.*
159. See William Polk, *The United States and the Arab World* (Cambridge, Mass.: Harvard University Press, 1965).
160. Personal communication with officers, later retired, who administered the province.
161. Ibid.
162. See *France-Observateur,* 1 November 1956, and Lacouture, *L'Égypte en Mouvement,* "La Reforme Agraire."
163. Little, *Egypt,* chap. 15.
164. William McCord and Abdulla Lutfiyya, "Urbanization and World View in the Middle East," in *Essays on Modernization of Under-Developed Societies,* ed. A. R. Desai (Bombay, India: Thacker and Co., 1972).
165. Jacques Berque, *Les Arabes d'Hier a Demain* (Paris: Editions du Seuil, 1960).
166. See Gen. Mohammed Neguib, *Egypt's Destiny* (Cairo, Egypt: Govt. Press, 1954).
167. See editorials in *Al-Misri* and *Rose el-Yousef,* Cairo (1954).
168. Little, *Egypt,* p. 233.
169. William Polk, *Arab World.*
170. Philip Dorn, "Stalemate in Egypt," *Peace News,* 9 July 1965.
171. Ibid.

172. Ibid.
173. Ibid.
174. See David Holden, " 'Hero of the Crossing,' they shout, 'Where is our breakfast?' " *New York Times Magazine*, 1 June 1974.
175. Ibid.
176. Ibid.
177. According to *Le Monde*, students at both the University of Cairo and Alexandria rioted for different causes (Aug. 1974).
178. Dorn, "Stalemate in Egypt."
179. Holden, "Hero of the Crossing."
180. Ibid.
181. Personal observation, William McCord, 1 April 1965.
182. Personal observation, William McCord, 1 April 1965.
183. Dorn, "Stalemate in Egypt."
184. Holden, "Hero of the Crossing."
185. Dorn, "Stalemate in Egypt."
186. Holden, "Hero of the Crossing."
187. Statistical Dept., *Annwaire Statistique*, Cairo (1975).
188. See, for example, any of the standard accounts of the Russian, French, German, and Italian revolutions.
189. Ibid.
190. Brinton, *Anatomy of Rèvolution*, p. 264.
191. Ibid.
192. Ibid.
193. Ibid.
194. Ibid.

SUGGESTED READINGS

Crane Brinton, *The Anatomy of Revolution* (New York: Vintage Books, 1962), and Lyford P. Edwards, *The Natural History of Revolution*, Heritage of Sociology Edition (Chicago: University of Chicago Press, 1970) remain classic works in the analysis of history's most important revolutions.

For more information on Cuba see Hart L. Phillips, *Cuba: Island of Paradox* (New York: Ivan Obelensky, 1959), and for a different point of view, Jean-Paul Sartre, *Sartre on Cuba* (New York: Ballantine Books, 1961). *Masses in Latin America* (New York: Oxford University Press, 1970), ed. Irving Louis Horowitz, contains many well presented cases of social change in Brazil, Peru, Mexico, Argentina, Central ica, and Cuba.

Personal descriptions of the Irish situation may be found in Bernadette Devlin, *The Price of My Soul* (London: Pan Special, 1969), and Liam de Paor, *Divided Ulster* (Harmondsworth, Middlesex, England: Penguin Books, 1970).

Dispassionate explanations of the Egyptian revolt are contained in Jean et Simone Lacouture, *L'Égypte en Mouvement* (Paris: Editions du Seuil, 1962) and Charles Issawi, *Egypt in Revolution* (London: Oxford University Press, 1963).

See Richard Ned Lebow, *White Britain and Black Ireland* (Philadelphia: Institute for the Study of Human Issues, 1976) for an eloquent description of colonization policies as they affected both Ireland and Egypt.

chapter 8

Urban social conflict: conclusions

Sickness of American Society does not reside in the existence of problems; it rests in the nation's incapacity to deal effectively with them.

Arthur Schlesinger

Although there are many dedicated urbanites who remain in the city to enjoy "the good life," urban dwellers around the United States and the world have expressed concern with the quality of their lives. The specific issues that make up the concerns, however, differ. In Sweden the problems of environment, the individual's control over personal destiny in an organized society, and a general dissatisfaction pervade complaints.[1] Parisians disdainfully describe the rhythm of life created by the construction of "concrete jungles" in parts of their city, as, "Metro, boulot, dodo," (translated, "subway, job, sleep").[2] Urban Americans of the 1970s have replaced their fears and concerns of the 1960s with worries about fiscal pressures and concern about safety on the streets.[3]

In each instance the concept of quality of urban existence remains ambiguous. The term would appear to be determined by the impact of physical environment; however, the concern also could be interpreted to be the social organization that emerges in most cities. Each of the complaints suggests the necessity of exploring different types of solutions. It is the purpose of this chapter not only to summarize the material that has been presented, but to examine some of the questions implied by the concept of "quality of urban life." Regardless of the specific complaint posited by individuals, there are few, if any, problems that can be understood solely on the basis of immediate exigencies such as economic recession. It is usually necessary to provide an historical perspective as well as conceptions of some idealized or predicted future in the discussion of present problems.

DESCRIPTIONS OF THE CITY

In their assessment of the city during the first part of the twentieth century, Georg Simmel and Louis Wirth described their conceptions of the prevailing "quality of life."[4] They described the anonymity and impersonality associated with the frequency of secondary relationships in cities, the growth of impersonal mechanisms of control, and the provision of services through the mammoth bureaucratic machinery. Competitiveness inspired by commerce also was viewed as characteristic of the urban setting, and these sociopsychological mental states were thought to result in a lack of trust and suspiciousness of unknown "others."

There is little quarrel with the description of life in the city provided by these early sociologists. More recent work has suggested that in addition to these characteristics, other, perhaps more positive, characteristics can be added. Inkeles, for example, noted the autonomy exercised by most urban, as compared to rural, residents.[5] He also noted the optimism concerning their ability to control their environment as characteristic of most urban dwellers.

McCord and Lutfiyya's study of urban dwellers in the Middle East suggests that the lessons of the city are not learned immediately or at one time; hence, a diversity of attitudes is found in cities where migration is an ongoing process.[6]

While these descriptions provide information about dimensions of the urban milieu, there remain implicit questions pertaining to the linkage of psychological attitudes created by urbanity and social facts. For example, what effect does the rapidity of demographic change have on the attitudes and behavior of urban dwellers? How do migrants learn to cope with the lessons of the city? What are the factors related to the emergence of groups of people who exercise power in urban areas? What are the factors related to the form and intensity of conflict experienced in urban settings?

Population shifts and the physical environment

In chapter 1 we presented some facts about the rate of urbanization around the world. These facts, combined with those in chapter 3 for United States cities, suggest that the problems of concern to urban dwellers will continue for some time.

Within the United States, for example, a recent leveling of migration to urban centers has been recorded.[7] There has been some indication that minority group members are slowly dispersing into suburban residential areas.[8] Moreover, a movement of a few former urbanites toward relatively uninhabited regions of the country has been reported.[9] Attempts also have been made by many urban planners and developers to draw middle-class families back into the city.[10] In spite of these indicators, there is little evidence that implies optimism regarding the cessation of "problems."

Rapid growth of any area places a heavy strain on the existing resources and conditions of life in terms of housing, water, education, transportation, and sewage. Given the possibility of economic expansion, however, the strain on the city and the newly arrived migrant need not deteriorate into a permanent condition. In fact, given these conditions, individuals and groups probably will experience success in their search for a better life. Such was the case for many groups of migrants to American cities in the late nineteenth and early twentieth centuries.[11]

More recent migrants have not been as fortunate as their predecessors. In spite of statistics that indicate urban migration patterns have altered, there remains a large population of people confronted with few hopes for success in the foreseeable future. Census figures demonstrate that the gap between urban and suburban dwellers has increased within the past decade. Whereas the median income among families in central cities grew from $5,950 in 1960 to $11,379 in 1974, the median income for families in the outlying portion of metropolitan areas increased from $6,707 to $14,056 during the same period. In other words, between 1960 and 1974 the gap in income between urbanites and suburbanites grew from $767 to $2,677.[12]

The problem for many urban centers in American cities is the concentration of poor members of society. The move of industrial firms and the more affluent to outlying areas means the removal of taxes. Hence, combined with little prospect for massive industrial growth in the future, the demand for jobs and services (ranging from welfare, housing, health care, and education to garbage collection and police protection) cannot be met easily. The quality of life in the city and the resultant urban milieu apparently will not have been altered from the somewhat dismal picture portrayed by Wirth and Simmel. Rather, the current issues confronting people in many urban areas indicate a threat to the optimism relayed in the Inkeles description of modern or urban man. For many the opportunity of industrial expansion may have passed.[13]

Innovation, however, has been a hallmark of the urban setting. As we have noted, the reform of specific institutions—prisons, mental hospitals, and education—as well as entire societies has sprung from the minds and work of urban dwellers. Perhaps it is not overly optimistic to propose that the solutions to current problems may be forthcoming.[14]

The social environment: coping

The state of the physical environment and factors such as the quantity of migration and density of population from our point of view are most significant in terms of their effect on the social environment. The social environment for an individual consists of the personal relationships developed. These relationships can serve as buffers and help the migrant to cope with the strains inherent in relocating not only place of residence but identity as well.

With the possible exception of Mexican-Americans who already lived in the border states[15] and American Indians,[16] migrants have arrived at their destination in the United States with a mixture of anxiety, insecurity, hope, and optimism.[17] These emotions were described by S. N. Eisenstadt in his study of Jewish immigrants to Palestine and Israel.[18]

The emotions experienced by immigrants are not unexpected. Lifelong friends, family, familiar surroundings, and even language and culture are often left behind. Once in the new environment the immigrant also commonly encounters hostility, frustration, ridicule, and even outright rejection.[19] Yet, most of them persist, upheld perhaps by their optimism rather than the reality of their experiences. This attitude is poignantly expressed in an essay submitted to a competition organized by the Committee for Immigrants in America in 1916. It acknowledges that for some the immigration to the United States meant "a fairy promised land that came out true, or a land which gives human rights, a land that gives morality through her churches and education through her free schools and libraries."[20]

Most recent migrants to urban centers in developing countries and the industrialized nations share the sense of insecurity and heightened expectations of the older generation of migrants.[21] Urban centers are held to be the land of promise for many people who were raised in the small towns and rural sections of the world. The move promises a mode of escaping persecution or racism, diminished opportunity, and boredom.[22]

In the past, the heightened expectation was relayed to those who had remained behind through personal correspondence or the arrival of money from members of the family who had migrated.[23] Today, mass media and some degree of education operate to create expectations, however illusory, pertaining to life in the city. The interplay of the level of these expectations and the frustrations encountered have been suggested by our cases to play a role in the emergence of collective action.

Before summarizing the role of expectations and other factors involved in the development of social conflict, the formation of groups in the urban setting should be reassessed. On the one hand, these groups serve as the vehicle of coping with the new environment, thus alleviating personal conflict; on the other, they may, under specifiable conditions, promote social conflict.

Buffer groups. Immigrants, old and new, have been aided in their adjustment to cities by persons with whom they could identify. In the United States, for example, immigrants from one place did not all come at the same time. Therefore, the earliest immigrants helped to organize more recent immigrants. German immigrants organized their self-help programs as early as 1800; Irish agencies could be found in every seaport on the Atlantic coast by 1850.[24] Similarly, the Pan-Hellenic Union, the Lithuanian mutual benefit society, the Polish National Alliance, and the Italian Immigrant Aid Society all contributed to the adjustment of their people. The nature of the aid afforded by these organizations is expressed in a description of the Pan Hellenic Union by the Report of the Massachusetts Commission on Immigrants written in 1914:

> In addition to the payment of sick and death benefits the Union has outlined a comprehensive program of bettering the conditions of Greeks in America by creating a spirit of self-help, by protecting the Greek immigrants and laborers, by aiding in the furtherance of the political ambitions of their much loved mother country and, at the same time, by instilling in the Greeks of the United States veneration and affection for the laws and institutions of America.[25]

The tide of European emigration to the United States reversed as Europe was drawn into World War I (1914–18), and black migrants were urged to move North to provide labor for industries. More than fifty thousand black people moved to Chicago between 1910 and 1920. The exodus from the South was so rapid that efforts were made by southern states such as Florida, Georgia, Alabama, and Mississippi to halt the movement through the imposition of fines and the licensing of recruiters.[26] The Urban League was created in 1917, and other organizations such as the YMCA and the YWCA also set out to "train the peasant folk in the ways of urban life."[27]

Ethnicity, nationality, religion, and other characteristics of identification, then, served to bind groups of individuals. The process was facilitated by ecological factors. That is, individual migrants not only were aided by formal organizations, but more commonly turned for help to members of their extended family or friends from "home" who had preceded them. As we have noted, similar language and eating habits also tended to draw persons together.[28]

Rural black Americans migrated to northern cities largely during the twentieth century.[29] Although they spoke English, they too gravitated first to those areas of the city where rent was cheap and friends were available.[30] The concentration of black people has grown in most major American cities such as Chicago, Los Angeles, New York, and Detroit. Competition for space, cheap housing, and the blockage of movement out of certain areas of the city have led to the development of black ghettos. The history of the growth of these segregated areas differs little by locale. It has been most completely chronicled in Chicago by Drake and Cayton.[31] As we have noted, however, unlike earlier migrants, black and other racially visible minorities have suffered a special, common fate:

> If individuals within [a ghetto] are able to change the telltale marks of poverty, name, foreign language, or distinctive customs, they may move out and lose themselves in middle-class, native-born neighborhoods. This, Negroes wearing the badge of color, cannot do. Negro areas must either expand as parts of a constantly growing Black Belt, or stagnate as deteriorating slums.[32]

In summary, economic and social factors interact to concentrate migrants of similar ethnicity. Communities, once founded, may initially serve as a buffer; eventually, however, they may also serve as prison.[33]

A paradigm developed by S. N. Eisenstadt[34] for the study of comparative migration suggests that another factor must be considered in the adjustment of migrants: "[the] institutionalization of migrant behavior with particular reference to the adaptation of new roles and the emergence of new leaders." The specific mechanism of adaptation, however, has differed for various groups of migrants.

Literacy provided one tool for the adjustment to urban society. Those groups possessing a literate tradition (even though they came from predominantly rural environments or spoke a different language) have found it a means of obtaining some degree of success in most nations. Thus, the Japanese (usually of the peasant class) who came to the United States possessed not only a heritage of familial and national solidarity but benefited also from the series of reforms that provided a high level of literacy in Meiji Japan by 1890. Literacy and a stress on education have been used as tools for relative social mobility in the United States despite a racial badge and an otherwise foreign cultural background.[35]

The valuation of literacy may be interpreted as a subdimension of an orientation toward achievement. Bernard C. Rosen[36] has documented with empirical evidence some differences in motivational values and educational-occupational aspirations between Greeks, French Canadians, Italians, blacks, and white Protestants. He concludes:

> . . . achievement motivation is more characteristic of Greeks, Jews, and white Protestants than of Italians and French Canadians.[37]

The differences between the groups were attributed to socialization practices, traditions, and life experiences. The findings also supported Rosen's observation of the rapidity with which Greeks, Jews, and Protestants have obtained middle-class status.[38]

Cultural shuttling demonstrates another mode of coping with the urban environment and the diversity of urban experiences by different groups. In some societies, certain groups have established a heritage as "migrant" urbanites. They come to the cities for a period of time to make their fortune and then return to a village environment. Today, many of these migratory urban men bring with them skills that help them adjust to the urban setting. They never totally absorb or experience conflict with urban values.

At least three groups can be cited as cultural shuttlers: the Nubians in Egypt,[39] the Mohawk Indians in Brooklyn,[40] and many New York Puerto Ricans.[41] Nubians have long followed a tradition in which the men go to Cairo or Alexandria to work as servants, learn the language of the city, and then return after approximately five years to their original families in the desert. The Mohawk Indian men live in Brooklyn and return to their wives and families in Canada on weekends or during periods of nonwork. Many Puerto Ricans come to New York City to work as skilled or semiskilled labor and return periodically to their families on the island. In large part this phenomenon is facilitated by the ease with which movement is possible between Puerto Rico and the mainland of the United States.

Shuttling suggests a number of interpretations about migration not usually considered by those who study populations on the move. First, it suggests the flexibility of some people to adapt to different cultures. Second, in some instances cultural shuttling also negates the assumption of a necessary conflict between rural and urban existence. Further, it indicates the complexity of describing urbanites and their problems of adjustment or acculturation. Perhaps the question of adjustment is most germane to those concerned with the formation of consensus in society through the internalization of values.[42]

Previous experiences in urban areas of many successful migrants have facilitated their adjustment. The Jews in the United States,[43] the Chinese from Yunan (now scattered from Hong Kong to San Francisco),[44] and the Ibos in Nigeria[45] all arrived at their eventual point of destination with experiences in preindustrial or industrial urban environments.

As discussed in chapter 2, however, urbanity is an attitude that has invaded the ideas and experiences of most rural residents in industrialized countries. The idea of women obtaining equity in pay and working conditions in the coal mining regions of the United States and the entry of civil rights workers into Mississippi support the notion that urbane attitudes can be relayed vicariously.

Two important instruments of socialization are schools[46] and television.[47] Both are ubiquitous in industrial societies; both also can create options through relaying information beyond an individual's immediate experiences. The socialization effected by the schools tends, for the most part, to concentrate on maintaining traditional values.[48] The mass media, on the other hand, has been analyzed in terms of both its legitimation and delegitimation effect.[49] In the first instance the media has been viewed as a means of disseminating reality as it is defined by decision makers.[50] Molotch and Lester, however, have shown that events such as the Santa Barbara oil spill may be interpreted by an insurgent political group (i.e., environmentalists) as access to the media for presentation of an "alternative" interpretive framework of social events (e.g., oil companies are acting against the public interest by exploiting the environment).[51] Such groups may even create events to deliberately pressure the media to present divergent viewpoints.[52]

In summary, almost any point of identification that serves to unify loyalties can result in conflict. When scarce resources are threatened (territory, jobs, or education) or ideological differences emerge and clash, existing bonds designating the "in group" and the "outsiders" are clearly drawn.

CONFLICT

Conflict in the form of reform movements, riots, or revolutions stems from urban areas where collectivities share similar sets of ideas and have at least the rudiments of some social bonds with others.[53]

The form and intensity conflict takes depend on several factors: (1) the degree of isolation of a particular group from participation in the broader society; (2) the economic state of the society; (3) the gap between expectations and the real attainment of a population; (4) the existence and role of a secondary elite in society; (5) the role of a third-party influence; and (6) the history of violence.

The degree of isolation of groups

Strife within urban areas of a substantive, cultural, or ideological nature can be expected when a segment of the population is restrained from participation in the broader society. The range of participation for different groups spans complete integration to separatism. In complete integration the interaction between peoples is free within all institutional spheres. Separatism denotes the development of parallel institutions that require no interaction. The free participation of persons of Northern European backgrounds in all American institutions at all levels represents complete integration; the Amish in Pennsylvania[54] and the blacks in South Africa[55] provide examples of separatism within a society.

Between the extremes of participation can be located other types of situations. For example, cooptation may be said to occur when power and control are maintained by one group but participation is allowed "outsiders" in most (but not all) social spheres. Participation in this instance usually is restricted to select members of the "outsider" group. The samurai in Japan in the mid-nineteenth century and the Jews[56] in the United States are examples of this situation. Cooperation, on the other hand, describes a situation in which control of one institution (such as the economy) is held by one group and politics may be controlled by another group. Power in this instance is fairly equally distributed and both parties remain dependent on the other. The relationship between the Dutch and the English in South Africa provides an example of this type of situation.[57]

At times, persons outside the group in power are allowed participation in certain institutions (such as the economy). The outsiders, however, almost always are placed in a subordinated position. Other activities such as religion, education, and family life for the subordinated members of society are conducted in separate institutions. The majority of blacks in American society and the Algerian workers in Marseilles, France,[58] provide examples of this type of participation.

The case material presented in this volume repeatedly has supported the conclusion that social strife is not usually the action of the most oppressed or completely segregated members of society. The factors that appear to be associated with the place migrants occupy in urban life include the traditions of the group, timing of migration, and the receptivity of the host population.

Even under the condition of partial separatism, ideologies developed by those in power to legitimate their position may not be completely effective. When a group is isolated in many spheres of their lives for an extended period of time, beliefs about substantive issues (as well as subcultural attitudes and values) different from that of the ruling group can be expected. Such was the instance of urban black Americans since class and caste factors served to reinforce boundaries of differential social participation.[59]

Beyond the visibility factor (which has already been discussed), black Americans have had many other problems finding success in northern urban areas. Racism has been institutionalized since the days of slavery.[60] Further, Southern blacks commonly lack appropriate skills for a technologically advanced society.[61]

The very large concentration of this sizable population in major American cities, however, gives blacks potential political power.[62] Moreover, the unification of the black population and the civil rights movement of the 1960s encouraged attention to their plight and brought some legal surcease. The case of black Americans is not complete in historical record; the final outcome is yet to be learned.

Of course, variations in beliefs and ideologies are not enough to effect social movements. They do serve as the setting against which the various types of battles between groups are fought: at times through the legal channels of society (e.g., courts or other mediating agencies); at other times through direct action, as in the instance of riots. The attempt to effect change through channels like the courts can only occur when this is viewed as an acceptable and legitimate means of resolving conflict. The more strident forms of strife, on the other hand, occur when ambiguity abounds in the means of resolving the conflict or when the long range goal is nebulous or multifaceted.[63]

Direct action or selected legal battles, even when successful, usually do not bring much relief when the problem is complex. Effective leadership, organization, and some form of power usually are necessary to bring about social change.

The economic state of the society

The more successful immigrants to urban areas, as we have discussed, arrived in urban areas during periods of expansion when economic opportunities (even for unskilled laborers) were open. For example, most European groups, emulating the Mohawk Indians, entered areas of economic expansion. In turn, if they desired, they were able to consolidate their economic position and move on to other new opportunities. Of course, the circumstances surrounding the timing of migration to an area usually are beyond the control of migrants.

Urban strife of all forms would appear to occur during what W. W. Rostow defined as the period of economic "takeoff" and the "drive to maturity."[64] Economic "takeoff" is the point at which an economy decisively shifts from a rural to an urban base, the rate of effective investment and savings increases from perhaps 5 percent of the national income to 10 percent (or more), new industries are created, and compound interest becomes built, as it were, into its habits and institutional structure.[65] Rostow pictures this period as normally requiring about twenty years. The "drive to maturity" period occurs during the next forty years and is marked by an even higher rate of investment, the acceleration of new industries, and an expansion into international trade.

These periods are crucial to urban society in several respects. They are times when new classes of entrepreneurs and industrial workers are created whose economic importance begins to surpass that of the established elite. To match their economic gains, these groups may attempt to enter new political and social strata to consolidate their position in society. Entrepreneurs commonly demand political power and social status, workers unionize against management, and the army equipped with modern weapons often sees itself as the carrier of a new civilization.

Migrants enter urban areas with high expectations; often, as we have already noted, with higher expectations than those who have already achieved some measure of success. Despite handicaps, many of the transitional urbanites prosper in the cities, compared to their counterparts who remain in rural situations.

If (as in the instance of women and minority groups in American cities and the samurai in Japan) economic development results in a major improvement in the new urbanites' position, a reform movement bent on the equalization of social or political position may ensue. If the reformers possess some form of power (e.g., numerical, economic, political) and do not prove overwhelmingly threatening to the power holders, then their demands are met with relatively little violence. Thus, the samurai sought and obtained political power; women sought equality of opportunity and have met with some success; and urban minorities in their search for social equity effected a broader based student population in the New York universities.

If, however, during the period of economic expansion and raised expectations in cities the economy should stall in its growth, the disillusionment of many different groups of urbanites is bound to be profound. When the economy, for example, has been growing at the rate of at least 8 percent annually for ten years or longer and a depression (zero percent growth) follows for a period of perhaps four years (or more), then riots or attempted revolution can be expected.

The specific type of collective action depends, in large part, on which particular group suffers the most from the depressed economy. If the economic burden falls primarily upon the lower classes who were slowly improving their lot, we can expect riots but little real change in the social situation of these people. On the other hand, if the drop in the economy imperils a variety of economic groups, including those who were relatively successful, this may serve as background to revolt or revolution.

The general principle of the effects of an altered economic situation applies to several types of urban conflict we have described. Ulster, for example, enjoyed a period of great prosperity during the armament period of World War II. After the war the introduction of the welfare state brought about an aura of continuing prosperity. As a group, Ulster's Catholics received improved housing, jobs, and higher salaries from 1940 to 1960 than they had ever enjoyed before.

The early 1960s, however, marked a distinct downturn in the Ulster economy: the armament expenditures of England in Belfast dried to a mere dribble; unions closed their doors against Catholic apprentices; and housing allocations reverted to the traditional pattern of Protestant privilege. The beginnings of protest and attempted revolution in Ulster occurred immediately after the period of economic stagnation: a time when Protestant groups still prospered but urban Catholics were left by the wayside.

Similarly in Cuba, the middle classes had steadily gained influence after Cuba had shaken the yoke of Spanish control. Until 1945 the urban middle classes prospered. Then sugar prices fell on the world market, and with them the newfound prosperity of the middle classes. In terms of deprivation, the rural and lower-class urban residents remained as exploited and passive as ever. At first, the middle classes welcomed, or tolerated, the coup d'etat of Batista. When he failed to salvage them, they turned to the more revolutionary figure of Fidel Castro.

The secession of Biafra from Nigeria, which we have not detailed in this volume, also fits the general pattern described.[66] Ibos (later "Biafrans") who migrated to northern Nigerian cities had dramatically improved their economic situation between 1950 and 1963.[67] Their progress, however, came to a resounding stop in 1966 as economic and political opportunities were closed to them.[68] It was at this point that riots, revolutions, counter-revolutions, and secession attempts burst upon Nigeria.

These examples could be further reiterated in the sequence of events in Egypt, East Saint Louis, and Watts. In each of these examples we have described the period of economic progress, subsequent urbanization, and a disruption in the economy followed by strife. Let us now look for the way in which economic downturn operates to promote strife.

Gap between expectation and attainment

Economic progress (preceding its disruption) usually has spawned new classes of urban entrepreneurs and industrial workers. To some degree, all populations share a similar fate when a depression occurs. It is not the objective situation, however, that can be assumed to be conducive to conflict; rather, it may be speculated that the gap created between the raised expectations of urban people and their standing during the depression is most important.

This consequence has been described by social scientists such as Crane Brinton[69] and Louis Kriesberg.[70] We suggest, however, that special attention focus on the attitudes and position of the urban secondary elite since it is they who are in the best position to subvert or overthrow the old regime. Generally more educated, articulate, and possessing other resources, this group can provide leadership and initiate action that triggers a consensus of opinion necessary to move collectivities of disgruntled, frustrated individuals. Individual discontent or unfocused crowd behavior is never sufficient to mobilize massive reforms or revolution.

Kriesberg has distinguished between three types of "gaps" between expectations and attainment.[71] Of course, we realize that the distinction between the types may be clear for only a given time. In fact, they may become blurred over the process of a particular historical event. Nonetheless, from our own case studies, each would appear particularly appropriate:

1. A situation where attainment drops but expectations remain stable
2. An environment where expectations increase drastically but attainment remains stable
3. An emotional climate in which expectations exceed attainment

The first situation is exemplified by a sudden drop in the economy, as discussed in the preceding section. For those most impoverished, an attitude of fatalism may mitigate consequences from the economic change. The attitudes of many rural peasants and urban "down and outers" provide examples of this situation.[72]

The second instance, where expectations have been greatly increased, is typically an urban dilemma. This was the situation for some groups in each of the cases presented in this volume. In East Saint Louis, whites had just begun to taste the fruits of unionization when they were threatened by black laborers; blacks in Watts had been exposed to the hopes of the national civil rights movement initiated in the late 1950s; and Houston police expected to enforce the norms of their region of the country. The expectations of the Cuban middle class, the Egyptian middle class, the Ulster Catholics, the samurai, women, and young minority group members also were raised prior to the social strife described.

In each of the situations presented a climate of frustration and discontent was a consequence of expectations exceeding attainment. This type of discrepancy, of course, can be the result of either lowered attainment, raised expectations, or inconsistent status on different social dimensions (e.g., political, economic, prestige).

In any instance, for those in power who wish to avoid violent action, our cases would indicate that it is perhaps unwise to initiate reform that will only partially satisfy the expectations of a group. By raising expectations, a government that improves in part the lot of some citizens may succeed only in increasing the chances of overt, violent action or the demand for change.[73] From a Machiavellian position, the proper policy for a ruling group would be to impose strict control over the population. The fact that the citizens of Watts (who were doing well by most standards of the black man's existence in the United States) broke into riots while the majority of Mississippi blacks (who were more systematically repressed) remained quiet and passive during the 1960s (before the invasion of civil rights workers) suggests the truth of this cynical observation.

In a similar fashion, Hitler rose to power only when the Weimar Republic failed to exercise strict controls over the Nazis;[74] Poland, Hungary, and Czechoslovakia revolted against Russian domination only after the "thaw" entailed by Stalin's death;[75] and Nasser initiated his revolt when Faruk lost his power over the military.[76] In each case, hostile outbreaks against the ruling group followed a period of attempted reform, an era when expectations were increased, and a time when military control over the populace was relaxed.

The gap between expectations and reality is affected by the simple rate of urbanization. The more rapidly a metropolitan area expands its population, the more likely it is that the people will feel disappointment, disillusionment, and anger. In a typical city undergoing a fast transition, "old-timers" and newcomers usually do not share the same values. Moreover, they must compete for jobs, housing, services, and privileges offered by the burgeoning city. Thus, the extent and violence of social conflict would appear to increase in step with the rapidity of urbanization. Belfast and Cairo, Houston and Los Angeles, and Havana and East Saint Louis experienced high rates of growth during a short time.

Contrasting riotous situations and those involving attempts at broad social change, we find that in the latter instance the secondary elite (that is, those close to the ruling group in political, economic, administrative, or military power) were most likely to initiate a revolution.[77] During eras where cities are undergoing rapid growth in population, however, and discontent is unfocused and multifaceted, collective behavior such as riots can turn into revolutions only when the dissidents can call upon the help of the secondary elite.

The secondary elite: status inconsistency

The leaders of some types of urban social movements have long been recognized as those who are relatively high in the socioeconomic stratum of society.[78] As Louis Kriesberg has cogently argued, the secondary elite take the lead in revolutions because "such persons are in some ways marginal; they do not fit clearly in the low ranking nor high ranking strata."[79] They are in a position to be particularly responsive to a change in expectations and social conditions. This statement would certainly be true of all the cases of reform and revolution we presented. For example, Egyptian military officers held a rank toward the top of their society; the Cuban middle class enjoyed many privileges and had captured the presidency; the samurai in Tokugawa Japan manned administrative and business posts; a few Ulster Catholics were college graduates; many women had long been employed in jobs outside the home; and some minority group members were gaining some success in terms of court decisions. Each of these groups also held an inconsistent status in their particular society. They were high on some dimensions, having made some gains, but low on others (e.g., political, prestige, economic).

Status inconsistency, as many social scientists have pointed out, is a major source of discontent.[80] One of the more important, if relatively neglected, consequences of such inconsistency is that a group with high status in one sphere but denied congruent status in another may turn to reform or revolution as a solution to its dilemna.

Our emphasis upon the primary role of the secondary elite in determining the course of reform or revolution runs contrary to the views of both classical Hegelianism and Marxism. Contrary to Hegel, we have argued that many rather nameless individuals composing the secondary elite may be swayed by frustration or lack of fulfillment of their expectations and attempt to change history. Unique "world historical individuals" may play a passing role or perhaps symbolize a given revolution, but an individual's impact on history cannot be compared with reforms initiated and supported by groups such as the samurai in Japan.

Our views differ from those of Marx in several ways. The working class, even in industrial-urban nations, is apparently of little importance in determining the course of social changes. Even in those situations where the urban proletariat plays some role, it is commonly a matter of fighting other poor people, or serving merely to legitimate the leaders of the revolution.

Further, Marxism (with its focus solely on the economic dimension), if accepted, can seriously blind leaders to the most effective actions. In Mississippi, for example, it probably would have been far wiser for the leaders of the attempted reform to solicit help from the Southern urban middle-class rather than to try to form alliances with poor rural whites, as they did. Aside from the direct economic threat each group posed for the other, even the poorest of white persons joining with the black movement entailed an intolerable status inconsistency in terms of a salient caste position. A similar situation also can be cited in the instance of the Irish Catholic attempts at seeking assistance from poor Irish Protestants to further their cause.

The rather simple concept of status inconsistency, then, provides some utility in an analysis of social strife, its origins, and manifestations.

Third parties

For the most part, we have concentrated on the character and experiences of conflicting groups. Because of technological advances that shorten travel between nations and continents to a matter of hours, the role of third party intervention has been heightened for conflict situations in modern times.

Third parties (that is, those who are not initially overtly involved in the conflict) can affect the nature of strife in several ways. First, third party intervention may help to initiate conflict. Such was the instance of Perry's declaration in 1854. The intrusion of this third party was inadvertent. It forced into the open a conflict that had been festering in Japan over a long period of time.

Second, third parties or even potential third parties to a conflict can embolden a weaker party to use force as a mode of resolving ongoing conflict. Dissidents in Warsaw (1954) and Hungary (1956) counted on outside aid in their insurrection.[81]

Third, even the rumor of forthcoming assistance from a third force can intensify conflict. In East Saint Louis, for example, false rumors that an armed black army was advancing from Chicago inflamed the hatred of the white rioters.[82] In Watts, similar rumors of massive black assistance to the rioters offered hope to the black population and intensified the passions of the white population.[83]

Fourth, the actual intervention of third parties can help prolong an ongoing conflict.

Each side in this instance would count on continuing help from its allies and thus fight on with intensity. This almost commonsense observation about the possible consequences of third party intervention has been supported in research by Ted Gurr, who found that external aid to dissidents correlates .37 with the length of any given civil strife.[84]

Fifth, a third party can, of course, serve as a mediator between conflicting parties. This is best exemplified by The Federal Mediation and Conciliation Service established in 1947 for public employment labor-management disputes, and the Human Relations Commissions formed between 1930 and 1950.

Alternatively, depending on the nature of its power and relationship to combatants, a third party can also impose its will upon the combatants. In Watts, for example, the forceful intervention of the National Guard between black rioters and white policemen quieted the situation.

The effects of third party intervention on the form and intensity of conflict depend on the role assumed by the third party. James H. Laue suggests the following five types of third party interventionists:[85]

1. *The activist,* who usually works closely with the powerless or nonestablishment party in a conflict
2. *The advocate,* who is not a member of a disputing group but serves as an adviser or consultant to that group
3. *The mediator,* who has an organization base acceptable to both parties
4. *The enforcer,* who represents power to enforce conditions on conflicting parties irrespective of their wishes
5. *The researcher,* who independently provides an evaluation of a given conflict situation.

Although these role types were developed on the basis of an examination of community conflict, Laue's typology can be extended to third party interventionists at any level of social conflict. The first two types of interventionists would serve to prolong or perhaps intensify strife. Further, these role types probably would be important to all kinds of social strife: reform, revolution, or riot. The latter three role types probably would play their most important role during the resolution phase of urban conflict. The mediator role is possibly most common in situations of reform where the enforcer role is probably most commonly associated with riotous situations.

A heritage of violence

When an urban neighborhood, an entire city, region, or nation possesses a long history of violence as a solution to social conflict, the likelihood of violence in a particular situation is greatly increased. Ted Gurr, among others, has pointed out this historical factor. In his study of 114 nations, Gurr found that civil strife in the 1960s was correlated .29 with historical levels of strife.[86]

Similarly, we have noted that urban centers possessing a tradition of violence are likely to erupt in violent civil conflict. East Saint Louis, Houston, and Watts were noted for their extremely high rates of violent crime (particularly murder) long before the reported riots took place. Cuba, Egypt, and Ulster also provide examples where violent social action was conducted in the setting of a heritage of violence.

Violence is even more likely to occur if a professional military class has traditionally involved itself in the solution of social strife.[87] In Egypt and Cuba, as well as in France (1958), Germany (during the Weimar Republic), and Biafra (1960s) an elite military class felt free—in fact, obligated by a mission—to intervene in an essentially civilian affair. The use of military force has not occurred in areas that have strictly separated military and civilian powers. It also has not occurred in areas such as the Scandinavian nations that maintain only a small officer corps.

Violent social action may serve many purposes. In the case of Watts, riots were almost cathartic and served to focus national attention on the problems of the black populations in urban centers of the North and the West. Violent action, in varying degrees, also has been used by some members of the women's liberation movement to draw attention to the plight of women.[88] On the other hand, violence expressive of frustration and severe discontent with the status quo can serve as signaling cues for an impending revolt or revolution. For the latter to occur, however, the history of violence and violent social action would have to interact with other factors we have discussed.

Table 5. Urban strife

Variables	Reform	Riot	Revolution
Agreement on basic values	Present	Relatively present	Absent
Nature of existing elite	Relatively open access	Relatively closed access	Closed
Use of violence	None	Confined	Unlimited

SUMMARY: THE FORM AND INTENSITY OF SOCIAL CONFLICT

In summary, the following generalizations are offered:

1. Urban reform movements arise when a discontented but already successful group articulates their expectation of equity in all spheres. They flourish in an environment of open expression, a lack of restraint by an inflexible elite, a professional military class, or severe repression. Many of the positive consequences of urbanization promote attempted reforms. The positive consequences include the urban mentality, actual gain along some dimension, and autonomy. Reform movements are not particularly violent.

2. Urban riots are uniquely lower-class phenomenon. They tend to occur during periods when some rather powerless group is suffering from real or perceived injustices. Many of the urban groups that initially serve as buffers for new migrants provide the basis of identification and different ideology that lead to riotous situations. Riots are, however, relatively ineffective in bringing about lasting social change, and this can be attributed to a lack of support from the secondary elite.

3. Revolutions may be viewed as a problem of sequential incidents. They are built on a foundation of discontent of a relatively powerful group as are reform movements. However, revolutions occur only after efforts at changing parts of the social system have been met with repression or failure. In Cuba, Egypt, and Ulster these situations were found to be true, as they were in classical revolutions such as the French, American, or Russian. Although Bastille Day usually marks the beginning of the French Revolution, previous actions such as bread riots, attempts to reform French society, and plans at revolt by Louis's brother had all failed before the revolution actually occurred. One could pick almost any point in the long sequence of events as the primary starting point of revolution.

To summarize this explication of urban social conflict, Table 5 graphically depicts different social movements along these dimensions:

Any given movement, of course, may take many of these forms. The task of abolishing slavery in the United States, for example, first expressed itself in abortive slave revolts (or riots), then emerged in the abolitionist reform movement and was finally resolved after the South revolted against the North. Abolition came only as a by-product of the North's war to preserve the union.

With this in mind, we have examined the different factors that produce particular urban movements and the elements that lead from one stage to another. Again, in a simplified fashion, the sources of urban social movements are summarized in Table 6.

Table 6. The sources and forms of urban social movements

Social factors	Reform movements	Riots	Revolutions
Predisposing factors			
A period of economic transition (the "take-off")	*	*	*
Unmet expectations among the urban masses	*	*	*
Conditioning factors			
A discontented secondary elite	*		*
Status inconsistency among the secondary elite	*		*
A heritage of violence		*	*
An inflexible elite		*	*
A professional military			*
Immediate factors			
Intervention by a third party			*
Severe repression			*
A sequence of prior failures in reform, rioting, and so on			*

Clearly, urban conflict does not necessarily lead to violence. There are many possible ways in which urban strife can be suppressed, defused, or escalated. For the practitioners of the political arts, a sense of the possible resolution of conflict as well as their determinants is of the utmost importance.

THE RESOLUTION OF URBAN CONFLICT

Conflict may be resolved in a number of ways. Any one resolution, however, brings with it other unintended and, in most instances, unanticipated problems. In the cases we have presented, six resolutions have been suggested:

Defeat of one party

Obviously, the most clear resolution to conflict is when one side wins and the other collapses in defeat. This occurs when a dominant power uses untrammeled force to ensure the downfall of its opponent. This resolution is exemplified in white America's suppression of rioting blacks, Russia's invasions of Hungary and Czechoslovakia, and Hitler's elimination of dissidents.

Anthony Oberschall has indicated in his review of social conflict that complete defeat of an opponent occurs when "public opinion favors repression during a period such as the 'red scare,' of nationalism and jingoism, of religious enthusiasm . . . during which members of a certain group have been labeled and targeted as 'reds,' 'traitors,' 'infidels,' or 'heretics.'"[89] Oberschall also noted that "if the protesters belong to a negatively privileged or 'pariah' social category, such as a racial or religious minority . . . who have not enjoyed full citizenship rights and have traditionally been kept in their place by the use of force, casualties will tend to be higher than if the protesters are drawn from more privileged groups."[90]

An all-out war will be declared against a combatant only when the group does not form an economic buttress for the ruling power. Similarly, dissenters usually do not attempt to dispose of an existing elite by unrestrained force if their own economic destiny is inextricably linked with them. Thus, in urban riots in the United States the whites generally dared not evoke the use of uncontrolled violence since their economic fate depended on the work of unskilled black laborers. Further, the white elite of particular Southern cities could not offend the sensibilities of the rest of the United States since commercial activities and their continued existence depended on the sentiments of the federal government.

Dependence, however, is a two-way relationship.[91] During the 1960s, blacks rejected suggestions by Martin Luther King that they undertake a boycott of white businesses.[92] They judged that a boycott would hurt black employees of white businesses more than it would aid the cause of the general black community. Mutual economic dependence of the antagonists would seem to be the best insurance against violent eruptions protesting inequitable circumstances.

Escapism

An *escapist* reaction occurs when one side simply disengages itself from the overt battle but quietly and privately continues its dissent. On an individual level, a schizophrenic who fails to convince others of the "reality" of his hallucinations follows this path. On a social level, such varied groups as American blacks,[93] German Mennonites,[94] and political dissenters in Nkrumah's Ghana also had chosen this alternative for a time.[95]

Why does the group in power allow the continuation of the dissent? Restraint is shown to a quietly dissenting group when those in power anticipate possible intervention by a third party or when they judge that overt battle would not be economically productive. For example, the English aristocracy stopped openly persecuting religious dissenters when it became clear that many of the persecuted were merchants or the pillars of the new industrialism.

Compromise

A nonviolent compromise is another possible outcome of social strife. It is the most common type of conflict resolution. Compromise occurs at all levels of social conflict: individuals must suppress some aspects of their personalities in order to function in society; husbands and wives must avoid clashing on every issue that confronts them in order to preserve their relationship; the samurai deposed the Tokugawa regime but continued to observe the sacredness of the emperor; and Egypt's free officers deposed Faruk but left much of the upper class intact.

Compromise may be a laudable solution to urban problems for it involves working with the opposition in a peaceful way to find mutually acceptable solutions to urban problems. It should be made clear, however, that compromise is by no means viewed as a panacea to urban problems since it may merely hide the real issues dividing opponents, or result in an eventually coercive decision.

Early compromises among whites resulted in the continuing degradation of American blacks following the Civil War—a war which eventuated in a series of compromises that merely continued slavery in a new form.[96] The Weimar Republic's early appeasement of the Nazis simply granted Hitler more power in the streets of Germany and resulted in dictatorship.[97] Compromise, therefore, is not suggested as an ideal solution. Its potential evils are as clear as its virtues.

A compromise solution takes place when both sides pragmatically assess the realities of a particular social situation and estimate that a continuing battle is not worth the effort. To summarize, antagonists reach a compromise position when—

1. Both sides perceive that the balance of violent force is approximately equal.
2. Both combatants admit that their economic or social interests would be damaged by continued conflict.

As noted earlier, acceptance of the demands of a reform movement depend upon a society's having already experienced changes. The contemporary women's liberation movement, for example, would be unthinkable in a rural or transitional economy. It was only when women had already achieved a measure of economic equality, opportunity for mobility, and an independent existence that they could effectively demand changes in their political, legal, educational, or social status.

3. Outside threats may compel a previously dominant regime to admit the indispensability of its putative enemy. The Tokugawa regime, for example, threatened by Perry's invasion, was compelled to call upon the lords for advice and aid. The focus of hostility had changed from an internal enemy to an external threat.
4. One side manages to quietly take away the actual power of its opponent without a direct confrontation and leaves the symbols of their former status intact.

Again, Japan presents a perfect example of such strategy. Similarly, the budding industrialists of England gained real political control through the House of Commons but left the remnants of the old regime (the monarchy and the House of Lords) untouched.

Actually, the defeat of a combatant, or the victory of the other combatant, is seldom complete. As Louis Kriesberg pointed out: "elements of compromise nearly always enter into an outcome."[98]

Conversion

Another type of resolution lies in conversion. This is where one side is made to accept the goals or values of the other. Often in urban areas, conversion occurs spontaneously and unconsciously. It is labeled acculturation.

Athens gradually absorbed the ideas of Alexandria; in its turn, Rome became hellenized by its Greek slaves; and Rome turned its eventual defeat into a triumph by Latinizing the Western world. In an analogous fashion, the United States has seen urban migrants gradually abandon their conflict with the "old stock" and accept the customs and language of the former opponent. Waves of Irishmen, Poles, Germans, Russians, and Italians have passed through United States cities. At first they found themselves in direct conflict with older groups. Gradually, "micks" have become Americans, the Mafia has been transformed into the Italo-American League, and many Jews have become Unitarians.

Such conversions occur when people on one side of the conflict believe that their cause has been lost, or when they perceive (as did the "rice Christians") that some concrete material benefit flows from having changed sides.

Intervention

Intervention by a third power may also resolve a conflict. On an international level this is exemplified by Britain's attempt to preserve Nigeria or Ulster.[99] In urban conflicts such as the East Saint Louis riots the appearance of a well-armed state militia finally resulted in the cessation of violence.

Moreover, as Georg Simmel and Lewis Coser have pointed out, the intervention of a third power may unify previously conflicting enemies.[100] They may come to view the interventionist as "the enemy."

The condition that prompts a third party to intervene is the perception that its own interests are affected and the belief that it possesses greater power than either combatant in the conflict situation.

Divide and conquer

A final possibility is that one side in a conflict is able to fractionate the issues that consume the other side. In some circumstances, it is possible to "divide and conquer" an enemy by spreading divisive rumors that split the issues which originally unified them. Thus, it was possible for Charles de Gaulle in 1962 to maintain his position. He controlled the mass media and separated the Algerian generals from other groups who opposed him.[101] Further, each of these groups had its own grievance: the urban workers desired better wages, the small capitalists wanted a fair share on taxes, and the farmers wanted better prices for their crops. Combined with the military leaders, all of these groups working together could have amassed an invincible opposition to de Gaulle. By playing one group against the other and by making the issues that concerned each group appear separate from the others, de Gaulle was able to deal with the revolts separately and in his own time.

DISCUSSION: URBAN SOCIAL CONFLICT IN RETROSPECT

Although recognizing that conflict is inherent to urban existence, we must also acknowledge that the inner discontent, cultural ambiguity, and anomie characteristic of cities are the bases of creativity. As Freud once argued, conflict within ourselves and with society is the price we pay for creativity.[102]

Perhaps our best hope is to encourage the growth of pluralistic urban centers—sophisticated societies that have developed many institutional channels for the expression of creativity and discontent. Without the various institutions unique to cities—trade unions, a free press, ethnic associations, neighborhood "communities," educational institutions, and a free judiciary—we would have drowned in the morass of urban discontent. The task of guiding urban conflict through equitable channels is complicated and grave; in such supremely important matters, the greatest sin would be to have never tried.

From Plato's Republic to contemporary times, man has dreamed of creating a society free of social conflict. As industrialization and urbanization have grown, so too have writings concerned with saving man from the torment and strife imposed by city life. In the nineteenth century, Marx and Engels, Proudhon and Bakunin, Tolstoy and Kropotkin pleaded for their own special solutions to the problems posed by the advance of technology and urbanization. In the twentieth century, their followers have urged a variety of solutions to the inevitable and in tense social conflicts.

Gandhi wished man to eschew all of the complexities of urban technological civilization and create a nonviolent civilization.[103] Although his philosophy played a major role in gaining independence for India, even his most ardent disciples would agree that India has not been able to follow his philosophical advice. Urbanization in India proceeds at an incredible rate, riots have torn Calcutta and Bombay, and Indian democracy balances precariously on the razor's edge.

Chinese Marxists such as Mao have become known as peasant heroes who have chosen to avoid the excess of heavy industrialization and urbanization. Mao was, however, the son of a rich landowner and received an urban education. Most of his prominent colleagues, such as Chou En-lai, were urbane "men of the world."[104] Their policies under Communism have been infinitely flexible and have reasonably encouraged agriculture. Yet, Shanghai and other cities continue to grow despite efforts to convince students and other urbanites to return to the countryside.[105] Dictatorship in China can suppress some of the more obvious characteristics of cities (such as the prevalence of prostitution or the open expression of severe discontent), but there is little evidence that the Chinese have eliminated the impersonality and bureaucratization so many observers have noted as intrinsic elements in the urban way of life.

Reformers and social philosophers in the United States have striven to improve the conditions of American cities. In many small but important ways they have succeeded. Some neighborhoods have been rejuvenated,[106] and particular cities that were dying economically have been saved.[107] The increase in crime rates has been cut, usually by a more efficient police force.[108] But this is not the dream of writers such as Erich Fromm, Paul and Percival Goodman, or B. F. Skinner.[109] These "anti-urban philosophers" have more grandiose aims.

Fromm, for example, would like to see the decentralization of cities, a dismantling of bureaucracy, and a return to life in small, self-governing, workers' communities. Skinner envisages small communities, detached from the metropolis, where human beings have been conditioned to desire and work for what is best for them. The Goodmans conceived of planning new cities designed to serve the highest ends of living and devoid of social conflict.

Alas, these dreams have not been fulfilled. Strife is endemic to the human condition: urbanization only serves to intensify it.

We can foresee no panaceas to the strife that is part of the world's cities and seems to increase in step with the metropolitanization of the entire world. There is no single solution, such as the returning of more than a few to "country life" or creating a new nonurban utopia. Once people "have seen the future" in the great cities of the world, they cannot return to a simpler, less urbane world with ease.

Economic forces, advances in technology, the growth of bureaucracy, the concentration of cultural and educational facilities in the cities, and even the lure of excitement, variety, and entertainment compel people to remain in the urban world.

In the foreseeable future, suburbs—commonly annexes and, increasingly, replicas of original cities—will probably multiply. A privileged few may escape to their summer homes on the beach or to desert or mountain retreats. For the vast majority of humankind, residence in some mammoth, sprawling metropolis is the most probable fate.

Realistically, we must face the fact that as metropolitan regions grow, so too will the incidence of interpersonal strife, feelings of anomie and alienation, and group conflict along with creative activity. There is little reason to believe that affluence in an urbanized society will bring complete satisfaction to humankind: there is less reason to believe that humankind can turn its back on the metropolis.

Issues for further discussion

1. Considering all of the relevant factors, is it possible to solve the urban problems of contemporary America?

2. What elements in contemporary American life would lead to a violent solution of urban issues? What might lead to a nonviolent resolution?

3. What are the major factors that affect the onset, nature, and intensity of urban social conflict?

4. Why do the most oppressed members of an urban society usually refrain from engaging in reform movements, riots, or revolutions?

5. How and why do changes in the economy affect the incidence of urban social conflict?

6. From the point of view of the ruling elite, should social, economic, or political reforms in urban society be allowed as a way of maintaining the elite's power?

7. In what ways can third parties influence the outcome of urban social strife?

8. What are the major predisposing factors that differentiate the various forms of urban social conflict?

9. What immediate factors lead to a revolution rather than to a reform movement or an urban riot?

10. What influences the outcome of an urban social conflict?

11. Does the theory presented in this book accurately portray the situation in such diverse events as the cultural revolution in China or the 1976 events in Beirut?

FOOTNOTES

1. Flora Lewis, "Urban Europeans Worry About the Quality of Life," *New York Times,* 26 March 1975, p. 10.

2. Ibid.
3. Ernest Holsendolph, "Urban Crisis of the 1960s is Over, Ford Aides Say," *New York Times,* 22 March 1975, p. 1.
4. Georg Simmel, *The Sociology of Georg Simmel,* trans. and ed. by Kurt H. Wolff (London: The Free Press of Glencoe, 1950), and Louis Wirth, *On Cities and Social Life* (Chicago: University of Chicago Press, Phoenix Books, 1964).
5. Alex Inkeles, "The Modernization of Man," in *Modernization,* ed. Myron Weiner (New York: Basic Books, 1966), chap. 10.
6. William McCord and Abdullah Lutfiyya, "Urbanization and World View in the Middle East," in *Essays on Modernization of Underdeveloped Societies,* ed. A. R. Desai (Bombay, India: Thacker and Co., 1967).
7. Holsendolph, *Urban Crisis Over,* p. 46.
8. Ernest Holsendolph, "Survey Finds Decline in Black Population in Capital, With a Sharp Rise in Suburbs," *New York Times,* 20 May 1975.
9. "The Growing Back to the Land Movement," *New York Times,* 8 June 1975.
10. Henry Schmandt and Warner Bloomberg, Jr., eds., *The Quality of Urban Life* 3 (Beverly Hills, Calif.: Sage Publications, 1969): 155.
11. Mario Puzo, "The Fortunate Pilgrim," in *A Nation of Nations,* ed. Theodore L. Gross (New York: The Free Press, 1971), p. 36.
12. Eileen Shanahan, "Study Finds Poor Blacks in Cities, Whites Outside," *New York Times* 30 August 1974, p. 14.
13. John Kenneth Galbraith, *The New Industrial State* (Boston: Houghton Mifflin Co., 1967).
14. Key issues and alternative solutions, for example, have been presented by William A. Caldwell, *How To Save Urban America* (New York: New American Library, 1973).
15. Joan Moore, *Mexican American* (New York: Prentice-Hall, 1970).
16. Murray Wax, *Indian American* (New York: Prentice-Hall, 1971).
17. Ernest Poole, "A Mixing Bowl for Nations," in *The Ordeal of Assimilation,* ed. Stanley Feldstein and Lawrence Costello (Garden City, N.J.: Doubleday & Co., 1974), p. 116.
18. Cited in Anthony Richmond, "Colored Colonials in the United Kingdom," in *Minority Problems,* ed. Arnold M. Rose and Caroline B. Rose (New York: Harper & Row, Publishers, 1965).
19. Jacob Riis, "How the Other Half Lives" (1891), reprinted in Feldstein and Costello, *Ordeal of Assimilation,* pp. 207–211.
20. "What America Means to a Russian Jewess," *Immigrants in American Review* (Jan. 1916), pp. 70–71, reprinted in Feldstein and Costello, *Ordeal of Assimilation,* p. 70.
21. See Claude Brown, *Manchild in the Promised Land* (New York: The MacMillan Co., 1965) and Gerald Breese, *Urbanization in Newly Developing Countries* (Englewood Cliffs, N.J.: Prentice-Hall, 1966).
22. Griffin Roscoe, "Newcomers from Southern Mountains," in Rose and Rose, *Minority Problems,* p. 55.
23. John Francis Maguire, "The Irish in America," in Feldstein and Costello, *Ordeal of Assimilation,* p. 59.
24. Feldstein and Costello, *Ordeal of Assimilation,* p. 78–83.
25. Ibid., p. 84.
26. St. Clair Drake and Horace R. Cayton, *Black Metropolis,* vol. 1 (New York: Harper & Row, Publishers, 1962), chap. 3.
27. Ibid., p. 64.
28. Feldstein and Costello, *Ordeal of Assimilation,* pt. 3, "The Slum as a Home."
29. John Hope Franklin, *A History of Negro America,* 3rd ed. (New York: Harper & Row, Publishers, 1962), chap. 3, and Edgar A. Toppin, "They Thought They Were as Good as We Are," *Christian Science Monitor,* 15 May 1969, p. 13.
30. See Drake and Cayton, *Black Metropolis.*
31. Ibid.
32. Ibid., p. 175.
33. Ibid., p. 34.
34. Richmond, "Colored Colonials," in Rose and Rose, *Minority Problems,* p. 76.
35. Audrie Girdner and Anne Loftis, *The Great Betrayal* (London: Collier-MacMillan, 1969), p. 459.
36. Bernard C. Rosen, "Race Ethnicity and the Achievement Syndrome," in *Minorities in a Changing World,* ed. Milton Barron (New York: Alfred A. Knopf, 1967), pp. 151–175.
37. Ibid., p. 172.
38. Ibid., p. 152.
39. Monroe Burger, *The Arab World Today* (Garden City, N.Y.: Doubleday & Co., 1962).
40. Wax, *Indian American.*
41. Joseph P. Fitzpatrick, "The Adjustment of Puerto Rico to New York City," *Journal of Intergroup Relations* (Winter 1959–60).
42. See, for example, Pierre L. van den Berghe, *South Africa: A Study in Conflict* (Middletown, Conn.: Wesleyan University Press, 1965).
43. See George E. Simpson and J. Milton Yinger, *Racial and Cultural Minorities* (New

York: Harper and Brothers, 1953), pp. 270–277.
44. See György Pálóczi Horváth, *Mao Tse-Tung* (Garden City, N.Y.: Doubleday & Co., 1963).
45. See Nnamdi Azikiwe, *Zik* (Cambridge, England: Cambridge University Press, 1961).
46. Don Adams, *Schooling and Social Change in Modern America* (New York: David McKay Co., 1972), chap. 3.
47. Eleanor E. Maccoby, "Effects of the Mass Media," in *Review of Child Development Research*, ed. Martin L. Hoffman and Lois Wladis Hoffman (New York: Russell Sage Foundation, 1964), pp. 325–329.
48. Robert J. Havighurst and Bruce L. Neugarten, *Society and Education*, 4th ed. (Boston: Allyn & Bacon, 1975), especially pt. 2.
49. W. R. Catton, "Value Modification by Mass Media," in *Violence and the Media*, ed. Robert Baker and Sandra J. Ball, report to the National Commission on the Causes and Prevention of Violence (Washington, D.C., 1969).
50. See, for example, John Twomey, "New Forms of Social Control over Mass Media Content," in *Violence and the Mass Media*, ed. Otto N. Larsen (New York: Harper & Row, Publishers, 1968), p. 174.
51. Cited in Henry Etzkowitz and Roger Mack, "Media, Social Researchers and the Public: Linkage of Legitimation and Delegitimation," *American Sociologist*, vol. 10, no. 2 (May 1975), p. 110.
52. "TV: Do Minorities Rule?" *Newsweek*, 2 June 1975.
53. Ralph H. Turner, "Collective Behavior," in *Handbook of Modern Sociology*, ed. R. E. L. Faris (Chicago: Rand McNally & Co., 1964).
54. Brewton Berry, *Race and Ethnic Relations* (Boston: The Riverside Press, 1958), p. 274.
55. Alan Paton, "Aparthied in Africa," reprinted in Barron, *Minorities in a Changing World*.
56. Ferdinand Lundberg, *The Rich and the Super Rich*, rev. ed. (New York: Bantom, 1969).
57. Pierre L. van den Berghe, *South Africa: A Study in Conflict*.
58. See Edward Tannenbaum, *The New France* (Chicago: University of Chicago Press, 1961).
59. Harold W. Pfautz, "The New 'New Negro': Emerging American," *Phylon* (Winter 1963), pp. 360–368.
60. Louis L. Knowles and Kenneth Prewitt, *Institutional Racism in America* (Englewood Cliffs, N.J.: Prentice-Hall, 1969).
61. See Whitney M. Young, Jr., and Kyle Haselden, "Should There Be Compensation for Negroes," *New York Times Magazine*, 6 October 1963.
62. James Q. Wilson, *Negro Politics* (New York: The Macmillan Co., 1960).
63. St. Clair Drake, "Violence and American Social Movements," in *Urban Riots: Violence and Social Change*, ed. Robert H. Connery (New York: Vintage Books, 1969).
64. W. W. Rostow, *The Stages of Economic Growth* (London: Cambridge University Press, 1960).
65. Ibid.
66. C. O. Ojukwu, *Biafra* (New York: Harper & Row, Publishers, 1969).
67. Ibid.
68. Ibid.
69. Crane Brinton, *The Anatomy of Revolution* (New York: Prentice-Hall, 1952).
70. Louis Kriesberg, *The Sociology of Social Conflict* (Englewood Cliffs, N.J.: Prentice-Hall, 1973).
71. Ibid., p. 206.
72. See, for example, Daniel Lerner, *The Passing of Traditional Society Modernizing the Middle East* (New York: The Free Press, 1958), and Samuel Wallace, *Skid Row as a Way of Life* (Totowa, N.J.: The Bedminster Press, 1965).
73. See, for example, Kurt and Gladys Land, *Collective Dynamics* (New York: Thomas Y. Crowell Co., 1961); Gerhard Lenski, *Power and Privilege* (New York: McGraw-Hill, 1966); and Seymour Lipset, *The Berkeley Student Revolt* (Garden City, N.Y.: Doubleday & Co., 1965).
74. Joachim Fest, *Hitler* (New York: Harcourt Brace Jovanovich, 1974).
75. See Edward Crankshaw, *Khrushchev Remembers* (Boston: Little, Brown and Co., 1970).
76. Jean and Simone Lacouture, *L'Égypte en Mouvement* (Paris: Editions du Seuil, 1962).
77. See Crane Brinton, *Anatomy of Revolution*, p. 110, and Lyford P. Edward, *The Natural History of Revolution* (Chicago: The University of Chicago Press, 1927), chap. 5.
78. Ibid.
79. Kriesberg, *Sociology of Social Conflict*, p. 12.
80. E. F. Jackson, "Status Consistency and Symptoms of Stress," *American Sociological Review* (1962), pp. 469–480, and Gerhard Lenski, *Power and Privilege*.

81. See Crankshaw, *Khrushchev Remembers.*
82. Elliott M. Rudwick, *Race Riot in East St. Louis* (Carbondale, Ill.: Southern Illinois University Press, 1964).
83. William M. McCord et al., *Lifestyles in the Black Ghetto* (New York: W. W. Norton & Co., 1969).
84. Ted R. Gurr, *Why Men Rebel* (Princeton, N.J.: Princeton University Press, 1970).
85. James H. Laue, *A History of Third Party Intervention in Community Conflict,* presented to the annual meeting of the American Sociological Society in New York City, mimeographed, 29 August 1973.
86. Gurr, *Why Men Rebel.*
87. See John Johnson, *The Role of the Military in Underdeveloped Nations* (Princeton, N.J.: Princeton University Press, 1962).
88. Miriam Schneir, ed., *Feminism* (New York: Random House, 1972), pp. 132–133.
89. Anthony R. Oberschall, *Social Conflict and Social Movements* (Englewood Cliffs, N.J.: Prentice-Hall, 1973), p. 338.
90. Ibid.
91. See J. W. Thibaut and Harold H. Kelly, *The Social Psychology of Groups* (New York: John Wiley & Sons, 1961), chap. 7.
92. See William McCord, *Mississippi: The Long, Hot Summer* (New York: W. W. Norton & Co., 1965).
93. Horace R. Cayton, "The Psychology of the Negro," in Barron, *Minorities in a Changing World,* p. 210.
94. Brewton Berry, *Race and Ethnic Relations.*
95. David Apter, *Ghana in Transition* (New York: Atheneum Publishers, 1963).
96. See John Hope Franklin, *From Slavery to Freedom* (New York: Alfred A. Knopf, 1967).
97. See Fest, *Hitler.*
98. Kriesberg, *Sociology of Social Conflict.*
99. See, for example, Andrew Boyd, *Holy War in Belfast* (London: Anvil Books, 1971).
100. Simmel, *The Sociology of Georg Simmel,* and Lewis Coser, *Functions of Social Conflict* (Glencoe, Ill.: The Free Press of Glencoe, 1956).
101. See Tannenbaum, *The New France.*
102. See Sigmund Freud, *Civilization and Its Discontents* (London: Cape and Smith, 1930).
103. See K. Shridharan, *The Mahatma and the World* (New York: Duell, Sloan and Pierce, 1946).
104. See Pálóczi Horváth, *Mao Tse-Tung.*
105. Ibid.
106. See William A. Caldwell, *How to Save Urban America* (New York: The New American Library, 1973), p. 41.
107. Ibid., p. 179, and Henry J. Schmandt and John C. Goldback, "The Urban Paradox," in Schmandt and Bloomberg, *Quality of Urban Life.*
108. See Donald Newman, *Criminal Justice* (Philadelphia: J. B. Lippincott Co., 1975).
109. Erich Fromm, *The Sane Society* (New York: Rinehart and Co., 1955); B. F. Skinner, *Walden Two* (New York: The Macmillan Co., 1948); and Paul Goodman and Percival Goodman, *Communitas* (New York: Random House, 1960).

SUGGESTED READINGS

A number of observers have undertaken the task of proposing solutions to urban problems. The following are among the more celebrated works offering alternatives to urban life and the strife it entails.

Charles Reich, *The Greening of America* (New York: Random House, 1970). In this volume Reich argues against contemporary culture and prophesies a new world.

Erich Fromm, *The Sane Society* (New York: Rinehart and Co., 1955) presents an eloquent plea that modern society is insane and that we should return to "communitarian socialism."

Robert Nozick, *Anarchy, State and Utopia* (New York: Basic Books, 1975) presents a "libertarian" solution to all social issues.

Walden Two, by B. F. Skinner (New York: The Macmillan Co., 1948) is a famous description of a utopian community that utilizes all of modern man's technology and yet, through behavioral conditioning, is able to help individuals preserve tranquility.

A symposium devoted to man's ability to survive advances in urbanization and technology has been edited by G. R. Urban, *Can We Survive Our Future?* (New York: St. Martin's Press, 1971).

Robert Heilbroner, *An Inquiry Into the Human Prospect* (New York: W. W. Norton & Co., 1974) offers little hope that urban social conflict can be resolved. Doris Lessing, in her novel, *The Memoirs of a Survivor* (New York: Alfred A. Knopf, 1975) presents an equally pessimistic view.

Index